Obsolescence

Obsolescence

An Architectural History

DANIEL M. ABRAMSON

The University of Chicago Press
Chicago and London

The University of Chicago Press, Chicago 60637
The University of Chicago Press, Ltd., London
© 2016 by The University of Chicago
All rights reserved. Published 2016.
Paperback edition 2017
Printed in the United States of America

26 25 24 23 22 21 20 19 18 17   3 4 5 6

ISBN-13: 978-0-226-31345-0 (cloth)
ISBN-13: 978-0-226-47805-0 (paper)
ISBN-13: 978-0-226-31359-7 (e-book)
DOI: 10.7208/chicago/9780226313597.001.0001

Library of Congress Cataloging-in-Publication Data

Abramson, Daniel M. (Daniel Michael), 1963– author.
   Obsolescence : an architectural history / Daniel M. Abramson.
      pages cm
   Includes bibliographical references and index.
      ISBN 978-0-226-31345-0 (cloth : alk. paper) — ISBN 978-0-226-31359-7 (ebook)
1. Architecture and technology. 2. Product obsolescence. I. Title.
   NA2543.T43A27 2016
   720.72—dc23

                        2015017854

♾ This paper meets the requirements of ANSI/NISO Z39.48-1992 (Permanence of
Paper).

For Karl and Eliora

Contents

Acknowledgments

Support for this book has come from the National Endowment for the Humanities, the American Council of Learned Societies, the Charles Warren Center for Studies in American History at Harvard University, the Newhouse Center for the Humanities at Wellesley College, the Paul Mellon Centre for Studies in British Art, the Graham Foundation for Advanced Studies in the Fine Arts, and Tufts University's Faculty Research Awards Committee, Deans' Office, and the Center for the Humanities at Tufts.

Always the best part of the project has been the opportunity to talk about it with others. I want to thank sincerely everyone who met and spoke with me; who invited me to lecture, write, and curate; who read the work in parts; and who generously shared their references and insights about obsolescence. Special communities of scholars have inspired me at the Warren Center and in the Aggregate Architectural History Collaborative. I am particularly grateful to those several colleagues and friends who engaged with the project in a sustained fashion over time—Robert Bruegmann and Florian Urban—and who read and commented sagely on the entire manuscript—Alice Friedman, Peter Probst, and Stephen Simon. All these people's contributions are woven deeply into the book.

Tufts University's Tisch Library has provided for many years an ideal work environment. At the University of Chicago Press, Timothy Mennel has been the most professional and supportive editor imaginable.

Friends and family have long encouraged me. My wife, Penley Knipe, especially, has provided endless patience and love, without which this effort truly would never have been possible. Lastly, this book is dedicated to my two beautiful children (who've been waiting for it their whole lives thus far). Eliora and Karl, my love for you will never be obsolete.

Introduction

In the heart of New York's financial district in the spring of 1910 hundreds of workers labored day and night to demolish one of the area's mightiest structures. Thirteen years earlier upon completion in 1897 the three-hundred-foot-tall Gillender Building had been the world's loftiest office block, soaring sixteen stories into the air. Now the modern steel and stone tower, still structurally sound, was being brought back down to earth, brick by brick, beam by beam, to make way for a larger skyscraper (fig. 0.1).[1] The brevity of the Gillender Building's life startled observers. The *New York Times* pondered the motives of those who would "sacrifice it as ruthlessly as though it were some ancient shack." This was, reported the newspaper, "the first time that such a high class office building, representing the best kind of modern fireproof construction, has been torn down to make way for a still more elaborate structure."[2]

The Gillender Building was not alone in its premature demise. In New York, the Grand Central Terminal (demolished in 1903), the Plaza Hotel (1907), the Western Union Building (1914), and the Tower Building (1914) were other major monuments razed after a generation or less. Elsewhere around the United States, Atlanta's thirty-year-old Fulton County Courthouse was wrecked in 1911. San Francisco's early skyscraping Mutual Life Building was gone in 1907, aged fourteen. Chicago lost a slew of pioneering skyscrapers at this time, from the nine-story Montauk Building (demolished in 1902) to the fifteen-story Champlain Building (1915), as well as the Continental Bank, Rand-McNally, and Trude buildings, all brought down in 1912. None of these Chicago buildings had stood for more than twenty-eight years. Back in New York, the Pabst Hotel "must about hold the record for speedy obsolescence," reported a real estate journal: the hotel lasted just five years (1898–1903).[3]

FIGURE 0.1. Gillender Building, New York, constructed 1897, demolished 1910.

What to make of this phenomenon, this "doctrine of the 'scrap heap,'" the magazine *Scientific American* editorialized in 1910 upon the occasion of the Gillender Building's end?[4] A real estate executive, Cecil Evers, offered that the Gillender had reached the "limit of its commercial life [. . .] no longer able to earn a proper return on the land it stands on."[5] In other words, the building's worth had dropped so precipitously that the only alternative appeared to be demolition and rebuilding. Evers in 1914 did not yet use the term *obsolescent*. But that was the process of sudden devaluation and expendability he described. In the 1910s, as this kind of obsolescence became endemic in American downtowns, real estate experts began asking pointed questions:

What caused architectural obsolescence? Were there principles and a logic to the process? What were its variables and variations? Could it be managed or even made beneficial? Faced with these questions, the American commercial real estate industry inaugurated study of architectural obsolescence. Basic answers soon began to be formulated.

Obsolescence, it was surmised, came about as a result of changing technology, economics, and land use, in which the new would inevitably outperform and devalue the old. Obsolescence's basic axioms were that architectural function and worth were quantifiable and necessarily decreased over time. Different types of buildings, it was also theorized, obsolesced at different rates—hotels, for example, faster than banks, since the former were more vulnerable to quick changes in style and taste. As an antidote, experts counseled that careful management of a building's design and adaptability might defer obsolescence. But it was still best to plan for replacement. It was noted, too, that there were ways to benefit financially from obsolescence within the depreciation allowances of the recent U.S. corporate income tax code by writing off the building investment as rapidly as possible to decrease tax liability. By the early 1930s the American commercial real estate industry felt it understood obsolescence, even if the process was essentially unpredictable. No prophecy was certain; the factors were too many, too complex, and too contingent. Still, the fundamentals were settled, especially regarding tax benefits. So the American real estate industry lost interest in the issue and never looked carefully at it again.

But this was hardly the end of the story. In fact, it was just the beginning. Presumptions of architectural obsolescence and shortened building lives had entered American popular consciousness in the 1920s through dissemination of the real estate industry discourse on the subject. Soon afterward American urban planners began applying the concept of obsolescence to neighborhoods and cities. When planners used it, the term *obsolete* designated substandard housing, health, and especially economic performance in entire urban districts. After World War II whole neighborhoods were explicitly deemed obsolete and primed for renewal, not just in the United States but in Europe as well, including in communist countries. Multiple conceptions of architectural obsolescence encompassed single buildings and whole cities, in capitalist and socialist societies alike. By 1960 nuanced and varied concepts of obsolescence had become ubiquitous worldwide in architectural thinking, a dominant paradigm for understanding change in the built environment. "The annual model, the disposable container, the throwaway city have become the norms," observed the American preservationist James Marston Fitch, who was fighting fiercely against demolitions at this time.[6]

How did architects and others react to the rise of the obsolescence paradigm? That is this book's key question. Just as there were plural conceptions of obsolescence (commercial and urban, capitalist and socialist, American and European), so there were multiple architectures of obsolescence, that is, different ways that design might respond. Engagement with obsolescence underwrote a diversity of mid-century architectural strategies, especially in the 1960s. Open-plan interior flexibility accepted and absorbed the changefulness of obsolescence. Modular megastructures joined together long- and short-life components. Visionary architecture that lasted a short moment embraced the promise of obsolescence, its opportunity for new choices, and its liberation from the past and convention.

Other responses of the 1960s were less accepting of obsolescence's logic. All over the globe, concrete brutalist buildings reasserted traditional values of permanence and durability. In the developed world, proponents of historic preservation, adaptive reuse, and architectural postmodernism revalued seemingly obsolete objects, finding new beginnings where others saw only endings. Ecological design sought to safeguard rather than discard existing resources. All together, these counterstrategies to obsolescence might be gathered under the heading of *sustainability*, in that they valued conservation over expendability. Today sustainability, which arose from the struggles over obsolescence in the 1960s, stands as the dominant paradigm for conceptualizing and managing architectural change. Yet obsolescence persists, as evidenced, for example, by the rapid pace of renewal in contemporary Chinese cities.

*

As prevalent as the notion of obsolescence has been in architecture and urbanism during the past century, its history has not been traced until now. This book maps the invention and rise of the obsolescence paradigm in all its varieties and then explores in detail the multiple architectural responses to obsolescence.

But first, how is obsolescence different from other effects of time addressed by architecture? Obsolescence has a particular temporality that differs from those of historical memory (in which new buildings are designed to look like those of the past), natural mutability (in which structures naturally change or decay), procession through space (in which we are aware of the time it takes to move through buildings), or even what the architectural historian Marvin Trachtenberg recently dubbed "durational building," which takes into account the time needed to construct the building. In contrast to all of these, obsolescence instead is principally engaged with the temporality of use—and disuse—that goes beyond creators' intentions or individuals' experience of place.[7] How does a building change over time in use and value? This is a distinctive species of impermanence. Much has been written about the idea of impermanence in architecture in relation to portability and adaptability; decay, weathering, and warfare; and ephemerality and the unfinished.[8] But the kind of impermanence found in obsolescence is a process of devaluation imposed upon architecture that is not intentionally short-lived, unfinished, or lightweight. Before the twentieth century, buildings were subject to obsolescence, to be sure: Renaissance fortifications, for example, became outmoded owing to developments in siege technology. But not until the twentieth century did obsolescence come to be understood as a general condition of change in architecture and cities as a whole—a relentless, universal, impersonal process of devaluation and discard.

When people have written about obsolescence they don't generally consider its architectural aspects. What literature exists on the subject focuses mainly on postwar twentieth-century consumer society and its flood of cheap, expendable commodities, with related attention to waste as obsolescence's "shadow world," the remainder that haunts modernity, as sociologist John Scanlan has written.[9] But architecture is not typically included in these studies. Nor has obsolescence received much more than passing mention in architectural history.[10] Understanding obsolescence has been the subject of some mid-century American urban history. Studies of "blight" and "creative destruction"—the latter being the very essence of capitalism, in the economic historian Joseph Schumpeter's terminology—have deepened our understandings of cities' redevelopment.[11] "It was the concept of obsolescence that redevelopers wielded as a weapon to remake downtowns," explains the historian Alison Isenberg.[12] Thomas W. Hanchett produced a provocative essay linking tax depreciation rates to 1950s shopping center construction.[13] By the middle of the twentieth century, accelerated devaluation and replacement was believed to be, in Max Page's words, a "self-evident, unquestionable, and inevitable" process of metropolitan change.[14] Obsolescence was not merely an economic condition, it could also vivify cultural growth and change. The critic Marshall Berman's *All That Is Solid Melts into Air: The Experience of Modernity* uses New York City's redevelopment to frame analyses of literary and artistic responses to accelerated change. Berman concludes that the "struggle of radically opposed modernisms gave the life of the 1960s much of its coherence and excitement."[15] Yet obsolescence has a much wider and deeper ambit beyond 1960s New York. It is a worldwide phenomenon that has found various expressions across time and space. If we had to pick an epicenter, a better case could be made for Chicago than New York as the capital of obsolescence. The Windy City's 1920s demolitions encoded American building life-span numbers in tax rules and the popular imagination. It was the setting for seminal obsolescence research, for vivid architectural work by Buckminster Fuller and Ludwig Mies van der Rohe, and for pioneering preservationist protests in the late 1950s against obsolescence's depredations.

Chicago's intensive engagement with obsolescence reflected its freewheeling capitalist economic dynamic, where business set the pace for quick change in the built environment. Correspondingly, the study of obsolescence offers particularly rich insight into the relation between architecture and economics, for the concept of obsolescence arose from nineteenth-century accounting and business practice before entering twentieth-century architectural thinking and design. Obsolescence's emphasis on measurable performance and quantifiable value applies fundamentally economic thinking to the built environment. Obsolescence may thus be considered what the critic Fredric Jameson calls "mediations between the economic and aesthetic," a way of interlinking the two spheres. Jameson famously analyzed late twentieth-century postmodern space's embodiment of capitalist globalization, in the case of John Portman's design for the Los Angeles Bonaventure Hotel.[16] The consideration of obsolescence expands and fine-tunes Jameson's approach. Obsolescence is both a broader theme, encompassing more of twentieth-century architecture, and a more closely focused one, concentrating upon a specific economic dynamic of capitalism, namely its process of rapid supersession and discard—Schumpeter's idea of "creative destruction."

Obsolescence as a process is almost by definition fundamental to capitalism. In the basic progression of money turned into commodities for sale, turned into more money to make more commodities—the endless cycle of M-C-M'—the old must give way to the new, or the process of accumulation fatally seizes up. The problem is particularly acute for capital in the form of architecture, which is not so easily discarded as machinery or consumer goods.[17] The capitalist built environment is a dynamic site of accumulation, subject to ceaseless disinvestment and redevelopment. Yet attitudes toward the fate of the physical fabric have changed. Alternatives to demolition discover the profitability of conservation. In architectural M-C-M', C does not necessarily have to disappear for reinvestment to take place.

What, specifically, does looking at obsolescence teach about the historical relationship between capitalism and architecture? Manfredo Tafuri's 1970s landmark *Architecture and Utopia: Design and Capitalist Development* examined modern architecture's service to capitalism in crisis, in which the author saw architecture as providing images of urban order in the face of metropolitan chaos. Likewise, obsolescence can be seen as a concept that brings order to the built environment, making sense of it by giving a name and logic to the seemingly irrational process of capitalist disinvestment and reinvestment. In his book, Tafuri argues that modern architecture lost its value to capitalism, as a conceptual pathfinder, in the wake of the Great Depression, when government technocrats, not urban visionaries, took charge of rebalancing economy and society: "Architecture as ideology of the plan is swept away by the *reality of the plan*."[18] Yet the story of architecture's ideological usefulness to capitalism, managing change and crisis, did not end with the inception of centralized state economic planning. Rather, architecture's postwar engagement with obsolescence continued to work through problems of capitalist redevelopment, finding a multiplicity of design solutions, eventually including sustainability, to accompany capitalism's continued evolution.

Part of architecture's ideological work in capitalist society involves helping people acculturate to capitalism's unsettling demands. "All fixed, fast-frozen relations, with their train of venerable ideas and views, are swept away, all new ones become obsolete before they can ossify," wrote Karl Marx and Friedrich Engels in *The Communist Manifesto* (1848). "All that is solid melts into air, all that is holy is profaned."[19] In this famous characterization of capitalist modernity, the process of obsolescence, the new ceaselessly superseding the old, seems to permeate experience. The eminent historian Eric Hobsbawm has asked, "How is it, then, that humans and societies structured to resist dynamic development come to terms with a mode of production whose essence is endless and unpredictable dynamic development?"[20] Part of the answer lies in the work of architects in their struggle with obsolescence, finding creative ways to acknowledge and even reconcile that fundamental contradiction between constancy and change, which Hobsbawm identifies as central to the capitalist life world. Subtle solutions as well as perplexities were found in architects' designs, more than in their words, to accommodate radical change, yet maintain a continuous identity. Architecture and its history have lessons to teach about coming to terms with capitalism.

More broadly, obsolescence concerns not just economics but philosophy, feeling, and expression. How do we face up to ends? How manage the grief of loss? What architectural values exceed measure? To grapple with these questions requires looking beyond the economistic logic of obsolescence— measurable performance, competition, supersession, and expendability— which offers no deeper human meanings. Opponents of obsolescence in the 1960s pressed at these blindnesses of the paradigm. They sought to rehabilitate the obsolete, to redeem its waste and revalue what exists. Sustainability thus emerged from the contradictions of obsolescence. One worldview shaded into another, exploiting its tensions, solving its problems, yet not completely superseding it either. As a result, obsolescence continues alongside sustainability.

*

This book is structured to look first at the circumstances, mainly American, that created perceptions of obsolescence, and then in the middle and later chapters at the architectural responses to obsolescence around the world. Chapter 1 surveys how change was perceived in Western architectural culture prior to the twentieth century. Then the commonplace demolition of recent buildings impelled the invention around 1910 of the idea of architectural obsolescence, most coherently in the writing of the New York engineer Reginald Pelham Bolton. The notion of determinate building life spans was further analyzed and propagated in the 1920s by the Chicago-based National Association of Building Owners and Managers, led by its executive, Earle Shultz, with the aim of securing favorable tax treatment. By the early 1930s the idea of architectural obsolescence had come to be widely publicized in the American popular imagination, coincident with rising consumerism in the 1920s, which also viewed expendability as inherent to progress.

In the 1930s and 1940s, chapter 2 shows, American city planners expanded the idea of obsolescence to the urban and social realms. Boston's West End neighborhood was an exemplary site for the articulation of urban obsolescence ideology in the 1950s at the hands of planner Frederick J. Adams, using evaluation methods produced by the American Public Health Association. Variant ideas of urban obsolescence were deployed by communist planners and were also present in Britain, Japan, and elsewhere. While most prevalent in America, all these discourses and practices of obsolescence contributed to the general perception, by the late 1950s, that obsolescence had become the primary framework for understanding and managing architectural change, on a scale ranging from individual buildings to whole cities, governed by principles of measurable performance, competition, supersession, and expendability.

Ideas and design responses to obsolescence are this book's materials, not actual data on building life spans—in part because only in the rarest instances has such information been compiled (e.g., in Chicago in the 1920s and in London in the 1960s). The discourses of obsolescence have seldom been empirical; more usually they are rhetorical, repeating clichés and myth. "Nowadays almost every building becomes obsolete before it is ready to fall down," went one mantra, voiced by the British obsolescence researcher Peter Cowan.[21] Much of the discourse on architectural obsolescence was frankly fantastical. Despite the widespread use of fixed building life-span numbers, for example, buildings do not disappear on predictable schedules. Nor does progress constantly accelerate and supersede the old, as other tenets of the paradigm presumed. The historian of science and technology David Edgerton writes, "We have been told that we live with an 'ever-increasing rate of change,' yet there is good evidence that it is not always increasing."[22] Edgerton cites coal, bicycles, books, and battleships as old technologies that have continued alongside the new, contradicting the axioms of obsolescence. Yet the myths of obsolescence had great power among architects and others. Faith in obsolescence, in quick-pace change and wholesale expendability, influenced multiple approaches to producing and designing, representing, and managing the built environment in the mid-twentieth century. Belief in obsolescence spurred equally fierce architectural innovation and counterreaction across multiple contexts.

Chapter 3 shows that architects responded to obsolescence at first by denial, holding fast to traditional values of permanence and finish. Only after World War II did they acknowledge obsolescence's promise, its apparent inevitability and potential gifts. All invocations of flexibility at this time reflected awareness of obsolescence. The British architectural historian and critic Reyner Banham preached an "aesthetics of expendability."[23] "What we need is more obsolescence, not less," declared the American industrial designer George Nelson in a well-known article from 1956.[24] At the University of London, the architect Richard Llewelyn Davies organized extensive academic studies of obsolescence. Just as there had been numerous discourses on architectural obsolescence outside the discipline—in real estate, planning, and industrial design—so multiple outlooks also emerged within architecture. It was not in words, though, but in design that architects ultimately engaged most profoundly with obsolescence.

If the guiding modernist dictum of Louis Sullivan—"form ever follows function"—was to remain relevant in the age of obsolescence, the hard question arose: what happens to form when function changes?[25] The 1960s was the decade of the most intense confrontation with obsolescence, as chapter 4 shows. Architects of all stripes and nationalities sought to fix obsolescence in function and image through design. Some of those who engaged most fruitfully with obsolescence were architectural history's usual midcentury modernist heroes, like Banham. Ludwig Mies van der Rohe's Berlin National Gallery embodied the factory-shed solution to obsolescence, allowing great internal flexibility that was meant to ensure continued usefulness in a variety of metamorphing conditions. The American Louis Kahn's Salk Institute pioneered the interstitial system, which stacked one factory loft space atop an-

other. Megastructures, with plug-in capsules and long-life frames, often associated with the Japanese Metabolists, harmonized differential rates of change
and replacement. Experimental visions like the Britons Peter Cook's Plug-In
City and Cedric Price's Potteries Thinkbelt sought to image the process of
obsolescence in design itself. Equally important in the history of obsolescence were more eccentric figures from the 1910s through the 1960s, like the
American engineer and obsolescence theorist Bolton, the building manager
Shultz, the city planner Adams, the American architect Ezra Ehrenkrantz
(who devised flexible school-building systems), and the British architects
Richard Llewelyn Davies and John Weeks, who theorized and designed for
expendability. Llewelyn Davies and Weeks's immense Northwick Park Hospital allowed for growth and attrition in the overall form as it might obsolesce.
The various architectures of obsolescence ran the gamut from accepting that
obsolescence *would* happen to believing that obsolescence *should* happen,
embracing its liberation from history and habit.

But just as many others were horrified by obsolescence's implications,
its transience and waste, and sought obsolescence's reversal, as chapter 5 re-
counts. Increasing numbers of buildings ancient and recent were falling to
the wrecking ball, including landmarks of industrial civilization just a few
generations old, like New York's Pennsylvania Station and London's Euston
Station. Internationally, it seemed an age of "historicide," as Rudy Koshar, a
historian of Germany, has written.[26] In response, critiques of obsolescence
emerged in American culture, as in the writings of the urbanist Jane Jacobs
and the journalist Vance Packard. Similarly, architectural countertactics to
obsolescence gathered steam across the decade of the 1960s. Permanence was
the virtue of concrete brutalism like Paul Rudolph's buildings in New Haven,
Connecticut. Revived historic preservationism, adaptive reuse, and gentrification throughout the developed world, along with the stylistic postmodernism of Kahn and the Italian Aldo Rossi, all had in common the revaluation
of the architecturally obsolete. In the 1960s a contest of ideas and tactics was
thus waged between those who accepted obsolescence's logic and those who
did not. The sides were arguably balanced, equally intense and imaginative,
until the early 1970s, when the weight of internal contradiction in the obsolescence paradigm combined with historical circumstances to terminate the
dominance of that paradigm, highlighted by the 1973 oil crisis, which ended
an era of abundance and futuristic optimism.

Subsequently, obsolescence gave way to its ostensible opposite: the paradigm of sustainability, defined here as all those tactics intended to conserve
rather than expend existing resources, natural and manmade. Buildings like
the 2005 German Federal Environment Agency in Dessau feature energy

conservation, renewable materials, and sensitivity to historical context. Thus we see emerging from mid-century engagements and struggles with obsolescence a prehistory of sustainability. Yet even as sustainability ascends, the two paradigms coexist. Sustainability inherits obsolescence's obsession with measurable performance, now for energy efficiency. The obsolescence mentality persists, too, in Chinese cities' and American suburbs' demolitions, in the work of the architect Rem Koolhaas, and in other contemporary architecture. What we learn from obsolescence, in the book's concluding chapter, is not just the historical background of sustainability, but, more important, that paradigms of change are themselves changeable creations. The idea of architectural obsolescence was invented to solve problems of capitalist redevelopment. Sustainability in turn addressed the blindnesses of obsolescence. What then, we might ask, of sustainability itself? What difficulties does it leave unresolved? What might this worldview's contradictions be, the forces acting upon it, and sustainability's fate for the future?

The overarching presumption of this book is that architectural objects reflect history and theory, but also work against their grain. There are tensions and struggles in design and building that go beyond illustrating simple historical or theoretical conclusions. Instead, form points to deeper, more conflicted levels of thinking about obsolescence and change than is otherwise verbalized. Price's Potteries Thinkbelt project, for example, represents a profoundly ambivalent meditation upon obsolescence, welcoming its gifts yet recognizing its limits. The purpose of this book, ultimately, is to address the open questions of historians like Hobsbawm, asking how people "come to terms" with modernity—here by looking at the built environment. In other words, what can architectural history teach history that might not in other ways be learned?

Inventing Obsolescence

Before Obsolescence

Prior to the twentieth century, conceptions of architectural time in the Western tradition prioritized permanence and gradual change. The past persists visibly in centuries-old monuments, such as the ancient Roman arch of Septimius Severus, illustrated by the famed eighteenth-century printmaker Giovanni Battista Piranesi (fig. 1.1). Nature and history worked their slow decay, the same picture shows. At the same time, human reuse adapted gently to the past, as we can see in the middleground, where the ruined Temple of Saturn is repurposed to mundane ends. And new architecture hewed to deep time as well. The seventeenth-century baroque church of Santi Luca e Martina, in Piranesi's background, features classical columns and a symmetrical composition, which echo antecedents from centuries before. Ruinscapes like these parade architectural continuity. Time proceeds slowly. The past endures. Even when the nineteenth-century English architect John Soane famously had his monumental Bank of England building pictured in an exhibition watercolor as a ruin, with its roofs and walls sheared away, he did so not to promote the value of transience but to underscore his and the institution's dream of immortal, Romanlike grandeur.[1]

Aesthetically, classical design, the dominant Western tradition since the Renaissance, strove for ideals of fixity and permanence. The Italian theorist and architect Leon Battista Alberti, in his seminal fifteenth-century treatise, defined formal perfection as "that reasoned harmony of all parts within a body, so that nothing may be added, taken away, or altered, but for the worse."[2] According to Alberti's prescription, a building was beautiful only when it appeared unchangeable and finished in time. Architects followed this vision for centuries. Constructions of permanent stone, like Santi Luca e Martina in Piranesi's print, are embellished with centralizing motifs, like temple

FIGURE 1.1. *Remains of the Temple of Concord, Rome*, Giovanni Battista Piranesi, late eighteenth century. © The Metropolitan Museum of Art. Source: Art Resource, NY.

fronts or triumphal arches, and framed at their ends by projecting stonework or columns. These conventions of centralized, framed arrangement embodied an aesthetic of symmetry, hierarchy, and completion, implying an eternal order in their very composition.

Temporal continuity and stability was valued beyond the classical tradition. Mid-nineteenth-century British medieval revivalists esteemed historical "development"—"continued, gradual, tranquil" change, explains the architectural historian David Brownlee.[3] The Gothic revival philosopher and critic John Ruskin extolled the virtues of permanence. "Architecture is always destroyed causelessly," he proclaimed in *The Seven Lamps of Architecture* (1849).[4] Other nineteenth-century observers, who accepted modernity more readily than Ruskin, still wished for traditional architectural endurance. "We are not like our fathers, building for a short time only," the American critic Mariana Griswold van Rensselaer wrote in the *Century Illustrated Magazine* in 1884 about modern commercial New York. "Their structures have proved but temporary, while for ours a life may be predicted as long as the city's own."[5] Van Rensselaer acknowledged the explosive initial development of a modern city but wished to see it slowed down in maturity, returning to architectural longevity.

To be sure, impermanent structures had always existed. Festivals, pageants, coronations, and fairs throughout history stood just for a moment. Famously in Japan, the wood temples at Ise have for centuries been reconstructed identically every two decades. But Japanese material impermanence fixes permanent principles; each generation internalizes the religious and architectural lessons of the past. The buildings may be deliberately transient, but the goal is eternal values. Occasionally, a building type in history had to face up to modern-style obsolescence—rapid, continuous devaluation and supersession engendered by external factors of innovation and competition. Renaissance fortifications, for instance, had notably short lives owing to improved siege technology. But this was unusual. Durability was the norm in building and values. It was only in the twentieth century that obsolescence became understood as a universal condition of built environment change—permanent and ceaseless replacement of structures and habits, applicable to all building types, regardless of function, form, and cultural meaning.

Another historical antecedent of modern obsolescence might perhaps be found in past large-scale urban renewals caused by natural disaster, war, or politics. The famous mid-nineteenth-century redevelopment of Paris, led by Baron Georges-Eugène Haussmann, impelled the poet Charles Baudelaire at the time to lament, "Alas, a city's face changes faster than the heart of a mortal."[6] But no one at the time envisioned Haussmann's redevelopment to be endless, rebuilt again and again, ad infinitum. Only in the twentieth century did a pace of unending, ceaseless change in the built environment come to be understood as the new normal.

In nineteenth-century culture the possibility of permanently shortened building lives and cultural values was recognized but not yet accepted as a desired end. Nathaniel Hawthorne in *The House of the Seven Gables* (1851) has the youthful "wild reformer" Holgrave declare provocatively, "It were better that [our public edifices] should crumble to ruin, once in twenty years, or thereabouts, as a hint to the people to examine into and reform the institutions which they symbolize."[7] Fixed building lives would reflect and impel radical change in each generation, Holgrave prophesies. By novel's end, however, Holgrave has reversed himself. He admits that "the happy man inevitably confines himself within ancient limits." And he imagines that he himself would "build a house for *another* generation" (emphasis added), not a short-life building.[8]

The romantic ideal—invented in the nineteenth century and ultimately disavowed by Holgrave—that each age produces its own architecture was influentially voiced in France by Victor Hugo. "This Will Kill That," reads a famous chapter title in Hugo's novel *Notre-Dame de Paris* (1831), one technology superseding another. He hypothesized that the printed page had replaced architecture in the fifteenth century as "the principal register of mankind."[9] In Hugo's time, some contemporary structures did appear to satisfy the desire to express architecturally the industrial character of the age. But spectacles like the vast 1851 Crystal Palace glass-and-iron exhibition pavilion in London were not considered proper architecture precisely because of their evident impermanence, even as they housed and embodied the latest marvels of machine civilization. Other aspects of the nineteenth-century Industrial Revolution did indirectly inspire the idea of architectural obsolescence and can be credited more directly with increasing the pace and scope of creative destruction generally.

The quickening business world, especially the cutting-edge railroad industry, which involved ever more people, goods, information, equipment, and capital, took an increasingly "deep and vested interest in a rigorous definition and measurement of time," explains the geographer David Harvey.[10] From this arose a new class of professional experts, including engineers, economists, and accountants, who sought to master not just space and nature, but that key factor in industrial productivity and profit management, time itself. Time's effect on value was of particular concern to modern accounting. By 1840, historians report, "the concept of depreciation was widely known and the need to recognize wear and tear explicitly discussed in publications available to British and U.S. textile mill owners and managers."[11] Assessing financial losses due to material wear and tear allowed industrial enterprises to value more accurately their capital assets for taxation, financing, and sale purposes, taking into consideration the dimension of time. Depreciation thus represented "a rational tool for management facing diversity and complexity."[12]

Obsolescence emerged alongside depreciation as a financial risk management tool. Yet whereas depreciation resulted from slow, more or less predictable, physical wear and tear, obsolescence was different. It "was the loss which is constantly arising from the superseding of machines before they are worn out, by others of a new and better construction," said Karl Marx, citing an 1862 English source.[13] He called this process "moral depreciation," but the more common term was obsolescence, from the Latin *obsolescere* (to grow old). The term was used first in sixteenth-century England to describe human speech "growne out of use," then in the nineteenth century to describe an organism's loss of function, before also encompassing inanimate machinery's loss of utility. In this newly understood process an object's material integrity holds fast—it is still young and operates as intended—but its functional worth has declined. Something better has come along to devalue and supersede it, to make it expendable and disposable. By the early twentieth century the accounting distinction between depreciation and obsolescence was well established. "Depreciation in its narrow sense, is physical—obsolescence economic," defined the real estate taxation expert Joseph Hall in 1925.[14]

In architecture, application of the idea of physical depreciation emerged in late nineteenth-century America as a product of insurance and builders' estimates. The popular 1895 *Architect's and Builder's Pocket-Book*, by Frank E. Kidder, in its twelfth edition offered readers detailed life-span charts for a whole range of structures and materials, from frame to brick, dwelling to store, plaster to porches, with paint the shortest-lived component (five years) and sheathing the longest (fifty).[15] The basis for these charts was an 1879 fire underwriter's paper, which in turn was founded upon eighty-three builders' reports from eleven western states. But economic obsolescence distinct from physical depreciation did not factor into Kidder's life-span numbers, which were simply material wear-and-tear rates.

Before 1900 the notion of obsolescence was thus absent from architectural thought. Buildings were expected to last for generations, along with the values and habits they embodied. Structures might wear out, but that process was slow, regular, and remediable. Rapid urban change might occur at one moment, but redevelopment would not be ceaseless. No one imagined a state of permanent expendability in the built environment. That idea had yet to be invented.

New York and Reginald Bolton's Theory

The concept of obsolescence, in the English language, was first applied to the built environment around 1910. Lower Manhattan was the early epicenter for the invention of the idea of architectural obsolescence. In the 1890s New York property corporations began investing tens of millions of dollars in large new structures to accommodate the growing numbers of lawyers, accountants, bankers, managers, and other white-collar workers servicing the new corporate American economy. These tenants drove demand for the latest plumbing, heating, and elevator technologies. Their ever-changing desires had the effect of devaluing even the most recently constructed accommodations. The scope of the demand required new kinds of institutions and organizations to finance construction. Previously real estate investment dollars had been gathered from individuals or small groups. But big buildings needed big money. New joint-stock real estate investment companies collected capital through stock issues from scores of individual investors and came to combine under one roof construction, finance, and real estate, such as that of the United States Realty and Construction Company. Moreover, these novel development entities used the existing money markets to innovate mortgage bonds, in effect cutting mortgages up into hundred- or thousand-dollar increments to be publicly sold to even more investors, making it possible to raise for building amounts of money heretofore unimaginable. As the professional building manager Earle Shultz wrote of later, similar Chicago developments, "Replacement of old, obsolete buildings was made possible by the flood of money provided by the bond houses."[16]

The result of all this cash and credit flowing into commercial real estate was intense market volatility. Growth and speculation hastened demolition and new construction. A boom-and-bust environment developed, with demand rising even as oversupply threatened investment values. The risk of catastrophic loss was profound, and as a result real estate capitalists faced harrowing unpredictability. This was the context then for the unsettling demolition of the thirteen-year-old Gillender Building in 1910 and the disappearance of numerous other short-lived commercial structures across the United States. As the author Henry James wrote in 1907, shocked upon seeing New York after years away, "One story is good only till another is told, and sky-scrapers are the last word of economic ingenuity only till another word be written."[17]

In this seemingly chaotic economic and built environment there appeared between 1904 and 1915 several books by New York real estate experts whose purpose was to explain the dynamics of downtown commercial development to real estate investors, for whom buildings were "capital invested for the sake of income [. . .] essentially utilities," as the mortgage company executive Cecil Evers put it in 1914.[18] The most comprehensive of these treatises was *Building for Profit: Principles Governing the Economic Improvement of Real Estate*, which went through three editions between 1911 and 1922. This pioneering work was authored by Reginald Pelham Bolton (fig. 1.2). Born in London in 1856, Bolton had come to America as a young man. He trained in civil engineering and specialized in elevator technology, writing a pamphlet on the subject in 1908 as well as other articles on office building construction. Bolton lived in the Washington Heights neighborhood of northern Manhattan, where he also conducted extensive archaeological digs, joined the recently founded American Scenic and Historic Preservation Society, and wrote prolifically on New York's colonial architecture and life in such works as *Washington Heights, Manhattan: Its Eventful Past* (1924) and *Indian Paths in the Great Metropolis* (1924).[19] Immersed in new and old New York alike, Bolton endeavored in both areas to steer modernization while sustaining established values. In *Building for Profit* the particular problem was the "financial deterioration" or "financial decay" of commercial architecture—what Bolton called, just once in his book, "obsolescence."[20]

FIGURE 1.2. Reginald Pelham Bolton, author of *Building for Profit*, 1911.

Bolton listed his ideas about obsolescence's causes, all extrinsic to a structure's physical condition. Among these were "the influence of fashion, change of habit, competition, development of new territory and shifting of the centres of population and business, altering of lines of transit."[21] Each individually was unpredictable, its particulars uncertain, full of chance and risk, in a word (though not his), contingent. But Bolton was certain that obsolescence would happen in the built environment, produced by large-scale urban change. Population growth, social transformations, technical innovations, and market competition—all these would inevitably work together to degrade properties' utility and value, leading to early demolitions and ceaseless rebuilding. Modern cities, Bolton hypothesized, would predictably renew themselves, a "process of reconstruction occurring about three times in a century."[22] Bolton's theory synthesized chance and regularity; the conditions under which this renewal would vary, but it would happen.

Bolton also proposed a theory of differential obsolescence. In a table titled "Economic Existence of Buildings," he ranked structures of various functions by "life in years," based upon projected changes in use, technology, and fashion (fig. 1.3). The longest-lived, banks, received forty-four to fifty years, offices twenty-seven to thirty-three years, and hotels fifteen to eighteen years. The most short-lived "taxpayers" (twelve to fifteen years) were one- or two-story buildings, the income from which could cover the taxes on a site until more lucrative development could occur.[23] Bolton additionally tabulated physical durability, different than economic life, component by component—from sixty-six-year masonry down to seven-year paintwork—arriving at a hypothetical 48.36-year "mean life" for a steel-frame office building's total material fabric.[24] These were largely theoretical exercises to encourage building owners to consider property in terms of time, money, decreasing worth and, ultimately, reinvestment and replacement.

Building for Profit offered several general principles of architectural obsolescence. First, as the life tables illustrated, economic obsolescence ran faster than physical decay. Second, obsolescence was inexorable. Third, it was always accelerating, according to Bolton. "The useful or economic existence of all classes of buildings, in the rapid march of modern conditions, is constantly shortening."[25] Against obsolescence, Bolton advised investors to build moderately on cheap land, to avoid extravagant stylistic "novelty in construction," and to be sure to set aside funds against an asset's "limited life of usefulness."[26]

Bolton's theory of architectural obsolescence was conjecture, based on experience and guesswork rather than detailed research. But it had the ring of truth in turn-of-the-century New York, where buildings lasted for decades, not generations. Bolton's theory offered the consolation of explanation. In his formulation, obsolescence was not waste. Rather, it embodied the overall logic of markets, innovation, and urban dynamics, governed by principles of competition, measurable performance, supersession, and expendability.

TABLE D

ECONOMIC EXISTENCE OF BUILDINGS

Type of building	Life in years
"Taxpayer"	12–15
Hotels	15–18
Apartment-houses	18–21
Store buildings	21–25
Tenements and flats	25–27
Office and business buildings	27–33
Lofts and factories	33–37
Residences	37–44
Banks and institutions	44–50

FIGURE 1.3. Economic Existence of Buildings, from Bolton, *Building for Profit*, 1911.

Architecture's value was financially quantifiable. The functionally innovative new would outperform the inadaptable old, making it worthy only for demolition. Bolton's insights would be echoed in the following decades by a host of others in the real estate industry: appraisers, agents, insurers, and developers.[27] Yet the general historical significance of Bolton's theory would have been constrained, limited to a small circle of real estate people, but for the kind of contingent external forces identified as fundamental to obsolescence itself. In this case the unpredictable factor catalyzing obsolescence's import for history was the introduction of the U.S. federal corporate income tax, whose deductions included "a reasonable allowance for obsolescence."[28]

Taxation and Obsolescence

The U.S. federal income tax's enactment in 1909, enshrined in the Sixteenth Amendment of 1913, was the result of a long populist struggle to force American elites and business to bear more of the cost of national modernization, from social services and farm relief to public works and imperial expansion. The income tax was at first a largely symbolic victory, the initial rate a mere 1 percent. Even here, grudging corporations, flexing their political muscle in Congress, were allowed deductions from income for the expense of doing business. This mirrored how modern accounting practice figured net profit income. Among these deductible costs, the tax code recognized the devaluation of income-producing equipment, like buildings, due to physical wear and tear and also, significantly, economic obsolescence, which was recognized as a distinctive phenomenon. The fact that the U.S. tax code allowed obsolescence-related losses of value, "apart from physical depreciation," as the Supreme Court noted in 1932, reflected a particularly American business and political history.[29]

By the late nineteenth century large modern U.S. corporations had developed sophisticated accounting systems that factored losses of value due to obsolescence into the assessment of investments for insurance, sales, borrowing, and other purposes. These advanced accounting techniques were thus available to taken up under the 1910s tax code. In characteristic American fashion, businesses were able to use this concept to wring successfully from the state what amounted to public subsidies for private investment. Such was the case with the depreciation allowance in the tax code. Such allowances, as historians have noted, "originated in the desire of governments to encourage capital expenditure in manufacturing," and they were of great value to businesses to offset tax obligations.[30] The higher the rate of depreciation allowed, the less income would have to be reported; thus, less tax would be paid, and owners would keep more of their money. In further deference to business, the U.S. tax bureaucracy did not itself impose standardized deductions. Rather, rates were left open for negotiation between government and industry leaders, sector by sector. Businesses therefore had an obvious interest in establishing the highest depreciation rates plausible. Allowing industry to argue for and prove the most beneficial deduction rates was to have important consequences for dissemination of the idea of architectural obsolescence.

Shortly after the corporate income tax's introduction, America entered World War I. To cover the war's unanticipated costs, tax rates soared, first to 6 percent in 1917, then to 12 percent a year later. Now the corporate income tax was more than symbolic. It was economically real and even onerous for businesses, who sought all the more to maximize deductions for depreciation and obsolescence. But what would those allowances be? There were no national rules and standards. Confusion and uncertainty reigned. Everything was case by case, with no predictability or certainty, left to the varying judgment of local representatives of the federal tax agency. Over how many years could a corporation recoup the loss of an asset? In the eyes of the state, what was a building's legal "lifetime"? These were open questions from the late 1910s on, impelling expanded attention to the issue of architectural obsolescence.

Chicago and NABOM's Analyses

Into the breach stepped the Chicago-based National Association of Building Owners and Managers (NABOM), invited by the Commissioner of Internal Revenue in 1917 to suggest "reasonable rates" of deduction.[31] Through the 1920s and into the early 1930s NABOM closely studied architectural obsolescence. It surveyed commercial building owners nationwide about local obsolescence conditions. It sponsored in-depth engineering analyses of recent structures undergoing demolition, which NABOM called building "autopsies." And it compiled building life-span data into persuasive statistics for submission to federal tax authorities. The result of all these efforts was the broad dissemination of the idea of architectural obsolescence and the concept's integration into American society.

NABOM had been established in 1907 as a confederation of local chapters that represented large downtown office building owners and managers "whose pocketbook was being stepped on," in the words of Earle Shultz, an Association executive.[32] NABOM lobbied governments, guided labor relations, and, above all, promoted exchange and concord among its membership in the interest of "a sound and orderly rental market," according to Shultz.[33] Like many national trade organizations formed in this period, NABOM's purpose in promoting industry cooperation was to minimize risk in a volatile economic environment—to mitigate "periods of feast and famine," as the National Association of Real Estate Boards put it.[34]

From its inception NABOM was preoccupied with the risks of obsolescence. At the Association's 1913 national convention, Reginald Bolton himself came to speak and warned, "Many of the skyscrapers in New York are monuments of uselessness."[35] A 1914–15 special NABOM Committee on Depreciation and Obsolescence concluded that "many a physically sound building will be wrecked, and at great expense, before it is thirty years old."[36] In the face of wartime tax increases, and in response to the 1917 invitation of tax authorities to suggest set rates, NABOM gathered expert opinion into the 1919 volume *Valuation and Depreciations of City Buildings*, which began with the tax authorities' letter of solicitation and then quoted at length from accountancy textbooks, judicial opinions, and Bolton's *Building for Profit*, to represent the range of thought, if not hard facts, on the subject.

The Association's own sponsored research into obsolescence commenced shortly thereafter, spearheaded by Shultz (fig. 1.4). Shultz had been born in 1884 and attended Ottawa University in rural Kansas, originally established by Baptists to school the local Indians. After college Schultz ventured to Chicago, where in 1905 he settled into a career in the rising field of property management. By 1914 he was in charge of the prominent Commonwealth Edison headquarters building, home also to NABOM's national offices, on La Salle Street in Chicago's downtown business Loop district. Clearly ambitious, Shultz aspired to establish his and his field's professional standing. For NABOM, he first conducted research on cost cutting and cleaning efficiencies, discovering, for example, that emptying a wastebasket took on average 0.081 minutes.[37] Shultz was applying to building management the scientific management techniques of Frederick Winslow Taylor, quantifying performance to maximize profit and burnishing Shultz's own professional credentials.

Shultz studied obsolescence in a similarly empirical and precise manner. His national survey for NABOM of 155 office buildings from forty-three American cities resulted in the 1922 report *The Effect of Obsolescence on the Useful and Profitable Life of Office Buildings*, published as a twenty-page supplement to the Association's *Bulletin*. Shultz's purpose was to educate NABOM's membership and to "obtain conclusive facts upon which to establish a claim for obsolescence" from the government.[38] By the time of Shultz's 1922 report, obsolescence—defined by Shultz as "a falling off in the value or usefulness of a thing from causes outside of the thing itself"—was now standard terminology, thanks to the tax code.[39]

The Effect of Obsolescence identified factors of obsolescence that were

FIGURE 1.4. Earle Shultz, executive of the National Association of Building Owners and Managers.

similar to those cited by Bolton: changes in fashion and district character, new buildings with better services, neighbors blocking light and air. Shultz attended as well to the architectural aspects of obsolescence. He alleged that wastefully wide corridors, inflexible office dimensions, and insufficient retail space rendered investments "entirely obsolete." Symbolic "publicity value" could also be "immediately destroyed" by the work of more prominent competitors.[40] Shultz's research made him skeptical, too, of emerging design antidotes to obsolescence, such as movable office partitions, which he judged a poor investment: costly at the outset and expensive to utilize. Ultimately, Shultz asserted, twenty-eight years was "the useful and profitable life of an office building during which it is earning an adequate return on the investment." Thereafter "it is only a question of time when it will have to be torn down."[41] The best that could be done was to build "on the edge of the present business center in the path of future growth," and, above all, to "set up and invest a fund sufficient to replace our buildings in thirty years."[42] *The Effect of Obsolescence* studied architectural obsolescence empirically, offered modest recommendations for amelioration, and set the stage for further analysis.

Shultz and NABOM followed up *The Effect of Obsolescence* with so-called

OFFICE BUILDING OBSOLESCENCE

A Study of the W. C. T. U. Temple, Chicago

OPENED
MAY 1st
1892

WRECKED
AUGUST 1st
1926

A Special Report of

THE NATIONAL ASSOCIATION OF BUILDING OWNERS AND MANAGERS

FIGURE 1.5. Women's Christian Temperance Union Building, Chicago, constructed 1892, demolished 1926.

autopsies of specific lost Chicago landmarks to detail further the causes of obsolescence. The buildings studied were the recently demolished Women's Christian Temperance Union (WCTU) Building, the Marshall Field Wholesale Store (designed by Henry Hobson Richardson), and the pioneering skyscraper Tacoma Building. A common factor, engineers commissioned by Shultz discovered, was thick load-bearing walls, like those supporting the thirteen-story WCTU building (fig. 1.5). This structure, next door to Shultz's and the Association's own offices, was completed in 1892 and demolished in 1926. The WCTU tower's heavy base and formidable piers expressed durability. But its bulk reduced rentable interior space and decreased window areas, diminishing its desirability to tenants and hence the owner's income. The structure's signature high-pitched roof proved equally uneconomical. It accommodated only cramped, skylit aeries, which "were rented to architects who could make use of the overhead light," the autopsy noted.[43] Altogether, inferior rental space was costing the building's owner $53,383 per year, calculated NABOM.

Similarly, the landmark Marshall Field Wholesale Store possessed a massive granite-faced base for an admired look of permanence (fig. 1.6). But the monumental design rested on primitive foundations unable to handle heavy loads, which resulted in sloping floors that resembled the "gentle hills and valleys of Nebraska," as the NABOM investigator noted.[44] Moreover, the first floor, six feet above sidewalk level, proved unadaptable for retail use once wholesale trading moved out of the district. "The Marshall Field Wholesale building was obsolete probably ten years after it was completed," concluded NABOM. Finished in 1886, it was demolished in 1930. The site was left a parking lot for years after, generating enough income to cover taxes while awaiting more profitable redevelopment.

Even in a more modern structure, like the innovative partial steel-frame Tacoma Building of 1889 by the leading Chicago architects Holabird and Roche, poor planning could accelerate obsolescence, NABOM discovered. The interior load-bearing walls, which supplemented the metal frame, impeded "effective sub-division of floor space," accused NABOM's 1929 autopsy, costing $579 in unrealized annual income per floor (fig. 1.7).[45] Elevator equipment was "probably the most notable instance of obsolescence in the Tacoma

FIGURE 1.6. Marshall Field Wholesale Store, Chicago, constructed 1886, demolished 1930.

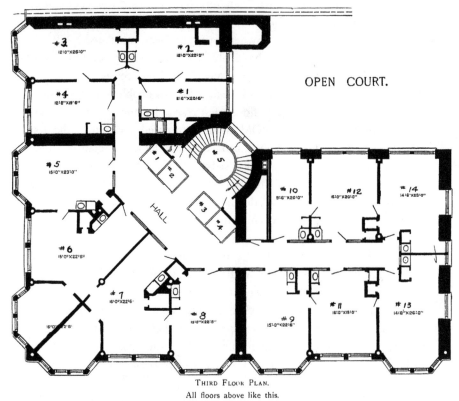

THIRD FLOOR PLAN.
All floors above like this.

FIG. 5—THIRD FLOOR PLAN. ALL FLOORS ABOVE LIKE THIS. NOTE ROOM SIZES AND LAYOUT

FIGURE 1.7. Tacoma Building, Chicago, third floor plan, constructed 1889, demolished 1929.

Building."[46] Small, slow, old-fashioned, open-top cabs dropped grease upon unsuspecting passengers but were too expensive to replace. "Although the building was earning an adequate return on the investment," explained the building's manager to NABOM, "the return figuring present market values of the property was very small."[47] Ultimately the Tacoma Building's accumulated obsolescence proved too much for its owner, the University of Chicago. The financially underperforming twelve-story landmark, antiquated at age thirty, was sold to a developer and demolished in 1929. Soon afterward it was replaced by a forty-eight-story tower, which could more lucratively exploit the site in its proprietors' interests.

NABOM's decade of empirical obsolescence research substantiated Bolton's earlier hypotheses. Even the most up-to-date monument, the Association warned, "may be so affected by obsolescence within a period of thirty-five years that its demolition becomes an economic necessity."[48] The report continued: "It is quite likely that the design of 1925 will be just as obsolete in 1960, when the modern buildings have reached the venerable age of thirty-five years."[49] NABOM was educating its membership about obsolescence. But it had not yet achieved its ultimate goal of a standard maximum federal tax deduction.

In 1927 the Department of the Treasury invited further NABOM data. An Association delegation, including Shultz, met Treasury officials in late 1930 to lay out the evidence. NABOM sensed its moment. Its lawyer reported, "I have been engaged in Obsolescence matters some part of at least every other day, and I have written (or received) almost one thousand letters."[50] NABOM's presentation to Treasury featured data from its home base of Chicago. According to a NABOM chart, fourteen of the major Loop structures demolished between 1902 and 1932 were only thirty-two years old on average (fig. 1.8). Another NABOM table showed that the mean age of all Chicago office buildings extant between 1885 and 1930 was never more than twenty years—and had been declining to less than eighteen years since 1926 (fig. 1.9). These statistics formed the basis of NABOM's request for formal "recognition of the fact that 30 years was the average expectancy of life of a new building."[51]

But Chicago was an anomaly, even an extreme. Nowhere else in America, perhaps the world, experienced greater architectural change after World War I than NABOM's home territory. A booming economy, easy credit, and

CHART 1.
CHICAGO OFFICE BUILDINGS DEMOLISHED TO MAKE WAY FOR NEW STRUCTURES

Building	Stories	Erected	Wrecked	Age
Montauk	9	1883	1902	19
Continental Bank	10	1884	1912	28
Rand-McNally	10	1884	1912	28
*Home Insurance	11	1885	1931	46
Board of Trade	10	1885	1928	42
Royal Insurance	15	1885	1920	35
Mallers	12	1886	1920	34
Tacoma	14	1888	1929	41
Chamber of Commerce	13	1890	1928	38
Champlain	15	1894	1915	21
Women's Temple	12	1892	1926	34
Willoughby	8	1892	1928	36
Trude	14	1897	1912	15
*Standard Trust	12	1900	1932	32
			(Total.....449)	
			(Average... 32)	

*Definitely scheduled to be torn down.
The first 6 buildings on this list represent 6 of the 8 buildings existing in 1885.

FIGURE 1.8. Chicago office buildings demolished, National Association of Building Owners and Managers, 1930.

CHART 2.
AVERAGE LIFE OF BUILDINGS
EXISTING EACH YEAR

Year	No. of Bldgs.	Years Av. Life
1885	8	1 1/2
1886	11	2
1887	11	3
1888	13	3 4/7
1889	14	4 3/7
1890	16	4 3/4
1891	19	5
1892	26	4 2/3
1893	33	4 2/3
1894	38	5
1895	42	5 4/7
1896	45	6 1/4
1897	48	6 5/6
1898	49	7 3/4
1899	49	8 3/4
1900	50	9 1/2
1901	50	10 1/2
1902	53	10 3/5
1903	54	11 2/5
1904	57	11 4/5
1905	60	12 1/6
1906	66	12 1/6
1907	70	12 4/7
1908	72	13 2/9
1909	72	14 2/9
1910	78	14 1/6
1911	84	14 2/7
1912	87	14
1913	94	13 7/8
1914	100	14
1915	102	14 2/3
1916	107	15
1917	108	15 4/5
1918	109	16 2/3
1919	110	17 1/2
1920	111	17 3/4
1921	111	18 3/4
1922	115	19 1/4
1923	124	19
1924	131	19
1925	135	19 1/2
1926	141	19 4/7
1927	159	18 1/3
1928	167	18 1/8
1929	178	17 1/2
1930	186	17 5/6

It took 16 years (1901) for the average life of existing buildings to reach 10 years; 31 years (1916) to reach an average of 15 years; 37 years (1922) to reach 19 years; and in the entire 45 years, the maximum average age has not reached 20 years.

FIGURE 1.9. Average life of Chicago buildings, National Association of Building Owners and Managers, 1930.

the 1923 loosening, at developers' instigation, of building height restrictions turned Chicago's low-rise, turn-of-the-century office blocks into seriously devalued assets. Previously these could reach no higher than 264 feet. Now they could be replaced by larger and more profitable structures, with towers 600 feet and higher. Between 1923 and 1930, amidst the din of wrecking balls, Loop office space nearly doubled from 18.5 million to 30 million square feet.[52] "The heart wood of the organic Chicago is constantly replacing old tissues with new ones," wrote the famed Chicago land economist Homer Hoyt in 1933.[53] The city was arguably the world capital of architectural obsolescence at this time, a crucible of expendability and its analysis, whose urban dynamism drew close attention not just from NABOM. For example, the renowned Chicago School of sociologists in 1925 named obsolescence as a factor catalyzing neighborhood transformations.[54] Northwestern University was the site of significant academic research on the subject as well.[55] Moreover, the city was "headquarters to most of the nation's real estate, city planning and housing organization" (like NABOM), the historian Jennifer Light reports.[56] Their discourse was naturally shaped by the extreme local conditions experienced as normal. In this context, Shultz's NABOM investigations were one Chicago endeavor among many to try to comprehend and manage change in the urban built environment, and they likely influenced his fellow Chicagoans.

The political achievement of the NABOM studies was to establish Chicago's extreme obsolescence numbers as a national norm for tax purposes. In 1931 the building owners just about got their wish for thirty-year life spans. New federal tax tables of combined depreciation and obsolescence allowances categorized commercial structures by modes of construction: the shortest life of twenty years for wooden mills and warehouses; the longest of fifty years for fireproof homes and stores. Roughly in the middle came office buildings: forty years if fireproof, twenty-five if wooden.[57] NABOM had gained its long-sought objective. Government publications established obsolescence as a norm for building devaluation: inevitable, universal, and predictable. NABOM officials took proud credit for suggesting "almost verbatim" obsolescence's causes in the new guidelines: "the erection of newer buildings of radically different styles, involving greater efficiency of layout," and so on.[58]

This was also the end of NABOM's study of obsolescence. No more reports on obsolescence appeared after the early 1930s. The political need was gone once the rules were settled, and with it organizational support for research evaporated. This is typical of the history of obsolescence. Politics plus institutional support equal fresh knowledge. Otherwise nothing new happens in the discourse. Old ideas and clichés merely repeat. Not until the 1960s in

Britain would a similar level of obsolescence research be achieved, in very different political and institutional contexts.

Obsolescence Culture and Contradiction

The broader cultural achievement of the downtown real estate industry discourse was to help establish the idea of architectural obsolescence in the American imagination. While the discourse strongly reflected Shultz's Chicago, its impact was national. In 1922 NABOM distributed 2700 copies of Shultz's *The Effect of Obsolescence* report to Association members nationwide as well as to unaffiliated bankers, public officials, and media as part of a "campaign of education, as NABOM called it."[59] Far beyond Chicago—from Florida to California to Alabama to South Dakota—newspapers in large and small towns alike ran advice columns for building owners based upon NABOM publicity, which explained architectural obsolescence and its tax implications.[60]

Subsequently, the Association's Chicago building autopsies and life-span statistics were also publicized in the popular and professional presses. "Thirty Years Average Life Span of Modern Skyscrapers," trumpeted a 1931 *New York Times* headline. That same year the journal *Architect and Engineer* declared the "Obsolescence of Modern Skyscrapers." "An Object Lesson in Obsolescence," instructed the magazine *Literary Digest* two years earlier. *Collier's* and the *New Republic* also ran articles on the topic, the latter in 1930 entitled "Waste—The Future of Prosperity."[61] A 1935 real estate appraisal bibliography listed some 125 entries on the subject in lay and expert journals.[62] Other building industry sectors, from steelmakers to elevator manufacturers, produced their own commentaries based upon NABOM's insights, further propagating the idea of architectural obsolescence, and fixed particularly upon the figure of the determinate building life-span number.[63] The underlying politics of the tax code remained largely unobserved by the new adherents to the ideas of architectural obsolescence.

In its broader dissemination, obsolescence also came to be seen as transcending commercial real estate. The *New York Times* quoted a banker's claim in 1931 that "modern needs, he says, have reduced average life of a *home* today to thirty years" (emphasis added).[64] The National Association of Real Estate Boards proposed fifty-year lives for fireproof single-family residences. This group in fact commissioned its own detailed 1925 obsolescence study inspired by NABOM analyses. "Blessed word," wrote the author of the Realtors' report, the economist W. C. Clark, "which the income tax has forced upon our acquaintance and which we delight to roll upon our tongues because of its euphonious length and the impression of technical competence which its free use seems to convey."[65]

The professional real estate discourse on architectural obsolescence took hold of the popular imagination because it resonated with a public awareness across America of seemingly epidemic building demolitions. As Clark suggested, the precision, quantifications, and set life-span numbers of the obsolescence discourse offered reassurance in a world of risk and uncertainty. The idea of architectural obsolescence composed order out of chaos. Its invention rationalized capitalist redevelopment when the pace of change appeared unprecedented. So many cities possessed major structures young in years but razed for reasons of obsolescence, from Atlanta's thirty-year-old Fulton County Courthouse, demolished in 1911, to Detroit's fifteen-year-old Hotel Pontchartrain, wrecked in the early 1920s.[66] First speculation, then the Depression in the 1930s further hastened demolition. In boom times, promise of profit from newer buildings fueled feverish redevelopment. Later, in the crisis years, difficulty in paying property taxes in the absence of sufficient rental income led owners to abandon or demolish their wasted assets. By 1937, it was estimated, a quarter of downtown Detroit consisted of vacant lots. Philadelphia witnessed hundreds of demolitions annually throughout the 1930s.[67] A 1936 study found 42 percent of downtown Chicago to be distressed: vacant, razed, or foreclosed buildings, often replaced by parking lots awaiting redevelopment.[68]

The process from construction to demolition now spanned less than a generation, no longer centuries. The architect Peter B. Wight of New York and Chicago told the historian Thomas Tallmadge in the mid-1920s "that he had lived to see every one of his buildings destroyed to make way for a great construction."[69] Louis Sullivan, another famed Chicago architect, reportedly said, "If you live long enough, you'll see all your buildings destroyed."[70] This was the "golden age of the house wrecker," reported *Collier's* in 1929, quoting President Herbert Hoover, who claimed that "of all the buildings which stood in this country at the turn of the century at least half have been torn down. [. . .] And many architects believe that in another fifteen years the remaining half, with a few notable exceptions, will have been razed to the ground."[71] The *New Yorker* eulogized the demolition man Jacob Volk as the "greatest wrecker of all time," responsible for the Gillender and thousands of other jobs: "Jake knows that everything that goes up comes down."[72]

Obsolescence came to appear ceaseless to the American popular imagination, short building life spans inevitable. "We are demolishing the cities of yesterday and putting up the cities of tomorrow," pronounced *Collier's* in 1929. "After that we will proceed, I dare say, to take them down to make way for something newer and better."[73] Later, in the depths of the Depression, obsolescence appeared to some a means of salvation. The architect Knud Lönberg-Holm promoted "time-zoning" buildings to spur reconstruction and economic recovery. By this he meant establishing state-regulated limits to building life spans, in effect socializing the built environment's production and pace of replacement. Similarly, the New York real estate broker Bernard London published a 1933 pamphlet entitled *Ending the Depression through Planned Obsolescence*, calling on government "to assign a lease of life to shoes and homes and machines. [. . .] New products would constantly be pouring forth from the factories and marketplaces, to take the place of the obsolete, and the wheels of industry would be kept going and employment regularized and assured for the masses."[74]

This welcoming of innovation and replacement undergirded the acceptance of architectural obsolescence. Popular notions on the theme coincided with concurrent ideas about consumer goods' "progressive obsolescence," which were trumpeted by the efficiency expert Christine Frederick, author of the popular *Selling Mrs. Consumer* (1929). Progressive obsolescence meant "a readiness to 'scrap' or lay aside an article before its natural life of usefulness is completed, in order to make way for the newer and better thing," Frederick explained.[75] As industrial expansion fueled middle-class incomes, advertisers and retailers offered an expanded array of consumer goods to newly prosperous families. The 1920s marked a turning point in American consumer culture. Firms competed for market share by offering the newest, best-performing, and most enticing models. Obsolescence was a mainspring for individual consumer desire and general economic development. Habits of sustained use, of keeping and maintaining an object as long as possible, were superseded by forces of expendability and convenience, novelty, prosperity, and marketing. Famously, General Motors in the mid-1920s, in imitation of the fashion industry, conceived of a regular triennial model change for its products, to contrast with Ford's unaltered Model T, both exploiting and stoking boredom with Ford's monotony. The vice president of GM, Charles F. Kettering, even addressed the 1927 NABOM annual convention in Detroit on their great subject of mutual interest—obsolescence: "We, the men interested in research, are never so happy as when we are creating obsolescence."[76]

In this milieu of consumer-driven economic growth, architectural obsolescence appeared partnered with progress. President Hoover, upon the occasion of the 1931 opening of the new Waldorf-Astoria Hotel in New York, opined, "I have faith that in another fifty years, the growth of America in wealth, science and art will necessitate the institution's moving again to an even finer and more magnificent place and equipment."[77] Obsolescence was coming to be seen as quintessentially American. W. C. Clark, in his 1925 report for the National Association of Real Estate Boards, identified the "chief causes" of obsolescence in architecture, industry, and consumption as "those broad economic and social changes which are due to the dynamic nature of our American civilization and which are, therefore, largely or wholly beyond the control of the individual."[78]

The idea of built-environment obsolescence was in many ways an analog in architecture to the Austrian economist Joseph Schumpeter's famous 1942 definition of capitalism as "Creative Destruction," a "perennial gale" of innovation and supersession, which Schumpeter derived from American experience.[79] Schumpeter had studied the development of modern American heavy industry to produce his theory, in which entrepreneurial experimentation destabilized existing modes of production, producing capitalism's continual self-renewal: new technologies, companies, and sectors constantly replacing the old. But Schumpeter may just as well have been describing the visible churning of the American built environment, as he would have observed it firsthand. Schumpeter initially encountered New York in 1912, stayed in Boston in 1927, and in 1932 settled permanently to work at Harvard University, where he penned his account of capitalism in flux. Schumpeter's experience of American architectural obsolescence may have influenced his famous doctrine of creative destruction. In any event, the two related paradigms— economic and architectural—mirrored each other in the United States between the wars. Architectural obsolescence had thus come to be understood as impersonal, a mechanistic creative destruction. In this, it differed from traditional processes of urban change, so often identified with a powerful personage or policy—for example, Baron Haussmann's remaking of nineteenth-century Paris. Rather, modern obsolescence appeared to function abstractly and collectively, out of the disembodied play of markets, competition, and innovation—"largely or wholly beyond the control of the individual," as Clark wrote. Economic forces in the obsolescence paradigm transcended politics, subjective interest, and the role of the state.

Architectural obsolescence was rhetorically naturalized as well, in a way that appeared to humanize obsolescence while reinforcing its apparent impersonality. Bolton used an anthropomorphic metaphor for structures that were "neglected in favor of younger rivals, as the still vigorous man or woman similarly circumstanced."[80] It appeared that aging and devaluation necessarily ran hand in hand, "as certain and ever-present as the forces of nature."[81] Wondered NABOM's Shultz, "The county provides a home for poor and aged human beings, but what shall we do with the obsolete and unprofitable office building?"[82] The effect of these naturalizing metaphors, though tied to the human aging process, was to further distance obsolescence from actual human agency. Bolton and Shultz's language makes obsolescence appear to be an inevitable and incontrovertible law of development and change—something that just happens to buildings—rather than the result of specific business practices and historical actors.

By 1930 the real estate men had been studying obsolescence's implications for more than a decade. They had formulated what they saw to be its principles and mechanisms. But they also understood, more subtly, its ambiguities and contradictions. They knew full well, for example, that the strict and concrete obsolescence life-span numbers were actually "guesswork," as George Mortimer, president of New York's Equitable Office Building Corporation, wrote in 1917.[83] Warned the real estate assessor Albert Noonan in 1936, "To use standardized tables for the measurement of obsolescence [. . .] is like putting your faith in the oracles of Delphi." Or, as Clark put it, "The experience of the past may not be the experience of the future."[84] Fixed life-span numbers, moreover, contradicted the intangibility and indeterminacy of obsolescence, which was rooted in contingent, abstract devaluation and not predictable, physical mortality.

Contradiction existed, too, between the finite building life-span numbers, propagated in the popular discourse of obsolescence, and the antidotes for obsolescence offered professionally to building owners and managers. Building lives could be extended. As Shultz later conceded, "With the development of buildings with more efficient layouts, it was finally realized that useful life, if they were properly maintained, could be at least 50 to 75 years."[85] Such admissions that rapid obsolescence was not actually inevitable, that it could be mitigated, could hardly be publicized by the real estate industry, much less reported to fiscal authorities, without compromising the favorable tax tables that happily enriched building owners. The original short building life-span numbers remained uncorrected.

Also obscured in the popular discourse on architectural obsolescence and its seemingly objective life-span numbers was the process's essential subjectivity. Devaluation could be as much a matter of fickle fashion as of cold financial calculation. "The market reaction toward outmoded structures is analogous to the feminine reaction to fashion," wrote the real estate expert John Burton in 1933.[86] The building-cycle economist Clarence Long in 1940 called this "the psychological life of a building."[87] In other words, how people *felt* about architecture impacted its worth. Tastes in design could change: from traditional to modern, for example, then back again. NABOM's rationalistic approach acknowledged but marginalized these factors of emotion, which were antithetic to the Association's hardheaded, functionalist outlook focused upon matters of technical performance, such as elevator technology and interior adaptability. The dominant discourse on architectural obsolescence, derived from the real estate industry, could neither measure nor value feelings about buildings: were they considered beautiful or ugly, were there cherished associated memories that could not be monetized?

Journalists and headline writers had reduced obsolescence's complications and ambiguities to the eye-catching figure of the building life-span number. The round integers that newspaper and magazines trumpeted endowed modernity with regularity and repetition, a permanent order amidst ceaseless change. But the calculations were imaginary, as the real estate men knew. Buildings don't magically disappear at thirty or forty years of age, as the popular press implied. Their fates are contingent, not biological nor determinate. The abstract tax-accounting practice of building life spans, whose expediency those in the real estate business understood, had in the public mind become something else, a seemingly hard fact that resolved modern life's complex changefulness into the single mythic figure of the building life-span number.

Some of these contradictions of obsolescence discourse were evident at the time. The *Journal of the American Institute of Architects* challenged the narrow economism of Shultz's 1922 obsolescence study: "But what the circular does not consider is the Social Consequences of all this unplanned growth, its frightful waste [. . .] its blind pursuit of individual benefits at the sake of social welfare."[88] A decade later, with the idea of architectural obsolescence ever more rooted in American life, another journal article of 1932, boldly titled "Some Fallacies of Obsolescence," argued that obsolescence was "a social phenomenon" and therefore "not amenable to physical nor to mathematical laws."[89] Its author, Eugene Church, accurately noted that NABOM's short building life-span numbers were generalized from extreme cases, could be mitigated by proper maintenance, and, moreover, represented the "claims of interested groups."[90] "If [obsolescence] is to be accepted as final," Church concluded rhetorically, "why not build cheap structures designed for a physical life of thirty or forty years?"[91] Or, as the English novelist Aldous Huxley, also in 1932, sardonically intoned in his well-known satire of compelled consumption, the dystopian *Brave New World*, "Ending is better than mending, ending is better than mending."[92]

Notwithstanding these contradictions, problems, and critiques, the paradigm of architectural obsolescence took hold in business and popular cultures arguably because it addressed fundamental issues of capitalism. As a worldview that offered a rationale for seemingly chaotic change, obsolescence solved certain key problems of capitalist development. The basic economic mechanism of capitalism is investing money to make and sell commodities, to make more money so as to invest in more commodities to make more money, to invest, to sell, to make more money, and so on and so on without end. Capitalism's characteristic restlessness and disequilibrium—its "economy of change," as the cultural theorist Evan Watkins puts it[93]—requires that commodities be exhausted of function or value, without which there are no new opportunities for reinvestment. The particular economic problem of capitalist property markets is managing the devaluation and replacement of a more or less permanent product. The geographer David Harvey calls this capitalism's "knife-edge path between preserving the exchange values of past capital investments in the built environment and destroying the value of these investments in order to open up fresh room for accumulation."[94]

New York investors circa 1910 knew instinctively what to do. They demolished without remorse the Gillender Building and other short-lived properties. But the process had no articulated logic until Bolton theorized it. Then, in the wake of new tax circumstances, Shultz and NABOM substantiated the idea empirically and publicized it broadly. Real estate businessmen had invented the idea of architectural obsolescence, giving the process a logic and a name. But beyond its inventors' intentions, the real estate discourse on architectural obsolescence became from the mid-1920s a more general paradigm for understanding change in the built environment. Obsolescence answered not just to the economic but also the cultural contradictions of capitalism, helping people "come to terms," in the historian Eric Hobsbawm's words, with the tension between, on the one hand, the human desire for constancy and, on the other, capitalism's "endless and unpredictable dynamic development."[95] Obsolescence answered a need for explanation amidst changeful times. It rendered disconcerting demolitions and devaluations as logical, beneficent, profitable, even progressive forces, and so softened the loss of permanence normally associated with architecture and society.

In the popular discourse on architectural obsolescence, the figure of the short building life span became an article of faith, a simplified avatar for the whole of obsolescence's complexities. This is consistent with how human beings engage with and render sensible life's experiences. A recent handbook on cultural theory defines mythical belief as the mindset that "transforms complex cultural process into apparently natural, unchangeable and self-evident ones."[96] Building life-span numbers, and in some ways the obsolescence paradigm itself, were just such mythical beliefs. As a worldview for comprehending change, invocations of building life-span numbers and obsolescence took the complex process of downtown capitalist rebuilding in the American context and transformed it into a seemingly inexorable, natural, and universal law of development. This rhetoric naturalized markets and depoliticized obsolescence, making both seemingly inevitable and disengaged from the agency and self-interest of powerful capitalists, who studied and promoted the notion of short-life buildings in part to gain favorable tax advantages.

The early story of obsolescence is particularly American, a confluence of urban redevelopment, consumer culture, and national tax policy that first birthed the idea in the real estate industry and then in the popular imagination. But what seemed self-evident in U.S. tax law about depreciation and obsolescence deductions was historically and nationally specific. In Great Britain, for example, where the tax code did not allow obsolescence deductions for buildings, no similar discourse evolved at this time. The British income tax had been established in 1842, seventy years before America's, and thus reflected different economic circumstances—more agrarian, with smaller-scale industry. It did not initially target corporations, commercial property, and capital gains, nor did it include the sophisticated notion of deducting working expenses. Even when depreciation allowances started to be allowed in British tax law, around 1900, it was for repairs and the replacement value of an existing piece of equipment. There was no annual write-off for obsolescence per se. Moreover, what depreciation allowances did exist in U.K. law were for industrial, not commercial, equipment and structures, like office buildings. And so there was no discussion of architectural obsolescence in the years around and after World War I, unlike in the United States, where the matter was of pressing national economic concern to well-organized corporate interests. As late as 1966 the British housing and taxation expert Adela Adam Nevitt complained, "The tax laws of the U.K. have taken no account of the fact that a dwelling has only a limited life."[97]

It was in America, then, by the early 1930s, that the idea of architectural obsolescence had taken root in both real estate economics and the popular imagination. Beyond its businessmen inventors' intentions, the worldview of obsolescence had become a primary mode for comprehending and managing architectural change. That the paradigm contained contradictions was noted, but muted. The idea of obsolescence solved more problems than it created in America between the wars. Subsequently, these plural notions of architectural obsolescence, in commercial real estate and popular culture, would spread from the scale of individual buildings to the city as a whole, engendering further additional concepts of urban obsolescence.

Urban Obsolescence

"An Obsolete Neighborhood"

In 1951 Boston's City Planning Board produced a comprehensive urban renewal scheme to redevelop fully one-fifth Boston's total land area. *A General Plan for Boston* detailed the city's woes, projected a better future, and invited federal renewal funding. Mostly, the sixty-six-page *General Plan* is filled with dry economic data. But a two-page spread stands out (fig. 2.1).[1] On the left, a black-inked map of Boston's West End district depicts a crooked maze of tightly packed blocks, alleys, and courts. Atop reads the title: "An Obsolete Neighborhood . . ." Across the page lies a pendant image, ". . . And a New Plan." Here, in lighter shades of gray, appears an imagined future, cleared of congestion—isolated slab blocks in a parklike setting.

Beneath the 1951 plan, statistics and a caption summarized the argument for the West End's obsolescence. The primary matter was the congestion of people and buildings: 112 families per acre, and 55 percent of the land covered by buildings that do "not allow sunlight and air to enter dwellings, and affords no possibility of a view."[2] These were densities, the *General Plan* noted, that "exceeded the standards set up by the American Public Health Association's Committee on the Hygiene of Housing."[3] Worse, continues the caption, "such an environment undoubtedly impairs the mental and physical health of its inhabitants." Ultimately, the text concludes, "there are indications that such an area is a deficit to the city in terms of cost of city services versus tax revenue." From physical congestion to ill health to economic liability: this was the logic of urban obsolescence.

A decade would pass before Boston's West End was infamously reduced to rubble. But once the neighborhood was designated "obsolete," its fate was largely sealed. How and why had the district earned this distinction? And what did it mean to denominate an entire area "obsolete"? How had the term

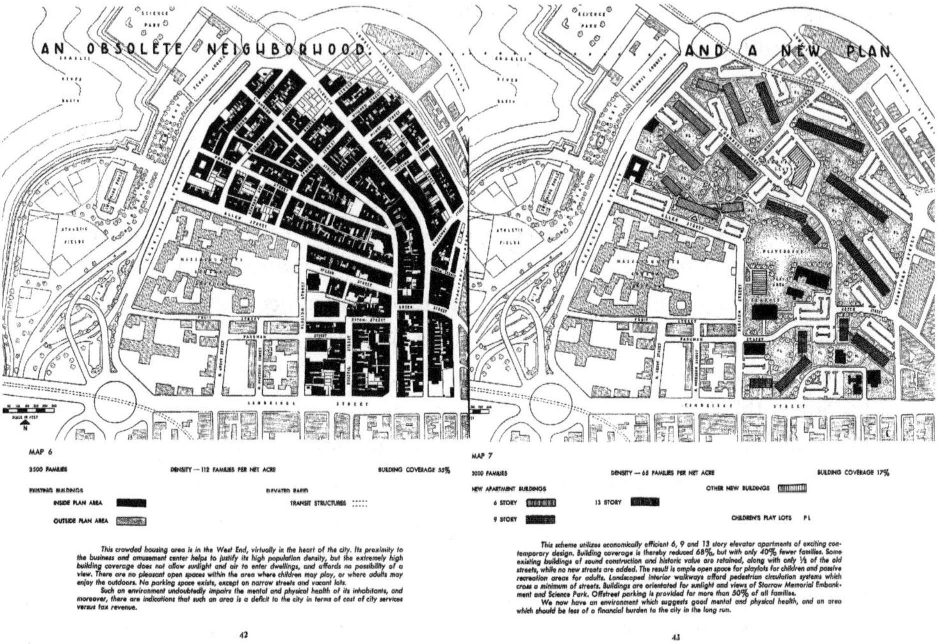

AN OBSOLETE NEIGHBORHOOD . . . AND A NEW PLAN
MAP 6
3500 FAMILIES
DENSITY — 112 FAMILIES PER NET ACRE
BUILDING COVERAGE 55%
EXISTING BUILDINGS
INSIDE PLAN AREA
OUTSIDE PLAN AREA
ELEVATED RAPID
TRANSIT STRUCTURES
This crowded housing area is in the West End, virtually in the heart of the city. Its proximity to the business and amusement center helps to justify its high population density, but the extremely high building coverage does not allow sunlight and air to enter dwellings, and affords no possibility of a view. There are no pleasant open spaces within the area where children may play, or where adults may enjoy the outdoors. No parking space exists, except on narrow streets and vacant lots.
Such an environment undoubtedly impairs the mental and physical health of its inhabitants, and moreover, there are indications that such an area is a deficit to the city in terms of cost of city services versus tax revenue.
42
MAP 7
2000 FAMILIES
DENSITY — 65 FAMILIES PER NET ACRE
BUILDING COVERAGE 17%
NEW APARTMENT BUILDINGS
6 STORY
9 STORY
13 STORY
OTHER NEW BUILDINGS
CHILDREN'S PLAY LOTS PL
This scheme utilizes economically efficient 6, 9 and 13 story elevator apartments of exciting contemporary design. Building coverage is thereby reduced 68%, but with only 40% fewer families. Some existing buildings of sound construction and historic value are retained, along with only ½ of the old streets, while no new streets are added. The result is ample open space for playlots for children and passive recreation areas for adults. Landscaped interior walkways afford pedestrian circulation systems which cross a minimum of streets. Buildings are orientated for sunlight and views of Storrow Memorial Embankment and Science Park. Offstreet parking is provided for more than 50% of all families.
We now have an environment which suggests good mental and physical health, and an area which should be less of a financial burden to the city in the long run.
43

FIGURE 2.1. "An Obsolete Neighborhood . . . And a New Plan," Boston City Planning Board, 1951.

migrated from commercial architecture to the urban realm? Who authored the idea of urban obsolescence, and how was it theorized and put into practice? What problems did the idea of urban obsolescence solve, and what contradictions did it leave unresolved? What were urban obsolescence's nuances in America and around the world, its multiplicities and their implications?

Theorizing Urban Obsolescence

American real estate assessors in the 1920s had initiated the idea of urban-scale obsolescence, which two decades later would frame the thinking for the redevelopment of Boston's West End. These assessors were seeking sophisticated means to determine the financial worth of land and buildings, as the vocation became more professionalized in its service to insurance companies, banks, and tax authorities who wanted to know present and, if possible, future values for properties. The larger purpose of these nuanced valuations was to rationalize processes of industrial and urban development, which were growing more complex in the early twentieth century. Real estate assessors' valuations helped businesses to maximize operations and profits and governments to maximize tax revenue. To arrive at their numbers, assessors employed detailed checklists of entire neighborhoods' physical and social conditions, which would presumably influence individual properties' worth. Their rubrics measured area factors such as economic stability, racial composition, family income, and adequate transportation. Whole districts that scored poorly were deemed in total to be economically deficient and thus obsolescent—regardless of the condition of individual properties—and so ineligible for lending, cut off from capital markets for investment and improvement purposes.[4] The assessors' procedures for measuring overall district obsolescence and value did reflect awareness of the office building owners' research on discrete commercial structures' dramatic loss of value owing to similarly complex combinations of external factors. Like the building owners' discourse, the assessors' outlook on obsolescence was widely publicized in the professional press to others in the real estate industry, including brokers and bankers. In the late 1930s the assessors' practices became de facto government policy, in the same manner, typical for the American state, that tax authorities had earlier turned to real estate businessmen to provide obsolescence figures. The private sector was believed to be authoritative in its realm of operations. The new Federal Housing Authority, seeking to promote home ownership and economic development in the Great Depression, adopted the assessors' criteria to determine eligibility for federal mortgage guarantees. Substandard neighborhoods by FHA guidelines were explicitly disqualified as "obsolete."[5]

Alongside pragmatic economic applications of the idea of urban obsolescence, pioneered by real estate assessors, more academic, theoretical investigations were taking place in other fields. In the 1920s the Chicago School of sociologists, studying overall metropolitan dynamics, identified a typical slum as a "zone in transition" or "zone of deterioration." This zone was believed to typically lie between an urban core (typically a downtown business district) and outlying residential neighborhoods. This zone was characterized by "intra-community invasions," noise, overcrowding, pollution, and rapid land-use and social change.[6] Compared to the real estate assessors' focus upon economics, the sociologists took a wider view of urban deterioration geographically and socially, looking at it as part of a broad metropolitan dynamic and focusing upon its human components. But the underlying presumptions were similar to those on which the assessors' outlook was based: identifying a process of measurable devaluation at the scale of a whole district that forebode further decline. The Chicago sociologists did not openly use the term "obsolescent," but their conceptualization of a "zone of deterioration" accorded with later uses of the word.

City planners took the lead in the 1930s, further developing an overtly named theory of urban obsolescence that combined the assessors' technical approach with the sociologists' broader outlook. By the crisis years of the Great Depression the planning profession had evolved its earlier emphasis on classically styled monumental layouts of urban centers and was instead developing quantitative methods of data analysis to solve broader societal problems of metropolitan decentralization and decay. As a subject, obsolescence, being about shifting numbers more than fixed form, fit this new planning schema. An early, 1932 collection of essays, "Obsolete Cities: A Challenge to Community Builders," edited by the housing reformer and planner Carol Aronovici, defined three stages of urban economic development—"pioneering, exploitation and obsolescence."[7] The chief culprit of obsolescence Aronovici identified as suburban competition, which was guilty of "leaving a considerable vacuum not only in the physical structure of the city but in its economic and social values [. . . to] result in a complete revaluing of the physical structure and equipment of our cities, a junking of what is obsolescent."[8] Cities, it was commonly argued, could not match suburbs' cheap land for new factories, single-family homes, and open roadways. Suburbs promised a new world of spaciousness, opportunity, and prosperity. In competition with suburbs, the urban built environment was losing its utility, attraction, and value and had to be rebuilt in order to compete, so the argument went. In other words, suburbs obsolesced cities. "Let the cities perish," thundered Aronovici, "so that we may have great and beautiful cities."[9]

The ideal urban condition was now "dynamic equilibrium," the historian Christine Boyer explains.[10] Processes of change, including obsolescence became the targets of study, with articles appearing regularly in the journals of planners, architects, and municipal law and financial officers, and later in the popular press as well.[11] Close investigation of urban obsolescence ensued. A "transition area" between the business and residential districts of St. Paul, Minnesota, was the focus of a 1935 planning journal article titled "The Obsolescence of Cities." "The first rented house is the beginning of obsolescence," the author, George Herrold, explained: "A different type of people gradually come in as owners move out. The character of the neighborhood changes and values recede for residential use."[12] Other social indicators of urban obsolescence included high rates of tuberculosis, crime, and juvenile delinquency; low incomes; declining family sizes; and a heterogeneous racial and ethnic population mix. As Herrold wrote, "The area slipped down another notch, and today it is inhabited by some eighteen different nationalities."[13] Housing reformers and planners such as Aronovici and Herrold demanded drastic measures to solve the problem of urban decline. Obsolescence analyses enabled planners to offer public policy makers plausible frameworks for managing change in troubled urban America.

Earlier campaigns to make cities less crowded, more healthy and virtuous, dating from the late nineteenth century, had focused upon addressing substandard tenement housing, primarily as a moral and social issue. But these efforts in the United States and Europe yielded scant results. It had not been enough to legislate new tenement standards (as had been done in New York and London a generation earlier), encourage private ownership to improve conditions, or demolish a few blocks here and there. The U.S. housing expert Edith Elmer Wood admitted in the 1930s, "Slum clearance, though much talked about, has been practiced very little."[14] A 1934 report confirmed that years of effort "has almost entirely failed to clear away old worn-out houses."[15]

The Depression heightened both the urgency and the opportunity to clear derelict areas, now framed by the economistic outlook of urban obsolescence. The quality and condition of housing stock had declined further, jobs were needed, and people more willingly turned to government for large-scale action. Moreover, whole cities were seen to be falling into decay and becoming devalued, not just isolated slums but potentially every residential neighborhood and commercial district. In this context, the idea of urban obsolescence augmented traditional slum-clearing agendas and named an overall, contemporary condition of wholesale urban crisis and change. Obsolescence was larger than just slum clearance, and its economic outlook became as important as, if not more so than, the concerns for morality that had shaped much of the rhetoric about redevelopment to this point.

When used in American planning literature of the 1930s through the 1950s, the word "obsolescence" was nearly synonymous with "blight," the terms interchangeable and often paired. A 1938 study, for example, estimated that 54,000 blocks in ninety-three American cities were "in an advanced state of blight and obsolescence."[16] Yet there were differences in emphasis between the terms. Blight bore naturalistic associations, familiar from traditional organic urban analogies of parks with lungs, avenues with arteries, or food markets with a city's stomach. In this respect "blight" connoted contagion and disfiguration, overlapping with disease metaphors. "There's only one way you can cure a place like the West End, and that is to wipe it out," declared a Boston banker. "It's a cancer in the long run to the community."[17] Obsolescence, on the other hand, bore more functionalist connotations of devalued performance, an accelerated emptying of usefulness and value caused by competition with something new and better. Obsolescence's economic outlook stood closer than blight to experts' characterization of the category. In the planning literature, blighted or obsolescent areas were marked *financially* by declining property values, where "old buildings are neglected and new ones are not erected," as a 1938 study titled *Urban Blight and Slums* defined it, "where it is not profitable to make or maintain improvements."[18] By contrast, slums were a "social liability," explained a 1932 federal Committee on Blighted Areas and Slums, where the poor inhabited *visibly* decayed, unsafe conditions.[19] Compared to a wholly obsolete slum, an obsolescent area, because it suffered less tangibly, was harder to spot. It was a not-yet slum, "one on the down-grade, which has not reached the slum stage," as a conventional definition of an obsolescent district ran.[20]

The planners' theory of obsolescence provided a refined technique for distinguishing wholly obsolete slums from merely blighted obsolescent areas. Degrees of obsolescence were in effect degrees of risk. Armed with such a diagnostic framework, planners triaged America's wounded cities, physically, economically, and socially. They offered detailed recommendations to policy leaders and the public, making their cases for urban redevelopment in highly dramatic terms. "Obsolescence is a challenge," declared the planner George Herrold; "it is a test of human adequacy to master its environs and to develop its own culture."[21]

During and after World War II the idea of urban obsolescence in America strengthened its hold upon the professional and public imaginations. The war years produced great faith in collective action and large-scale planning, as well as a sense of distance from the past, all key features of the urban obsolescence paradigm.[22] The nation had mobilized as never before, and in the wake of victory a new society seemed capable of being brought into existence by a similar all-encompassing effort. Obsolescence as a worldview that broke with tradition and projected an improved future resonated with this spirit. "Our cities have grown into obsolescence as a whole," declared the German émigré architects Walter Gropius and Martin Wagner at a 1942 Harvard conference, "their physical structures as well as their legal, economic, and administrative habits."[23] After 1945 a prosperous nation was ready to apply its developing urban expertise to the problem of city decline. A 1947 speech by the tax expert Mabel Walker opened with the declaration, "The American city is obsolescent."[24] "Every large American city is now physically obsolete," declared the city administrator of New York in 1956.[25]

Added to cities' postwar obsolescence problems, on top of suburban competition and internal sclerosis, was the threat of nuclear annihilation. Experts and the U.S. government promoted industrial and urban dispersal as "the most important if not the only answer to the threat of atomic aggression," argued the *Bulletin of the Atomic Scientist* in 1951.[26] "The anxiety about being bombed into oblivion" hung in the air, writes the architectural historian Anthony Vidler, contributing to the age's overarching sense of mutability.[27]

By the mid-1950s the idea of urban obsolescence had been scaled up in America from buildings and neighborhoods to the very form of the dense, centralized city itself. A 1959 Ford Foundation study suggested "that the physical city as it has existed for hundreds of years is not only undergoing a transformation but, like some factory buildings, is becoming obsolescent."[28] Decentralization appeared to have doomed the urban settlement. Nearly forty years after the discourse on urban obsolescence began, a policy expert in 1970 could still declare faith in "the basic message: the basic fact of life—which is that the city is functionally obsolete. There are very few things that it currently does better than an alternate location."[29]

Others, however, questioned just how far urban obsolescence had proceeded. Articles from the early 1960s in the popular magazines *Saturday Review* and *Atlantic Monthly* asked, "Are Cities Obsolete?" and "Are Cities Dead?"[30] The authors (one of them the New York city planner Robert Moses) answered in the negative, arguing for cities' adaptability. Indeed, a line of thinking emerged that perceived urban obsolescence not as pathological but as a normal even vital condition. The American housing expert Miles Colean's 1953 book, *Renewing Our Cities*, explained, "A city in which there were not at all times some worn-out or obsolete parts would not be a dynamic city."[31] Colean's ideal city was vibrantly obsolescent, never obsolete. Healthy development depended upon managing processes of differential obsolescence and small-scale expendability.

A multiplicity of urban obsolescences had thus been elaborated from the 1920s on, dramatically expanding the connotations of the real estate men's earlier discourse on commercial building obsolescence. The real estate assessors' outlook offered technically focused, culturally prejudiced measurements of neighborhood obsolescence, which excluded African American and other ethnic neighborhoods from capital markets. The Chicago School theorized wider spatial and social dynamics for urban obsolescence. City planners combined the two approaches—technical and social—in order to proffer their own professional remedies in the broad metropolitan context. Responding to Herrold's essay, the planner Frederick J. Adams wrote, "Would such blighted districts occur in a city that was comprehensively planned and administered?"[32] Earlier slum clearance strategy was now enlarged spatially and justified economically. Obsolescence refigured urban decline as a process of competitive progress, presenting the strong solution of wholesale replacement. And even as American urban obsolescence discourse developed in the postwar period, a strain of skepticism arose that doubted the doomsday pronouncements. Instead, obsolescence as a process of fast-paced urban change and replacement could be interpreted positively as adaptive and beneficial.

In all their nuances and varieties, ideas on urban obsolescence shared some fundamental aspects with the earlier real estate discourse on architectural obsolescence. Both accepted quantifiable measurements of built environment performance—variously financial, physical, and social—and presumed that the new would outperform and supersede the old, thus making the latter expendable. Out of all these plural obsolescences the term and idea had become part of the American vocabulary for comprehending and managing urban change, from individual buildings to whole cities, in professional discourse and the popular imagination alike. Accelerating human-made change appeared a permanent condition. A sense of everlasting transience came to permeate conceptions of the urban built environment. "In our cities we have launched on a desperate program of razing and rebuilding that gives promise of being *endless*," observed the planner Kevin Lynch in 1958, who did not altogether approve the process.[33] Obsolescence appeared to be here to stay.

Practicing Urban Obsolescence

This then was the theory of urban obsolescence in all its diversity from the 1930s through the 1950s. How did the paradigm play out in practice and politics? We can return to the case of Boston's West End, an L-shaped, forty-eight-acre area close by downtown that in 1950 was home to some twelve thousand people, mostly Italian Americans but also Jews, Poles, and others living on the cheap in turn-of-the-century tenements rising high along cramped sidewalks and streets. Ground-floor stores and luncheonettes were ubiquitous, trees a rarity. Fragmented socially by ethnicity and income—the poorest concentrated in the dense center—the West End was not necessarily a "cohesive neighborhood,"[34] according to the sociologist Herbert Gans, who was then studying and living in the district, though it could look so because of its dominant working-class culture, architectural uniformity, and defined boundaries of river, hospital, rail lines, and thoroughfares. Density and disorder are the qualities of the 1951 map (see fig. 2.1).

This plan had in fact been authored by one of the leading prewar exponents of the theory of urban obsolescence, Frederick J. Adams (fig. 2.2). Son of the famous planner Thomas Adams, the younger Adams, born in London in 1901 and trained in America as an architect, came to Boston in 1932 to teach at the Massachusetts Institute of Technology (MIT). Writing on the subject of urban obsolescence, Adams declared in 1945, "The basic pattern and a large

FIGURE 2.2. Frederick J. Adams, urban planner.

proportion of the structures in our cities are physically and economically obsolete."[35] To mitigate the problem, Adams, typical for the planning profession, proposed universal planning standards for light, air, space, and density regardless of citizens' class, race, and place of residence—the same in cities and suburbs. After World War II Adams helped found MIT's city planning program (up the Charles River from the West End) and served on the American Public Health Association committee, which produced the assessment rubric that would finalize the West End's obsolescence.

Even more directly, Adams was hired by the Boston City Planning Board to advise on its 1951 *General Plan for Boston*, which announced the West End's obsolescence. Adams's planning consulting firm, Adams, Howard & Greeley, offered clients, among other services, "advice on layout and design."[36] As a theorist and practitioner then Adams's fingerprints are all over the "obsolete neighborhood" designation, not least the graphic page-spread conjoining planning maps, density data, and public health rhetoric, all areas of his expertise (see fig. 2.1). Adams in effect authored the West End's obsolescence,

or rather its designation as an obsolescent neighborhood. The ideas and procedures planners like Adams had developed during the 1930s and 1940s to
address urban obsolescence were implemented by the city of Boston with
Adams's guidance, in the 1950s.

Subsequent studies of the West End from 1953 to 1955 filled in the argument for the neighborhood's obsolescence. All, with Adams's consulting advice, featured a comprehensive assessment of housing conditions painting a
dire picture. Out of 631 buildings surveyed 89 percent lacked rear stairs and
80 percent lacked fire escapes; 61 percent had trash strewn about, according to the assessors, and 60 percent showed signs of rat infestation. Of the
3671 dwelling units evaluated, 63 percent lacked washbasins and 64.8 percent
had "larger" or "extreme defects such as large holes in plaster walls and ceil-
ings, broken windows, damaged floors, etc."[37] The conclusions were sobering:
"Nearly 80% of all dwelling units in the West End rank as sub-standard or
only marginally standard."[38] The 1951 indictment of obsolescence had been
substantiated. This housing survey represented Boston planners' "main argument for describing the area as a slum," judged Gans—a description that
went well beyond the category of merely blighted.[39] The neighborhood was
now officially "decadent," according to state law, brought low by "obsolete"
buildings.[40]

Appraising Urban Obsolescence

The survey that in the mid-1950s made the West End's obsolescence offi-
cial was conducted by "trained field inspectors using the American Public
Health Association (APHA) technique," the report explained.[41] This was *An
Appraisal Method for Measuring the Quality of Housing* (4 vols., 1945–46).
Initially conceived to standardize wartime housing, the APHA's *Appraisal
Method* received its widest application in the wake of the federal Housing Act
of 1949, which required assessment of a city's housing stock before residential
areas could be renewed. By 1951 the APHA method to measure urban obsoles-
cence was being employed at redevelopment agencies in a score of American
cities, including Milwaukee, Philadelphia, Washington, Los Angeles, New
Haven, and St. Louis.[42]

The context for the *Appraisal Method*'s engagement with urban obsolescence was public health experts' desire, like that of city planners, to enhance
their professional relevance. "The public health of the future must be not only
an engineering science and a medical science; it must also be a social science,"
declared the chair of the APHA's Committee on the Hygiene of Housing,
C.-E. A. Winslow, also a professor at Yale.[43] This committee was active from

the late 1930s through the late 1940s. It received substantial support from the Rockefeller Foundation and the League of Nations and thus exemplified the mid-century "big research" approach to major societal and scientific issues, which brought together academic and other nongovernmental institutions of elite civil society, in this instance to combat urban obsolescence.[44] The particular APHA Subcommittee on Appraisal of Residential Areas, which specifically devised the *Appraisal Method*, included a statistician, sociologist, physician, and housing specialist, as well as the city planner Adams.

The goals of the APHA's *Appraisal Method* were to "map with accuracy the housing assets and liabilities of a city" and to provide a "concise and quantitative picture," "a summary picture that will be understood by the busy public official or the layman."[45] Earlier attempts to map urban obsolescence had been imprecise, based on large census tracts and just a few indicating factors. The APHA method, by contrast, employed dozens of criteria to produce a fine-grained analysis, building by building, block by block. First, field inspectors with printed appraisal forms canvassed a neighborhood to assess "penalty score points" on dozens of items ranging from toilet facilities and sleeping arrangements to heating equipment and overall structural condition (fig. 2.3). The entire district also would be subjected to a separate "environmental survey," in which penalty points would be assessed for factors such as land crowding, commercial nuisances, and inadequate community facilities. Office clerks then transcribed field scores onto punch cards and added together the environmental and dwelling unit penalty points to produce a neighborhood's sum total housing quality score, "the distinctive feature of the method" that expressed "complex relationships in a single figure."[46]

In the APHA's five-grade classification system fewer than 30 penalty points in a total housing quality score represented grade A, "good to excellent housing." Over 120 penalty points indicated grade E, "thoroughgoing slums."[47] Right in the middle stood the obsolescent area, a 60-to-89-point grade C score representing "mediocre housing districts in which extensive blight and obsolescence can be expected [. . .] which may involve serious problems of blight and shrinking values during the next ten or twenty years" (fig. 2.4).[48] Grade C obsolescent areas were not yet slums. But they required vigilance, "both as protection to the remaining unspoiled neighborhoods and as a safeguard to the city's tax base."[49] If a Grade C obsolescent area collapsed into a wholly obsolete slum, "there is usually no practical remedy except rebuilding," intoned the APHA manual.[50] Abstraction and bureaucracy characterized the APHA method for measuring urban obsolescence based on checklists and enumeration. The manual made the "determination of basic needs [. . .] a matter of quantitative measure"; "it becomes possible to put all

DWELLING SURVEY

City_____ State_____

UNIT APPRAISAL FORM
☐ Rooming Unit   Serial U_____

I. DESCRIPTION

STRUCTURE: Address_____

District No._____Block No._____Appr. Area No._____
Owner or Agent_____ Not Avail. for Occup. ☐
Number of Units: Dwelling_____Rooming_____Business_____
Stories_____Wood ☐ Attached ☐ Toilets_____Baths_____
UNIT: Floor_____Part_____Unit No._____
Rooms_____Occupants_____With Lodgers ☐ Nonwhite ☐
Occupied by: Tenant ☐ Owner ☐ Bldg. Employee ☐ Vacant ☐
Rent $_____per mo. ☐ per wk. ☐ Incl. Furn. ☐ Incl. Heat ☐
Monthly Income $_____ Rent: Rm/Mo $_____ Insp. by _____ Insp. Date _____

II. APPRAISAL

DEFICIENCY ITEM.	Penalty Score Points	Basic Defic.
A. FACILITIES		
1. STRUCTURE: Main Access	__ __	
2. Water Supply (Source)	__ __	__
3. Sewer Connection	__ __	
4. Daylight Obstruction	__ __	
5. Stairs and Fire Escapes	__ __	
6. Public Hall Lighting	__ __	
7. UNIT: Location in Structure	__ __	
8. Kitchen (or Special Rooming Unit) Facilities	__ __	
9. Toilet: Location____Type____Sharing____	__ __	*
10. Bath: Location____Type____Sharing____	__ __	
11. Water Supply (Location and Type)	__ __	
12. Washing Facilities	__ __	
13. Dual Egress.	__ __	__
14. Electric Lighting	__ __	
15. Central Heating.	__ __	
16. Rooms Lacking Installed Heater.	__ __	__
17. Rooms Lacking Window.	__ __	
18. Rooms Lacking Closet.	__ __	
19. Rooms of Substandard Area.	__ __	
20. Combined Room Facilities (items 16-19)____		
w____x____y____z____	__ __	
a. Subtotal: Facilities	__	
B. MAINTENANCE		
21. Toilet Condition Index.	__ __	
22. Deterioration Index: Struc____Unit____	__ __	*
23. Infestation Index: Struc____Unit____	__ __	
24. Sanitary Index: Struc____Unit____	__ __	
25. Basement Condition Index.	__ __	
w____x____y____z____		
b. Subtotal: Maintenance.	__	
C. OCCUPANCY		
26. Room Crowding: Persons per Room	__ __	__
27. Room Crowding: Persons per Sleeping Room	__ __	
28. Area Crowding: Sleeping Area per Person	__ __	
29. Area Crowding: Nonsleeping Area per Person	__ __	
30. Doubling of Basic Families.	__ __	
w____x____y____z____		
c. Subtotal: Occupancy.	__	
D. DWELLING TOTAL	__	__
E. ENVIRONMENT TOTAL w_x_y_z_v_	__	__
F. HOUSING TOTAL	__	__

Key to Sanitary Index (Item 24)
Yes: Rcd__Ga__Ora__Reported: Pl__Po__Wpl__Wfd__Hh__Wh__
Extreme: Rcd__Ga__Ora__Observed: Pl__Po__Wpl__Wfd__Hh__Wh__

Form DS-4: Copyright 1944, Committee on the Hygiene of Housing
American Public Health Association

FIGURE I.
APPRAISAL
FORM FOR
SCORING
DEFICIENCY
ITEMS OF
DWELLING
UNITS

FIGURE 2.3. Housing appraisal form, American Public Health Association, 1945.

AREA 12   AREA 12

GRADE C

FIGURE 2.4. Grade C obsolescent area, American Public Health Association, 1945.

the housing cards on the table, where every group concerned may consider
dispassionately its proper role in the reconstruction task."[51] Establishing an
"official designation of substandardness by areas will serve as a beacon to
guide the agencies of reconstruction."[52]

The Politics of Urban Obsolescence

Notwithstanding the scientific method, determinations of obsolescence
were fundamentally political, a tool whereby policy makers could rationalize and manage processes of urban redevelopment, disinvestment, and reinvestment. In the case of Boston, the designation of the West End as obsolete
came after the 1949 election of the reformist mayor John B. Hynes. He had
defeated the neighborhood populist James Michael Curley on a platform
of directing municipal policy away from Curley's wealth redistribution to
the working class through social services and jobs patronage, which critics
charged had been fundamentally corrupt. Alternately, the reformist vision
championed by Hynes promoted traditional wealth building for elite business interests, which in theory would benefit all Bostonians and reverse the
city's long-term economic decline. Already in Hynes's inaugural address the
new mayor promised a master plan to unleash federal renewal funding for
the decaying inner city. The West End's demolition would replace an ethnic
working-class constituency, requiring expensive social services, with reform-
minded, white, middle-class voters who paid taxes and had shopping dollars for nearby downtown. "Boston must 'provide pleasant accommodations
for the great American middle class, or perish,'" declared the chairman of
the Boston Finance Commission, echoing a familiar American mid-century
sentiment.[53] These changes were consistent with responses nationwide to the

fact that cities were losing their younger generations, who aspired to spacious suburbs of newness and abundance and were repelled by their parents' world of straitened, immigrant, tenement districts.

Urban renewal framed as obsolescence seemingly depoliticized the process of gentrification—a quality heightened in Boston both by Adams's "expert" mien and Hynes's reformist agenda. A neighborhood's "official designation of substandardness" appeared objective and irrefutable, redevelopment imperative. Measuring obsolescence framed urban change in impersonal terms of standards and competition, supersession and expendability. "Quantification is a way of making decisions without seeming to decide," historian Theodore Porter has written.[54] Or, as Boston authorities told critics in the 1950s, "To people who lived there for a long time the West End may not seem 'substandard.' But the preliminary studies made by the Housing Authority show that it is."[55]

Notwithstanding all the markers of impersonal objectivity, designations of urban obsolescence were deeply biased. What middle-class evaluators quantified as obsolete—crowded, noisy tenements and roads, mixed with stores and taverns, children playing in the streets—were for the West Enders themselves good places to play, socialize, and communicate, reinforcing ties of kinship and community. "Even the sense of adjacent human beings carried by noise and smells provides a sense of comfort," researchers noted of the neighborhood before its demise.[56] Not just homes but habits were deemed obsolete. Measurements of obsolescence indicted working-class culture as much as tenement housing. The West End's localism transgressed middle-class values of individualism and mobility. As the sociologist Gans observed at the time, "Obsolescence per se is not harmful; the judgment [is] merely a reflection of middle-class standards."[57]

Designations of urban obsolescence also screened political choices. In Boston, a half dozen other districts, authorities knew, possessed equal or worse density, devaluation, and dilapidation statistics. But the West End lacked the cultural cachet of the Back Bay's elegant if rundown townhomes and the political clout of the North End neighborhood, center of Boston's Italian American community. The vulnerable West End was in the wrong place at the wrong time. Downtown merchants desired its gentrification for middle-class shoppers. Nearby Massachusetts General Hospital disliked its working-class neighbor and coveted the land for expansion. Real estate developers prized the district's proximity to and views of the Charles River.[58] The West End was not actually Boston's most obsolete neighborhood, by the measured standards. But it was ripe for the picking.

The paradigm of urban obsolescence was thus never merely analytical.

It was always political, "wielded as a weapon," the historian Alison Isenberg writes of 1950s American downtown renewal efforts.[59] The West End's assessors admitted to the urban renewal critic Jane Jacobs that they'd fudged the 1952–53 housing survey, which confirmed the West End's obsolescence, with "pictures of sufficient dark and noisome spaces to justify that this was a slum."[60] The APHA *Appraisal Method* and the language of obsolescence became cynical devices of justification, which signaled a district's irrelevance to the present moment. Denominating a neighborhood obsolete placed it at a temporal remove from modern society, foreclosing its adaptability, and all the more easily designated for clearance. As a "chronopolitics" (a term coined by the anthropologist Johannes Fabian), urban obsolescence sorts society by positions in time.[61] Some groups and places are denoted progressive, modern, and up-to-date; others, underdeveloped, traditional, and stagnant in time. The designation thus embodies asymmetries of power, between those who render and benefit from the category and those who are forced to live under its logic, whose habits and habitations are deemed dysfunctional, valueless, out-of-time. Separation and domination are the objectives, obsolescence the means.

At the same time, the framework of obsolescence could promote consensus, in the American context of postwar urban renewal. Earlier, the first federal Housing Act of 1937 had reflected the social agenda of housing activists for the "eradication of slums" and provision of working-class public housing, while providing construction jobs during the Depression.[62] But business interests generally resisted, opposed to increased taxation, support for labor, and state intervention in the housing market. Twelve years later, however, the Housing Act of 1949 widened its purview to "the clearance of slums *and blighted areas* [emphasis added] [. . .] providing maximum opportunity for the redevelopment of project areas by private enterprise."[63] The 1949 law's inclusion of "maximum opportunity for [. . .] private enterprise," and the term "blighted"—synonymous with "obsolescent," and including commercial districts—thus elevated economic priorities to equal standing with social concerns. Federal funding would pay two-thirds of the cost of clearing land to be sold to a private developer, thus publicly subsidizing and accelerating the process of private capitalist reinvestment in decaying American cities.

Conceptualizing the problem of America's urban areas as obsolescence would thus have made strong sense to business interests. The law's inclusion of blight framed America's urban ills as economic, curable by an architectural version of Joseph Schumpeter's "Creative Destruction," the new superseding the old. Invoking obsolescence, in law and discourse, arguably helped render postwar federal urban renewal legislation palatable to businessmen who would otherwise be antipathetic to government social programs. Obsolescence worked as a concept now because it resolved for a time the conflict between American capitalism, labor, and the state over urban renewal. Obsolescence in 1950s America offered a mutually agreeable framework for managing change in the built environment.

Obsolescence at Mid-Century

The idea of urban obsolescence took root most generally in the context of a postwar American consumer culture charmed by notions of "planned obsolescence" and expendable commodities. Since the late 1920s, marketers had enjoined Americans to accept "progressive obsolescence," in the best-selling author Christine Frederick's phrase, "to make way for the newer and better thing."[64] In the postwar period, obsolescence was even more compelling, as the American economy tilted from industry to consumption. To maintain profits, businesses focused upon filling and refilling American homes and driveways with an unending stream of gadgets and innovations. "Obsolescence as a process is wealth-producing, not wasteful," declared the designer George Nelson in 1956; "it leads to constant renewal of the industrial establishment at higher and higher levels, and it provides a way of getting a maximum of goods to a maximum of people."[65] In mid-century America urban obsolescence's allure was overwhelming: a reflection of material abundance, progressive in its liberation from the past, promising a better future modeled on the spacious, car-centered suburban competitor that had apparently bested the traditional city economically and demographically. Like a marketer's vision, the 1951 Boston *General Plan* contrasts the congested disorder of an "obsolete neighborhood" with the genteel, modern openness of the pendant "new plan" (see fig. 2.1). This is the mid-twentieth-century dream ideal, the city suburbanized, new and improved, obsolescing the last century's model in performance and styling.

The paradigm of urban obsolescence was itself something new for the twentieth century. Its technocratic methods represented an evolution in tactics to clear and revalue urban land. As an impersonal, seemingly endless law of modern, economic urban development, obsolescence contrasted with the traditionally divisive, personalized politics of historic urban redevelopment. The massive rebuilding of Paris, for example, in the second half of the nineteenth century was "political from the very start," explains the geographer David Harvey, and always closely associated with the name of Georges-Eugène Haussmann, the region's governor, directed by Emperor Louis Napoléon.[66] The Haussmannization of Paris, which expelled tens of thousands from working-class districts, laid down ninety miles of boulevards to connect opulent monumental structures, and enriched hosts of capitalist financiers, also elicited the violent backlash of the Paris Commune of 1870. By contrast, twentieth-century urban obsolescence worked through a broad consensus of capital and the state, civil, and consumer societies, conjoining economic values of quantifiable performance with a social theory of progressive change. Moreover, no one believed at the time that Haussmann's Paris would itself become obsolete, gone and replaced within a generation. The new monuments were intended by their architects, builders, patrons, and users to last and embody permanent values. (Only in the years after World War I would the philosopher Walter Benjamin look back at nineteenth-century Paris's redevelopment as portending the modern process of continual obsolescence; Benjamin projected his own perceived conditions into the past.) By contrast, the twentieth-century paradigm of urban obsolescence presumed systemic impermanence: a ceaseless eradication of values and structures that would destroy the new all over again just a few decades on. Accepting obsolescence was part and parcel of embracing modernity.

Those subjected to the judgment of urban obsolescence in the midtwentieth century were nearly powerless against this dominant ideology. Overwhelmed by the weight of professional expertise, social bias, governmental policy, and bureaucratic technique, Boston's West Enders possessed few allies and had no language or strategy to counter the obsolescence worldview. Except for residents, "all approved of the development," recalled Gans, one of their few middle-class sympathizers.[67] In 1956, years after the die was cast, the West Enders belatedly organized opposition. But their demonizing of the developer Jerome Rappaport and Mayor Hynes missed the point that impersonal bureaucratic technique, more than individual agency, undergirded redevelopment. Rappaport and Hynes were instruments, not authors, of the process. They fulfilled economic and political roles within obsolescence's logic rather than singularly effecting change. Moreover, the West Enders' taking the fight to the city through a 1958 lawsuit, which claimed that housing survey statistics overstated the neighborhood's substandardness, did no good.[68] Arguing percentages of unsound buildings simply reinforced the paradigm's underlying validity; it did not allow for the possibility that the category of "unsound building" was itself problematic.

In the spring of 1958, the city of Boston seized the West End by eminent domain, taking private property for the public good of urban renewal. Demolition began in 1959 and was completed by 1962. Nearly two thousand families were evicted from the district. Nine hundred buildings occupying forty-eight acres were demolished, leaving a flattened wasteland of dirt, brick, and ghostly streets. Atop this rose, by the early 1970s, a modernist complex of middle-class-occupied towers, townhomes, and community facilities called Charles River Park, modeled upon the original 1951 "new plan." The renewed West End had emerged from the theory and practice of urban obsolescence that dominated the postwar American urban environment from the late 1940s through the mid-1960s in scores of American cities small and large. The Boston experience played out repeatedly in such places as New Haven, Philadelphia, St. Louis, and Washington, D.C. The case of the West End, however, was emblematic because of its explicit, dramatic designation as "obsolete" in the 1951 plan, as well as the vivid physical and social consequences of the vast demolition in the heart of one of America's best-known cities.

The Contradictions of Urban Obsolescence

The idea of urban obsolescence extended and deepened the earlier American downtown real estate discourse on architectural obsolescence. In like manner, it rationalized accelerated redevelopment using economic criteria. But now the concept was projected onto whole urban communities and classes by a wider professional and political elite, from planners and public health experts to mayors and social activists. What was in effect a proposition about the dynamics of change in the contemporary urban built environment—that the measurably new and better-made had to replace the insufficient old—came to be accepted as a reasoned, natural fact. And what had been in the 1920s an actuarial and political expedient for American capitalist office-building owners became by mid-century a pervasive paradigm for comprehending and managing change across the whole of the urban built environment.

Yet there were internal disputes and contradictions. Many presumed determinate fixes, like the authors of the West End's static "new plan," while others projected ceaseless change, like the housing expert Miles Colean, who equated continuous obsolescence with urban dynamism. Some deemed the very form of the dense, centralized city to be obsolete, while many rejected this verdict.[69] There was a real tension as well between, on the one hand, obsolescence's intangibility and unpredictability, and on the other, the concreteness of the statistical determinations and large-scale transformations it produced. Even more knottily, it was not apparent that the economic imperatives of the obsolescence discourse could be reconciled with the accompanying social agendas. Which took priority, economic renewal or community development? Moreover, there were multiple ways to perceive and add nuance to the processes of urban obsolescence. The precise definition of obsolescence itself was never fixed.

Further still quantifications of performance or of decay in residential districts obscured affective values—how a place *measured* was never equivalent to what it *meant*. When applied to domestic settings, the techniques for determining obsolescence confronted a fuller range of human architectural attachments than when simply applied to commercial buildings. Redevelopment raised critical questions about the ways the built environment might contribute to habits of sociability, emotional sentiment, and collective and individual identities through space, symbolism, and aesthetic satisfaction—how neighborhood residents felt, not just how many broken windows could be counted. These intangible qualities could not be measured by the paradigm of urban obsolescence.

Progressive ideals ran up against political reality. The APHA appraisal technique was meant for urban triage, but in Boston it was used ex post facto in the mid-1950s by planning bureaucrats against a district they had already in 1951 overtly indicted as an "Obsolete Neighborhood." Experts' tools ended up as weapons for wholesale clearance, beyond the theorists' best intentions. The ways that the discourse around urban obsolescence conflated the physical and the social led to confusion as well. In which realms was a neighborhood obsolescent: physical, social, or both? The distinction never comes clear, nor does a chain of causality. A member of the APHA's own Committee on the Hygiene of Housing acknowledged that "there is little evidence that substandard housing per se causes sickness and death."[70] Slippage between the physical and the social allowed obsolescence in one category to justify action in the other. The obsolescence framework both suppressed and exploited this ambiguity to impose social power from above in the guise of objective analysis.

Even more broadly, it was not at all evident how to square the contradiction between obsolescence's fundamental temporality, its unpredictable indeterminacy, and finished solutions like the West End "new plan." "Even the new projects with which we hope to redevelop the present blighted areas will, in their turn, become obsolete," admitted the American architect Louis Justement in 1946.[71] Boston's West End was rebuilt as Charles River Park by the early 1970s, just in time for an unanticipated postmodern backlash against modernism. In the early twenty-first century, some Charles River Park townhomes have been demolished for brick apartment blocks reminiscent of old West End tenements. What replaced the obsolete itself became obsolete. The complex's owners have even given back the district its old name, without irony, to trade on "the neighborhood spirit and electric energy of Boston's historic, wonderful and cherished West End."[72]

By the time the West End "new plan" began to be implemented in the mid-1960s, the phrase "obsolete neighborhood" was itself already obsolete.

The term was not used again after 1951 to describe the Boston district, and it dissipated generally in American planning discourse through the 1960s. "Blight," once interchangeable with "obsolescence," became the preferred term. Planners or commentators offered no explanation at the time for the eclipse of "obsolete." Perhaps it had become too revealing of a coldhearted logic of quantification and expendability, compared with blight's more naturalistic connotations of health and even reparability. The economistic inflections that arguably enhanced the political effectiveness of the idea of obsolescence in postwar America may ultimately have helped discredit obsolescence.

But maybe the most stubborn, destabilizing contradiction of all involved exceptions in practice to urban obsolescence, those structures exempted from a neighborhood's overall designation. In Boston's West End, five buildings purposely remained—two churches, a historic home, a school, and a social services agency (all shaded black in the "new plan"). Officially this was because of their structural soundness and community usefulness. But ideologically they were also the neighborhood's few elite-styled, historic constructions.[73] What survived served as a reproach to the dominant worldview. The remainders contradicted urban obsolescence's totalizing logic—the hardheaded calculation of an area's complete substandardness—and helped seed different options for the future. If these exceptions somehow had held their value and were worth preserving, then could not other structures in the same area also potentially be adjudged immune to obsolescence? The remainders imply the question, how might new and old coexist rather than conflict? The paradigm of obsolescence, with its prioritizing of supersession and expendability, had no answer to these questions. Urban obsolescence thus resolved certain tensions in the process of urban redevelopment—for example, facilitating business interests' and housing reformers' agreement on redevelopment—but at the same time it left other contradictions open, like what to do with its remainders. The unresolved contradictions, as we shall see, provided critics of obsolescence openings to formulate new frameworks for comprehending and managing change in the built environment.

International Obsolescence

Even as the idea of urban obsolescence was accepted within the United States—with all its nuances, multiplicities, and contradictions—outside the United States the concept gained traction, too, after World War II. The prospect of limited urban life spans figured in several European renewal programs. But the concept was differently deployed than in the United States, producing a further diversity of obsolescences worldwide.

Immediately after the war, the Swiss architect Hans Bernoulli theorized a city of the future's "constant organic regeneration," achieved by means of eighty-year district rebuilding cycles. Government would mandate time contracts for each building type, from thirty-year temporary structures, to forty-to-sixty-year industries and offices, to sixty-to-eighty-year housing. For the monumental or sacred, "the contract remains valid as long as the building stands."[74] Bernoulli imagined urban change as a process of legislated obsolescence, inevitable devaluation met by required replacement enforced by the state. Such socialism enforcing obsolescence would have been anathema in free-enterprise Cold War America and was never in practice taken up anywhere in the world, but the idea that cities possessed limited life spans was becoming ubiquitous.

In Britain, London's eighteenth-century Georgian fabric had been explicitly deemed "obsolete" in 1938 by the leading commercial property developer W. Stanley Edgson. The 1957 Housing Act, which required demolition of one old unit for each new construction, also possessed an "obsolescent" classification. And some British town planning literature of the late 1950s and 1960s applied the term to slum clearance and city center renewal, referencing "seventy-five years as the useful life of a building."[75] But in general, urban obsolescence was a "neglected" subject in Britain, as reported in 1954.[76] Wartime bombing had cleared areas for rebuilding, without the need to call them obsolete. Meanwhile, the postwar British welfare state focused upon social reconstruction, not capitalist profit, obviating the context for the economic logic of the obsolescence discourse and paradigm. Significantly, the London County Council's twenty-four-person planning research unit contained not a single economist.[77] In Britain the idea of urban obsolescence was present but never gained much traction, likely because planners were more focused upon social rather than economic priorities for urban change.

In communist Eastern Europe the term "obsolescence" was more widespread, as the historian Florian Urban has documented. Here the term took on social connotations more than economic ones. East German planners used the idea of obsolescence to condemn prewar tenement buildings for embodying capitalist social exploitation of the working class. Obsolescence justified the demolition of twenty thousand structures in East Berlin between 1961 and 1971. Going forward, the planners projected eighty-year life spans for the new buildings. These too would become obsolete, it was believed, as socialism advanced, with the eighty-year figure pegged to socialism's presumed evolution as a framework for living, continually improving citizens' conditions. Throughout the Soviet sphere, "the life span of a building was regarded as a scientifically proven fact," writes Urban, citing several 1960s Polish, Hungarian, Soviet, and Czech studies of "'obsolete building stock.'" Communist obsolescence was calculated not upon the amortization and flux of invested capital, but upon the anticipated and more or less endless pace of socialist development. Obsolescence would be a constant. Advancing technologies and social improvements would necessitate new architectures. "In both the Eastern and Western blocs," Urban concludes, "obsolescence was the catchword of the time."[78]

Still, evidence indicates that the idea of urban obsolescence was used more sparingly outside the United States. Why? Historically, the paradigm of architectural obsolescence had been developing early in the United States since the 1910s, longer than anywhere else, and had been popularized since the 1920s. In the following decades, American planners devoted themselves to theoretical refinements of distinctions between obsolescent and slum districts. In the postwar period, American urban obsolescence competed with levels of suburbanization exceeding those elsewhere in the world, strongly compelling American urban elites to name and confront the problem, as well as the possibility that the dense, centralized city might be obsolescent altogether. Moreover, postwar prosperity and consumer culture came sooner to America, strengthening the obsolescence perspective as urban redevelopment got under way.

By contrast, wider public ownership of land, in both Western and Eastern Europe, dampened the real estate speculation that had fueled American-style obsolescence. In Europe, too, traditions of adapting existing buildings tamped down obsolescence-driven demolition. Moreover, the impulse to replace what had been destroyed in the war could take precedence emotionally over deliberately demolishing the old for the new. Nations had their own distinctive obsolescence outlooks, too. In communist Eastern Europe, obsolescence referred to capitalist housing types, whose eradication signaled socialist victory. In Britain, echoes of obsolescence's economism, which promoted private financial interests, were muted by the welfare state's more public outlook. Elsewhere around the world, from New Zealand to France, the long-standing social objective of slum clearance was combined with more recent modernist architectural visions to organize urban rebuilding. These countries' architects, planners, and policy makers wanted tower-in-the-park developments as symbols of modern efficiency and social improvement. Yet despite some surface similarities, this occurred at a conceptual distance from the dynamics of American obsolescence. In the United States, renewal went beyond slum clearance, attacking overall metropolitan decay, and renewal was more economically motivated than elsewhere.[79] Nor did other nations' more nakedly ideological expropriations of urban land and buildings require obsolescence's relative subtlety as a logic of renewal. In South Africa the government notoriously cleared out sixty thousand people from multiracial District Six, Cape Town, beginning in 1966, to make way for a whites-only redevelopment.[80] The South African state did not need the economic arguments and technical measurements of obsolescence to impel and justify action. The ideology of apartheid was a blunter weapon.

Multiple Obsolescences

In all its diversity, obsolescence had become, by about 1960, an acknowledged concept worldwide for understanding and managing change in the urban environment. Diffused globally, the idea of urban obsolescence was present in variety, nuance, and emphasis, flexibly applied from capitalist America to communist Europe. It encompassed economic and social factors. It transcended slum clearance and was scaled from neighborhood to city, measured on a spectrum from incipient to wholly obsolete. Within the American context there had been assessors', sociologists', and planners' developments of the idea of urban obsolescence. There had been skeptics' views, too, from the mid-1950s, which did not see as dire the situation of aging cities, yet still accepted that they were obsolescing. Elsewhere, socialism countered the economism of American-style obsolescence. Yet across national boundaries a general presumption of short building life spans and fast-paced urban change strongly persisted.

The significance of the paradigm of obsolescence at mid-century lay not in its uniform application but in the ubiquity of its rhetoric and underlying concepts. Whether or not one believed the city to be terminally obsolete or in-process obsolescent, solutions to be final or provisional, expendability to be a virtue or a necessity, profit or socialism to be the goal, the framework of understanding was obsolescence. The ideas of shortened life spans, accelerating change, superseding innovation, expendable buildings, and obsolescent cities became myths of modernity, transcending local variations on the theme. Born in America and diffused around the world, obsolescence was the process that needed confronting and managing, a prime task for mid-century architecture. We now turn to the ways in which architects and others responded to this broad presumption of obsolescence.

The Promise of Obsolescence

How did architects react to the emergence of obsolescence in the 1920s and its solidification in the 1950s as a dominant paradigm for comprehending and managing change in the built environment? At first by denial—only later did they acknowledge its relevance and significance. And just as there were multiple discourses and outlooks upon the paradigm of architectural obsolescence (real estate and urban, commercial and social, American and European), so there would emerge multiple discourses within architecture on the subject of obsolescence. These would run the gamut from accepting that architectural obsolescence would happen to promoting that obsolescence should happen. The promise of obsolescence came to infuse much architectural thought. Nearly all believed in obsolescence's inevitability. Some even embraced its largest gift, the possibility that architectural transience could engender human freedom.

The Interwar Years

In the years before World War II, traditional and avant-garde architects alike held fast to established values of permanence and stability, paying little heed to obsolescence. Classical designers in the 1920s and 1930s continued to produce, as they had for centuries, monumental masonry landmarks such as the British architect Edwin Lutyens's capitol complex in New Delhi, India, or the French American Paul P. Cret's Federal Reserve Board Building in Washington, D.C. (fig. 3.1). In their qualities of balance and symmetry, unity and proportion, refinement and finish, these works followed the Renaissance architect Leon Battista Alberti's influential fifteenth-century ideal

FIGURE 3.1. Viceroy's House, New Delhi, Edwin Lutyens, 1913–31.

of complete "reasoned harmony." Change is unimaginable in this aesthetic, form fixed forever.

Meanwhile, more self-conscious modernist architects, notwithstanding numerous disagreements with tradition, similarly idealized "a profound projection of harmony," in the French Swiss master Le Corbusier's words, "a sure and permanent home," "the necessity for order," "a state of perfection."[1] Explained Walter Gropius, the founder of the Bauhaus, in Dessau, Germany, "We aimed at realizing standards of excellence, not creating transient novelties."[2] In Italy the famed 1914 Italian Futurist manifesto called for "expendability and transience [*la caducità e la transitorietà*]. Our houses will last less time than we do."[3] Yet the accompanying designs by the Futurist architect Antonio Sant'Elia, contrary to the group's stated principles, were in fact structures of massive, pyramidal immutability (fig. 3.2). Said Sant'Elia of his fellow Futurists' love of obsolescence, "Don't attribute this nonsense to me. You know that I believe exactly the opposite."[4] The famous 1923–25 townhouse in the Dutch city of Utrecht, a collaboration of the architect, Gerrit Rietveld, and the owner, Truus Schröder-Schräder, featured flexible partitions adaptable to changing daily uses (sleep, eating, entertaining), but did not imagine radical potential disruptions to its modern solution.

The interwar-period modernists expected "to pass the crisis," Le Corbusier wrote, emerging into a new world that, like the old, would be stable and secure, beyond obsolescence.[5] Le Corbusier, coming of age and professionally trained before World War I, was in many ways a man of tradition. His famous manifesto, *Vers une architecture*, written in the early 1920s, still believed in standards and order, fixed principles and geometries, even if these rejected older conventions of decoration and historical reference. Contradictory desires for change and order—belief in progress but not modernism's own mutability—were resolved in favor of certainty and permanence. As the architectural historian Reyner Banham noted in a postwar critique of 1920s modernism, it aimed for "perfection" and "stabilised types and norms," not "a high rate of scrapping."[6] The past might be obsolescent in modernist formulations. But the new, with its updated certainties, would not be. The modern would endure.

Exceptions of course existed. In America, architects of the 1933–34 Chicago World's Fair envisioned the general use of disposable prefabricated structures, "immunizing the world against the deadly atrophy of obsolescence," a contemporary report on the fair noted.[7] Again in interwar Chicago—the capital

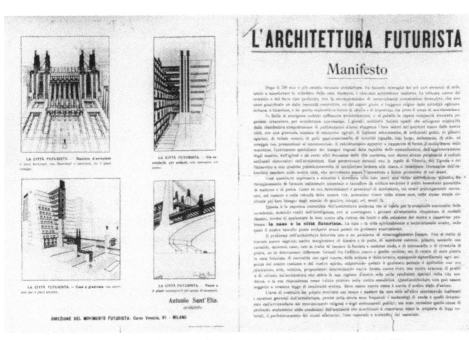

FIGURE 3.2. Project for La città nova (*left*) and Futurist Manifesto (*right*), Antonio Sant'Elia, 1914.

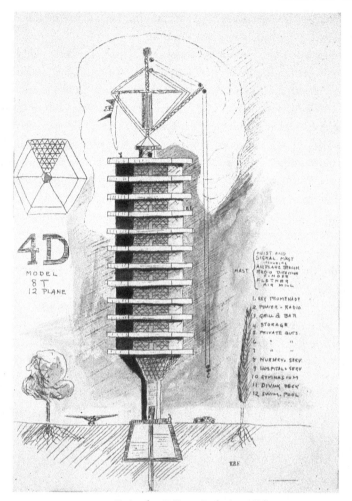

FIGURE 3.3. Project for 4D Tower, Buckminster Fuller, 1928.

of obsolescence at this time—the visionary designer Buckminster Fuller projected in 1928 a futuristic "4D Tower" (time being the fourth dimension), which featured a permanent rooftop crane hoisting in and out of place ever more advanced modular units (fig. 3.3). This was architecture accommodating its own obsolescence, the way "the modern automobile changes year by year," Fuller explained.[8]

Indeed, Henry Ford's automobile company treated its factories as disposable objects during these years. The revolutionary design of Ford's Highland Park plant in Detroit by Albert Kahn, with interior cranes to hoist supplies from railcar to assembly line, had hardly been completed in 1914 before the carmaker's agents in 1915 began buying suburban farmland for the newer, better River Rouge complex ten miles away. Ford's overarching objectives were to mass-produce low price automobiles and pay his workers high enough salaries to afford these and other consumer commodities. Ford believed American industrial prosperity, growth, and social stability would be guaranteed through standardized mass production combined with workers' high wages, an outlook that came be known as Fordism, adopted throughout the mid-century American economy. In pursuit of this ambition, Ford was "more willing than many industrialists to abandon an old building and build a new one," notes the historian Lindy Biggs, leaving obsolete structures to fall to ruin.[9]

Some Europeans at this time were also becoming conscious of architectural obsolescence. The Czech shoe manufacturer Tomáš Baťa, who in the 1910s had personally toured Ford's installations, explicitly railed against "obsolete houses that will strangle and suffocate the next generation." Instead, Baťa projected fixed twenty-year life spans for the factories and dwellings of his famed company town of Zlín, whose gridded architectural designs Le Corbusier himself on a visit praised for combining "diverse parts into a harmonious whole."[10] Elsewhere in Europe, a Swiss lakeside bathhouse was built to be extendable and dividable for changing needs. A Dutch sanatorium was made expandable, too, with an assumed thirty-year life span that foresaw tuberculosis's eradication.[11] In England, the editors of *The Architects' Journal* imagined that the ideal new school "is one which will be efficient for 30 to 40 years only"; and a British biologist in 1936 lecturing to architects suggested that "structures should be designed for a life of no more than 25 years" so as not to "stultify the development of the human organism."[12] But these, like the American cases, were eccentricities. In the 1920s and 1930s the promise of obsolescence remained too exotic for most architectural imaginations, too much at odds with traditional presumptions of permanence. Real estate experts and planners grappled with obsolescence in these decades, but the vast majority of architects saw no relation yet to their own thought and practice.

Postwar America

After World War II the possibilities obsolescence afforded architecture became more evident. In America, prefabrication and demountability using boom cranes, for disassembly and possible reassembly elsewhere, which had been pioneered for wartime housing, now seemed applicable generally "for outwitting extraordinary forms of obsolescence," reported the journal *Pencil Points* in 1944.[13] Articles on retail store obsolescence, bathroom obsolescence, and apartment and single-family home obsolescence also appeared intermittently in the American architectural press of the 1940s and 1950s. "Yesterday's house is as obsolete as yesterday's car," warned *House and Home* in 1959.[14] In these commentaries, obsolescence could be a matter of new technology superseding old (e.g., artificial lighting enabling offices away from windows); or of institutions evolving toward different accommodation (e.g., servant space made redundant in the home). In 1950, when Frank Lloyd Wright's famous Larkin company office building in Buffalo was demolished after forty-four years of life, the architect "reportedly said that the building had served its purpose and deserved a decent burial," remembered one of his associates.[15] Awareness and even acceptance of architectural obsolescence was on the rise, but it was not yet a preoccupation.

Elsewhere in American design culture, however, ideas about obsolescence took faster, stronger hold. In 1947 the industrial designer J. Gordon Lippincott forecast obsolescence as postwar America's "Keynote of Prosperity."[16] Obsolescence fueled American postwar capitalism, the argument went. Consumer desire for fashionable novelty, primed by advertising and design, quickened at expectations of easy expendability. In 1957 Brooks Stevens, a designer of Jeeps and Harleys, declared, "Our whole economy is based on planned obsolescence, and everybody who can read without moving his lips should know it by now."[17] Obsolescence kept factories occupied, labor employed, and corporations profitable, went the argument. It was essential to the engine of Fordism, encouraging workers and consumers to buy products the assembly lines churned out, keeping all well-paid and employed. "Without installment buying and obsolescence," claimed the commentator Paul Mazur, "large sections of our billion dollar industries would rust."[18]

In the context of the Cold War, this type obsolescence-driven prosperity symbolized capitalism's superiority over communism. American homes and driveways were filled with televisions and tailfins not through state control of the economy but via the agency of private ownership, markets and individual choice. The apparently egalitarian opportunity for possession of this stream of commodities, transcending traditional boundaries of ethnicity and class, offered a new, inclusive form of social identity and democratic citizenship, a "consumers' republic," in the words of the historian Lizabeth Cohen.[19] The same ideology of beneficent obsolescence, in which expendability represented progress, supported U.S. military superiority, President Dwight Eisenhower noted in 1956, "recognizing that obsolescence compels the never-ending replacement of older weapons with new ones."[20] Obsolescence underwrote Cold War American practices and values from economics to geopolitics. Thus the leading industrial designer George Nelson could boldly declare in an oft-republished 1956 essay, "What we need is more obsolescence, not less" —

accelerated, systematized, and scaled up. "The same holds for the cities," Nelson pronounced, explicitly bringing the built environment into the picture.[21]

American architects in the 1950s, however, were not yet up to the task. Even those who conceived of modern housing in terms of miraculous gadgetry and economical prefabrication, like the Harvard dean Joseph Hudnut describing a futuristic "refrigerator to-live-in," neither promoted nor predicted actual short-lived buildings.[22] Less engaged with consumer culture than industrial designers were, architects hewed longer to principles of longevity and fixed form (perhaps in answer to public expectations of what "home" and "architecture" should look like) and abjured an aesthetics of impermanence and mutability. A relative exception was the prominent American architect Eero Saarinen. Like the General Motors executives for whom he built a new headquarters in suburban Detroit, Saarinen believed in a new style for every job—a kind of annual model change in architecture that avoided set vocabularies—even if such "unique design solutions were inherently time-limited," as the architectural historian Alice Friedman has written about Saarinen's glamorous, image-conscious work, which other modernists derided as overly fickle and fashion oriented.[23] Still, the pump was being primed for more architects to engage with transience and expendability. Living in a culture of consumer obsolescence, a younger generation of American architects would soon respond to Nelson's challenge for "more obsolescence, not less."

British Engagements

Differently than America, in Britain consciousness of obsolescence entered architectural culture through other means. Postwar austerity made American-style consumerism at first a fantasy, illustrated in the collage dreams of the artist Eduardo Paolozzi (fig. 3.4). Paolozzi advocated "an alternative culture," with "more energy and excitement than official culture."[24] Soon after hearing Paolozzi lecture in 1952 at London's Institute of Contemporary Art, the young architecture critic and historian Reyner Banham, part of the Independent Group circle of artists, began preaching "an aesthetics of expendability" for the age's "throwaway economy" and "noisy ephimeridae" (fig. 3.5).[25] Obsolescence was liberation, in Banham's influential view. It should happen, dissolving "permanency, durability and perennity," and producing "an expendable, replaceable vehicle of popular desires," an architectural equivalent to the vibrancy of consumer culture expressed by Paolozzi. From prominent perches in media and academia, Banham would give voice to a British generation's embrace in the 1960s of obsolescence, its technophilia, consumerism, and Americanism.

FIGURE 3.4. *Dr Pepper*, Sir Eduardo Paolozzi (1924–2005), 1948.

    A second British engagement with obsolescence from a more analytical angle also emerged in the 1950s, centered on the figure of the establishment architect Richard Llewelyn Davies (fig. 3.6). In the mid-1950s he directed a large multidisciplinary study of hospital design in support of the new National Health Service, seeking efficiencies in the face of limited state funding. Without yet naming obsolescence as such, Llewelyn Davies's team, which included experts in statistics and management, sought to avoid feared future losses in hospital buildings' utility and value due to technological and service innovations. A short section of the study titled "Flexibility and Growth," likely authored by the young architect John Weeks, concluded that hospital wards should be planned "like branches on a tree, each with freedom to grow without disturbing the general pattern."[26]

Llewelyn Davies's analytical, multidisciplinary 1955 study reflected his social-, teamwork-, and research-oriented education at Cambridge University and the Architectural Association in the 1930s. His war years were spent on quick-assembly, prefabricated railway stations under the direction of Leslie

FIGURE 3.5. Reyner Banham, prophet of expendability.

FIGURE 3.6. Richard Llewelyn Davies, obsolescence researcher.

Martin, which honed Llewelyn Davies's scientific approach to architecture. After the war he and Weeks went to work on prefabricated, modular school designs, and then both went together to the research department of the Nuffield Provincial Hospitals Trust, which sponsored the major 1955 study. Llewelyn Davies's interest in growth and form also reflected a particular postwar cultural consciousness. A well-known 1951 London Institute of Contemporary Art exhibit, exploring "ordered complexity," gained inspiration from the biologist D'Arcy Wentworth Thompson's classic *On Growth and Form*, a book cited in a 1951 Llewelyn Davies article titled "Endless Architecture."[27] In this article, widely read at the time, Llewelyn Davies praised Mies van der Rohe's recent boxlike glass, steel, and brick buildings at the Illinois Institute of Technology for having achieved an ideal synthesis of "symmetry and infinite repetition" in its repeated-bay aesthetic. Mies's Alumni Memorial Hall, Llewelyn Davies asserted, possesses both walls conceived as "unbounded" without "stop-ends" at the corners, "extending infinitely into space," yet also restrained in the composition's subtle, overall symmetry, "giving it repose [. . .] the faintest possible steadying of the eye."[28] This was just the kind of accommodation to change within order that Llewelyn Davies hoped to emulate against obsolescence in hospitals.

Llewelyn Davies, like Banham, would emerge an influential figure in British obsolescence work, spearheading a decade-long research effort in the 1960s at the University of London. Llewelyn Davies and his colleagues presumed obsolescence would happen and sought accommodations to it. They were agnostic as to whether it should happen, unlike Banham, who openly promoted the process. Though coming from different vantages, the two men complemented each other in their work. The efficiencies against obsolescence sought by Llewelyn Davies for welfare-state services enabled the personal freedoms that Banham celebrated in consumer culture. In turn, satisfied individual desires would, we might suggest, make bearable for people at an everyday level the increasingly organized and straitjacketing British welfare-state society.

In 1950s America the situation differed. A weaker, decentralized state in terms of social services did not support extended obsolescence research like Llewelyn Davies's into hospital design. Consumerism was actual, not exoticized, so perhaps Americans were less inclined to fetishize expendability, as did the Englishmen Paolozzi and Banham. Moreover, the United States had no equivalent to the close-knit London artistic scene that stimulated architects' thinking about consumerism, growth, and form. The American architectural establishment in this period was still largely devoted to the technologically driven steel, glass, and concrete modernism of Mies, Le Corbusier, and Gropius. American architectural engagement with obsolescence would emerge through different channels. The U.S. and British cases do not exhaust the possibilities of studying national contexts for emerging architectural consciousness of obsolescence in the 1950s. They are two instances that can frame other national analyses of how cultural and politicoeconomic factors stimulated obsolescence awareness.

Avant-Garde and Establishment Discourses in the 1960s

Starting in the early 1960s, the density of obsolescence discourse intensified in architectural culture. In Britain, Banham's obsolescence campaign had been echoed since the late 1950s by the architects Alison and Peter Smithson, who took inspiration from throwaway consumer society, as did Paolozzi and other Independent Group artists. The Smithsons wrote about "an aesthetics of change" in 1957 and in 1960 coauthored another article that distinguished between long-life "architectural fixes" (public institutions) and short-life "architectural transients" (shops and houses).[29] The latter "transients" were embraced with a vengeance by a group of young London architects producing the magazine *Archigram*, the 1963 issue of which prophesied "Expendability: Towards Throwaway Architecture"—building as mass consumption, a "direct expression of a freedom to choose."[30] The new decade was getting under way with hopes of youthful change. As the architectural historian Elain Harwood writes, "The Sixties opened with an unquestioned belief in new technology, and in progress as a simple and continually upward curve."[31] Another young English architect, Cedric Price, writing in *Archigram* 2 (1962), promoted "an expendable aesthetic" and "planned obsolescence." Price characterized his own building designs as "short-life toys." "Nothing is to last for more than ten years, some things not even ten days,"[32] Price described his unbuilt 1964–66 Fun Palace project for a London entertainment complex, envisioned as a fantastic open framework of shiftable interior parts.

The embrace of obsolescence in avant-garde circles spread internationally in the 1960s. The Team X group of young architects from across Europe, who came together to theorize a new modernism, advocated "the possibilities offered by a 'throw-away' technology," wrote the Smithsons in 1962.[33] In Paris, the Israeli Yona Friedman imagined in the late 1950s a "mobile architecture" of interchangeable modules within a giant space frame, "expression of a constantly changing structure of society" (fig. 3.7).[34] Also in Paris, the Dutch artist Constant Nieuwenhuys's "New Babylon" experiments (1957–74) envisioned a similar utopia, where "every element would be left undetermined, mobile and flexible" to let people "play their lives in a variety of surroundings."[35] The

FIGURE 3.7. Ville Spatiale (Paris), Yona Friedman, 1959.

French intellectual group Utopie, which included the philosopher Jean Baudrillard, published in 1967 an extended analysis of obsolescence. "The ephemeral is undoubtedly the truth of our future habitats," declared Baudrillard.[36]
And in America, Robert Venturi and Denise Scott Brown learned from studying Las Vegas in 1968 to accept and even embrace the spectacle of obsolescence. "The most unique, most monumental parts of the Strip, the signs and
casino facades, are also the most changeable," they observed. From this Venturi and Scott Brown would devise the idea of "decorated shed" architecture,
generic buildings emblazoned with large-scale imagery.[37]

Meanwhile, in Japan, the Metabolist group of young architects, organized
together at a 1960 Tokyo design conference, saw in obsolescence opportunities for an indigenous Japanese modernism. Obsolescence embodied Japan's
new industrial-consumer society. But the ephemeral process also resonated
with native themes of architectural transience. Traditions of wood construction, Shinto shrine rebuilding, and Buddhism's cyclical life view seemed to
be aspects of an essential Japanese acceptance of evanescence, reflecting an
experience of visceral built-environment catastrophes that ranged from historic earthquakes and fires to recent wartime bombing. "There is no fixed
form in the ever-developing world," declared the critic Noboru Kawazoe in
the publication *Metabolism 1960: Proposals for a New Urbanism*; "we hope
to create something which, even in destruction, will cause a subsequent new
creation."[38] Illustrating Metabolist ideas, Arata Isozaki's 1962 "Future City

(The Incubation Process)" shows an unfinished concrete work of infrastructure bestriding the ruins of both past and present—an image of unceasing supersession and expendability (fig. 3.8).

Avant-garde engagements with obsolescence traveled widely. The Tokyo World Design Conference of 1960—launchpad of Metabolism—was attended by leading American and European architects, including Louis Kahn, Paul Rudolph, and the Smithsons. Reyner Banham's long 1965 article, "A Clip-On Architecture," was published separately in both the United States and Britain. The Yale University architecture school's leading journal, *Perspecta*, featured in its 1967 issue the work of Archigram, Team X, and the Metabolists. It also reprinted George Nelson's 1956 clarion call for "more obsolescence." In 1968 the London *Architectural Review* published a unique, broad-ranging essay entitled "Obsolescence" by the Italian architect Manfredi Nicoletti, which cited the Futurists, British obsolescence researchers, and Nicoletti's colleague Yona Friedman. In the contemporary unsettled life-world, Nicoletti wrote, "marked by an irresistible acceleration of obsolescence," there also, importantly, existed a contrary human need for "some degree of constancy [. . .] symbols of continuity." It would be architecture's job, Nicoletti argued, to provide "a consistent physiognomy" in the face of obsolescence's deformations.[39]

How to confront obsolescence was an abiding concern not just of avant-garde but of mainstream architecture, too. In England, Llewelyn Davies (knighted in 1963 for his service to state and profession) became head of the University of London's Bartlett School of Architecture, one of the country's preeminent institutions, where he hired none other than Banham to teach architectural history and theory. For himself, and perhaps typical of his slightly older wartime generation, Llewelyn Davies championed a technocratic, problem-solving approach to building, for the benefit of the British welfare state and society, and within which obsolescence would be combated more than embraced. Thus Llewelyn Davies established in 1964 a Joint Unit for Planning Research to pursue obsolescence work. With sustained government support, this group published in leading journals across the 1960s numerous studies of hospital, office, and other building types' functional performances over time, culminating in a major, multivolume 1970 report, "Obsolescence in the Built Environment."[40] "Nowadays almost every building becomes obsolete before it is ready to fall down," declared the lead researcher, Peter Cowan. In a graph from 1963 entitled "Functional Obsolescence," Cowan diagrammed and theorized obsolescence as an inexorable process of devaluation— performance always stepping down, a decline arrested just temporarily by rebuilding or adaptation (fig. 3.9).[41] Further analysis revealed obsolescence to be irreducible to easy prediction or analogy. "To impose patterns of natural

FIGURE 3.8. Future City (Incubation Process), Arata Isozaki, 1962.

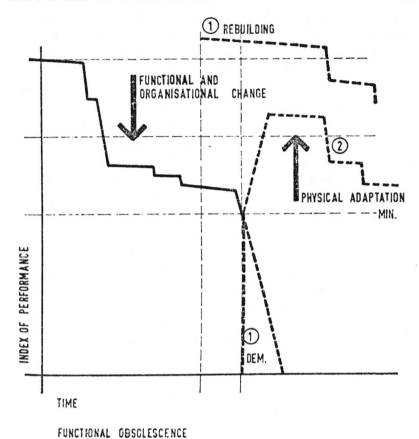

FIGURE 3.9. "Functional Obsolescence" graph, Peter Cowan, University of London, 1963.

growth upon buildings is not only irrelevant but wrong," concluded Cowan. "The vagaries of human social action" controlled change "in fits and starts at varying intervals of time."[42]

Mainstream architecture recognized that major building types, from factories to libraries to airports to offices, on both sides of the Atlantic faced challenges of technological and organizational obsolescence.[43] No less a figure than President Lyndon Johnson raised the alarm on hospitals in 1966. "General hospitals containing 260,000 beds—one third of our nation's—are now in obsolete condition," declared the nation's leader when seeking congressional funding to repair the problem.[44] One American study, commissioned by a Portland, Oregon, hospital from the West Coast architect Herbert McLaughlin, called for all new nursing units to "be designed for demolition and replacement" within twenty years, paced to anticipated obsolescence.[45]

In the realm of school building, the American architect Ezra Ehrenkrantz (inspired by his work and study in Britain) successfully promoted to California public officials in the mid-1960s a system of modular flexibility adaptable to change. "It sounded like a very appealing thing to them," explained the designer-as-marketer; "there was a nice inherent sales situation there."[46] And in the same year the Bartlett obsolescence studies culminated, two American architecture professors, William Zuk and Roger H. Clark, brought out a 163-page illustrated primer titled *Kinetic Architecture* (featuring Archigram and Buckminster Fuller), which promoted expendable, demountable, and disposable buildings. Zuk and Clark's arguments were based upon the now-conventional presumption that "very often, in fact, buildings are functionally obsolete before they are complete."[47] All invocations of flexibility at this time were in effect fears of obsolescence, awareness of which was at its most pervasive in the 1960s. Selling obsolescence, as Ehrenkrantz did explicitly, worked in an era beset by change, felt not only by school and hospital administrators, but by whole societies generally buffeted by political instability and the rapid renewal of the built environment.

Facilities management also began emerging in the mid-1960s as a distinct profession nurturing building longevity in the face of obsolescence. The British architect Frank Duffy recalled, "In New York in the Sixties, I first came across serious designers (who called themselves space planners and who were then despised as hacks by conventional architects) who understood something of the changing relationship between complex organizations and their stock of space."[48] The Herman Miller furniture corporation focused upon the modular, flexible production of office environments that could adapt over time. The conglomerates IBM and McDonald's, to extend building life, initiated post-occupancy evaluation studies of facilities' design efficiencies as their functions changed over time. In British academic circles, a pioneering Building Performance Research Unit that aimed to reconceptualize design as "a continuous process lasting as long as the building itself" was established by Thomas Markus in the mid-1960s, first in Wales and then at the University of Strathclyde.[49] All these efforts explicitly targeted obsolescence.

In the space of a few decades, centuries-old presumptions of architectural permanence had been overthrown. "Ours is an age of change, of dynamism, of unrest, of revolution," proclaimed the authors of *Kinetic Architecture*, echoing the era's dominant refrain.[50] A postwar generation raised in prosperity, consumerism, and seemingly limitless resources took innovation, supersession, and expendability to be a general condition of change. "Buildings which formerly took fifty years to fail, now fail in five," declared the firm of young avant-garde architects Candilis, Josic, and Woods in 1965.[51] Ubiquitous demolition made the process seem inevitable, natural, and universal. A 1964 cartoon in the American magazine *Look* wryly depicted a modern building cornerstone: "Erected 1964 . . . To Be Demolished 1975"—an echo of the 1920s, but now a generation or so later less wondrously, more sardonically observed.[52] Obsolescence would happen; it was the new normal for change in the built environment. Obsolescence had to be engaged in architectural thought. It might be rationalized for efficiency's sake, accepting that it would inevitably occur—the attitude of mainstream figures like Llewelyn Davies and his research colleagues. Or obsolescence might be wholeheartedly embraced for its liberating potential, for the idea that it should happen—the outlook given voice by Reyner Banham. School builders and hospital designers, quantitative researchers and visionary utopians, mainstream and avant-garde architects alike—obsolescence was the ocean in which all swam.

Disjointed Discourses

Yet, the circuitry between the multiple poles of architectural discourse on obsolescence in the 1960s remained unintegrated. Hospital investigators across the Atlantic knew little of one another's work. Banham accused American architects of lagging fifteen years behind his countrymen's grasp of indeterminacy.[53] Beyond the University of London, little sustained research was supported by government or industry. In America, only rarely did a private professional firm, like the Texas-based Caudill Rowland Scott (CRS), pursue a research program, but none of its dozens of reports focused specifically upon obsolescence.[54]

Even at the Bartlett School of Architecture, with its unique engagement with obsolescence, there were difficulties. Research analysts took at face value the short building lifespan figures they found in American tax tables, misunderstanding their fundamentally political—not scientific—derivation.[55] People equally preoccupied by obsolescence at the Bartlett ignored each other's insights. Banham, the prophet of expendability embracing obsolescence that *should* happen, dismissed the pragmatic Llewelyn Davies circle's "solid, plodding work," who merely accepted that obsolescence *would* happen.[56] Reciprocally, the latter never engaged Banham's cultural outlook and affirmation of obsolescence. Common interest in obsolescence failed to bridge architecture's deep-rooted establishment/avant-garde divide.

The result was a relatively underdeveloped and unintegrated architectural discourse on obsolescence. Clichés abounded, echoing one another: "nowadays almost every building becomes obsolete before it is ready to fall down"; "buildings which formerly took fifty years to fail, now fail in five." What architects verbalized went little beyond previous explorations. A half century after the engineer Reginald Bolton's pioneering but now obscure work, architects in the 1960s rediscovered that buildings obsolesced at different rates. Nor did they strive to correct their predecessors' blindnesses. Like the real estate man Earle Shultz of the 1920s, researchers in the 1960s emphasized quantification of building performance, disregarding affective values of fashion and taste, desire and memory. And like theorists of urban obsolescence since the 1930s, the next generation projected into the future the recent past's pace of change, presuming obsolescence's universality.

Still, there were glimmers of opportunity. The plural architectural discourses on obsolescence in the 1960s indicated contradictions in the response to obsolescence, in the tensions between seeking efficiency and embracing freedom, balancing change and constancy, between the woulds and the shoulds of obsolescence. However, these were difficulties to be worked out not verbally, but rather in design. Beyond the problems of intradisciplinary communication, architects generally pursued their deepest thinking in building, not writing (otherwise they would have been philosophers, not designers). The multiple discourses on architectural obsolescence of the 1960s set the conceptual contexts and problems. But answers and further questions would be formed through design, not words.

Fixing Obsolescence

A variety of architectural design fixes for obsolescence were worked out mainly in the 1960s. In this most intense decade of engagement, designing for obsolescence would mean first repairing, or rather preempting, obsolescence's degradations of utility, making sure a building worked regardless of functional change. In these cases, architects accepted that obsolescence would happen. But they strove to mitigate its effects by making buildings internally adaptable and therefore, hopefully, longer lived. A second-level fix for obsolescence sought to stabilize architectural form against obsolescence's deformations, ensuring aesthetic continuity. Here, architects more willingly accepted obsolescence's dramatic physical changes, yet still designed for some degree of aesthetic coherence over time. The third and most difficult fix for obsolescence entailed picturing in form itself the process of obsolescence; this meant not "fixing" in terms of repairing or stabilizing, but fixing in terms of capturing an image of a dynamic temporal process. This fix would consider obsolescence visually, not verbally, in order to plumb its depths and limits through architecture. In these rare, even poetic instances, architects believed not just that obsolescence would happen but that it should. They welcomed the fullness of obsolescence's promise, both its inevitability and its gifts. This kind of design hoped that embracing obsolescence—transience and expendability, the shedding of past and present, habit and convention—would lead to greater fulfillment of human opportunity and freedom.

These ideas found expression in built and unbuilt designs alike. They also came through in work made by avant-garde and establishment figures—both engaged obsolescence profoundly—and in work made around the globe, from America to Europe to Japan. Just as there were multiple discourses of obsolescence—real estate and urban, pre- and post–World War II, capitalist and socialist—so were there plural design responses to obsolescence. What follows is not an exhaustive account but a general schema of the architectures of obsolescence.

Factory Sheds

Architects' prime design solution to obsolescence in the mid-twentieth century was the open-plan factory shed. The prototypical 1937 Glenn Martin aircraft plant outside Baltimore, Maryland, by the firm of Albert Kahn, for example, anticipated planes with three-hundred-foot wingspans assembled under a vast support-free roof, made possible by innovations in steel-and-glass construction (fig. 4.1). The longevity of the structural shell would be maximized by its capacity for internal adaptability. As a postwar example of the same solution, in the 1960s, Team 4—the young husband-and-wife pairs of architects Richard and Su Rogers and Norman and Wendy Foster—adapted an open-floor factory-shed plan for the Reliance Controls electronics facility at Swindon, near London (fig. 4.2). Unlike prewar modernists, who used sliding partitions for spontaneity and freedom in domestic settings (like at the Dutch Schröder-Schräder house discussed in the last chapter), Team 4's focus in Swindon was flexibility to ensure functionality and productivity in the face of anticipated technological and organizational obsolescence, which

FIGURE 4.1. Glenn Martin Aircraft Assembly Building, Middle River (Maryland), Albert Kahn, 1937.

FIGURE 4.2. Reliance Controls Factory, Swindon (England), Team Four Architects, 1967.

had not been expectations of the 1920s avant-garde. Movable partitions at Reliance Controls enabled flexible division into various manufacturing, office, and canteen functions.

The factory-shed model's adaptability specifically to office design was most fully embodied at mid-century by the *Bürolandschaft* (office landscaping) movement (fig. 4.3), which originated in Germany. Low-slung, lightweight furnishings spread informally across open floor plates symbolized flexibility against obsolescence. *Bürolandschaft* planning presumed that obsolescence would happen—that changes in work technique would inevitably outmode fixed physical arrangements. A leading exponent of *Bürolandschaft*, the British architect Frank Duffy, explained, "The basic office building shell lasts 40 years; the scenery within five to seven."[1] School buildings also adopted the factory-shed model. In California, the School Construction Systems Development (SCSD) program, devised in the 1960s by Ezra Ehrenkrantz for some dozen high schools, employed beneath a broad steel roof demountable partitions, folding panels, accordion walls, and relocatable services (fig. 4.4). The concern was that "a given school's educational program may impose entirely different requirements in ten or even five years," explained Ehrenkrantz in 1964.[2] All was changeable internally against the threat of obsolescence.

The factory-shed response to obsolescence proved adaptable as well for more technically complex programs, like laboratories and hospitals, in North America and Europe. The renowned American architect Louis Kahn's Salk Institute (1959–65) in La Jolla, California, pioneered the composition of stacked open loft levels, in which every other floor held working lab or ward space, while the intervening decks were packed with piping and duct-work, as also in the San Diego Veterans Administration Hospital, completed by the firm of Charles Luckman in 1968 (fig. 4.5). Thus the habitable sto-ries were flexibly serviced and left unobstructed for reconfiguration in this so-called interstitial system "to create space that does not become obsolete," explained the Canadian architect Eberhard Zeidler about his sprawling Mc-Master Health Sciences Center in Hamilton, Ontario (1967–72).[3] Interstitial-ism's characteristic exterior box massing, as at London's Greenwich District Hospital by W. E. Tatton Brown and R. H. Goodman (1962–74), reflects the

FIGURE 4.3. Frederick Deckel Building, Munich, Walter Henn, 1961.

FIGURE 4.4. Sonora High School, Fullerton (California), William E. Blurock, 1966.

factory shed's typical truss construction (fig. 4.6). Yet the external rigidity
of the fixed frame belied the interior's endlessly divisible spatial mutability
(fig. 4.7). To architects for whom monumentality in modern form was a virtue, like Kahn, factory-shed planning possessed enticing attractions. Worlds
of transience and change were encased in stasis and permanence. This is the
design dichotomy of the factory-shed solution to obsolescence: to hold it at
bay by internalizing its deformations.

As a solution to obsolescence, interstitialism spawned cultural variants,
such as Paris's Pompidou Center for modern art (1970–77), known as Beaubourg. Here the interstitial principle is externalized and verticalized. The
service elements, rather than being contained within alternating horizontal
levels, are clipped upward to the outside frame (fig. 4.8). At Beaubourg, this
created clear-span interior loft exhibition floors, which thus become "a flexible

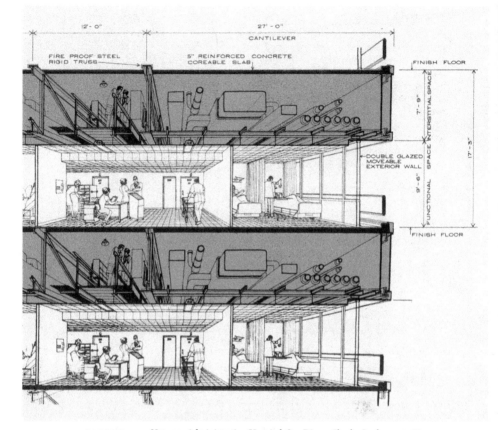

FIGURE 4.5. Veterans Administration Hospital, San Diego, Charles Luckman, 1968.

and evolutive space," resilient against obsolescence, the architects Richard Rogers and Renzo Piano explained. Indeed, Piano declared, "Beaubourg isn't built for 20 years, but for 300, 400, 500 years."[4] The force of Beaubourg's design lies precisely in its tension between permanence and transience. The thin structural lattice is static and contained whereas the clipped-on services and internal partitioning appear mutable and ephemeral.

Another museum variant of interstitialism, Ludwig Mies van der Rohe's New National Gallery in Berlin (1962–68), takes the type to its extreme (fig. 4.9). Here, all that services the institution and makes it work (permanent galleries, office, and mechanical systems) lies downward, out of sight, in the podium. The museum's visible identity stands as an open glass shed that could accommodate any sort of exhibition and layout. Mies had been experimenting with the type of the "single large room" since the early 1940s,

FIGURE 4.6. Greenwich District Hospital, London, W. E. Tatton Brown and R. H. Goodman, 1962–74.

not coincidentally upon leaving Germany and settling in Chicago, the capital of obsolescence. (One of his early photo-collage experiments in 1942 in fact took an image of the Glenn Martin factory shed and transformed it into an art gallery.) Clearly aware of obsolescence's threat, Mies cautioned, "The purposes for which a building is used are constantly changing and we cannot afford to tear down the building each time."[5] Mies's response, for any function, was a bare structural steel frame, which symbolically represented technological society and was also viable indefinitely, encompassing space provisionally partitioned in an open "variable ground plan," as Mies called it.[6] Thus, "the building lasts much longer than its function."[7] Less was not just more, to paraphrase Mies's famous dictum; it was forever. At the Berlin National Gallery, infinitely adaptable space, flexibly partitioned, seemingly extended indefinitely past columnless corners. But this was *virtual* adaptability, not the real thing, dependent upon the conventional rooms below, extension structurally impossible without those corner supports, and the whole firmly finished within the square plan's columns, roof, and glass. Mies's New National Gallery represents the symbolic essence of the factory-shed solution: obsolescence's flux absorbed within the perfect, fixed frame.

Initially provision has been made for general medicine with beds. It is hoped that the combination of clinical and non-clinical departments on each floor and their close proximity to each other—both vertically and horizontally—will encourage a 'therapeutic community' within the hospital, bringing different categories of staff into closer contact, breaking down traditional barriers between grades and between staff and patients. If the more than usually apparent cheerfulness of some of the staff—particularly at the less exalted end of the hierarchy—is anything to go

by, then the therapy seems already to be having the desired effect.

The ward

Each ward unit is planned so that patients' rooms are along the outside wall, with ancillary rooms between the ward corridor and the main 'inner ring hospital street'. In this

Detailed plan of second floor

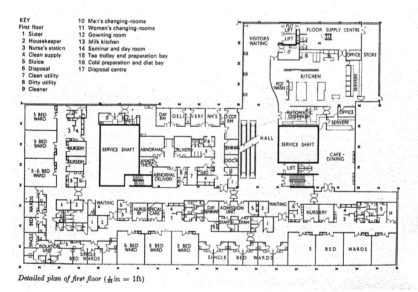

Detailed plan of first floor ($\frac{1}{32}$ in = 1 ft)

FIGURE 4.7. Greenwich District Hospital plans, from *The Architects' Journal*, 26 November 1969, p. 1373.

FIGURE 4.8. Pompidou Center, Paris, Renzo Piano + Richard Rogers, 1970–77.

FIGURE 4.9. New National Gallery, Berlin, Ludwig Mies van der Rohe, 1962–68.

Indeterminacy

Notwithstanding its apparent virtues and widespread adoption, the factory-shed solution to obsolescence had its critics on both practical and symbolic grounds. Complete flexibility was actually unnecessary and expensive, some argued. "The great majority of things in life," British obsolescence studies of the 1960s suggested, "are done in spaces between 100 and 200 square feet."[8] The factory shed's endless rearrangement of room sizes was thus superfluous. Rather, a few standard room types would do: "the ability to provide services at every point over the whole of a building is a luxury."[9] The factory shed's monolithic massing clashed symbolically, too, with the age's perceived dynamism. John Weeks rejected the impulse "to build architectural monuments, expensive, elaborate and, being monumental, necessarily finite."[10] Instead, he proposed in the early 1960s an "indeterminate architecture" as the best "solution to the problem of obsolescence."[11] As Weeks explained in a 1964 article: "Where buildings cannot last to necessary efficiency standards, even for the duration of one man's life, without almost continuous alteration and enlargement, the use of 'closed form' design rules is inappropriate. [. . .] A building for an indeterminate brief cannot then adhere to a finite geometric control system. The ideal of unity through constant relationships cannot be achieved. Such a building will be geometrically aformal."[12] Weeks's thinking about obsolescence and indeterminacy was particularly British, derived in part from detailed investigations into building obsolescence that were the product of British welfare-state research. In the United States, by contrast, the monolithic designs of Mies and Kahn held sway, uninflected by any empirical understanding of how change would deform fixed geometries. These were two different architectures of obsolescence. Both belonged to the paradigm, but each acknowledged it differently. Indeterminacy, as Weeks theorized and practiced it, more openly accepted obsolescence's deformation of form, as both a realistic fact of change and as a symbolization of modern dynamism.

Weeks had been trained beginning in 1938 at the Architectural Association and then after the war worked on prefabricated rail stations, where he met Richard Llewelyn Davies, as discussed in the previous chapter. After completing their 1950s investigations of British hospital design, the two opened together a private practice in 1960 whose first major commission, appropriately, was for a hospital at Northwick Park in suburban London (1961–76), the largest and most expensive British medical complex of its day (fig. 4.10). Here Weeks put into practice his theory of indeterminacy, the idea of open-ended, "aformal" design that could flex under the pressures of obsolescence.

FIGURE 4.10. Northwick Park Hospital, aerial view, Harrow (England), Richard Llewelyn Davies and John Weeks, 1961–76.

Northwick Park Hospital's interior layout of fixed room dimensions reflected the obsolescence investigators' findings that most hospital functions
could actually be accommodated in a narrow range of room sizes (100–150
square feet). This the architects called "duffle coat" planning, after the Royal
Navy's limited range of coat sizes provided to sailors.[13] For larger-scale adaptation Northwick Park Hospital was designed to modify its total shape.
The loose-jointed site plan's individual blocks could, if necessary, be demolished and updated without disturbing the functioning or overall unity
of the whole (unlike a monolithic factory shed). Many of Northwick Park
Hospital's edges also feature "growing ends," shown in the site plan with dot-
ted lines and arrows at the margins of several buildings (fig. 4.11). Here, demountable fire stairs and steel panels, which could be taken down and put
up again as needed, visibly anticipate extension (fig. 4.12). Thus the hospital's total form could flex in response to institutional change. Northwick Park
Hospital's potential shape-shifting reflects obsolescence investigators' insights
into different rates of growth and change among hospital departments—for

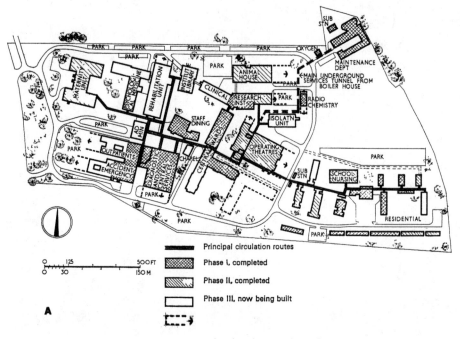

FIGURE 4.11. Northwick Park Hosptial, site plan.

example, that lab and research spaces evolved much more dramatically than patient areas.[14]

Weeks's approach expresses architecture's essential unfinished nature, its indeterminacy against obsolescence. In this Weeks's aesthetic also reflected contemporary general interest in the "open work," as the Italian philosopher Umberto Eco wrote in 1962, "to conceive, feel, and thus see the world as possibility," performing a "liberating role" from convention.[15] Weeks was a close associate from the early 1950s of such experimental artists as Adrian Heath and Kenneth and Mary Martin, who saw modern visual culture similarly, and with whom Weeks collaborated on the famed 1956 This Is Tomorrow exhibit at London's Institute of Contemporary Art.[16] Weeks conceived indeterminate architecture similarly to these artists' open-ended, abstract constructions of screens and walls. Northwick Park Hospital would have "no final plan," Weeks envisioned, being "forever unfinished."[17] The architect must "design a building that will inhibit *change* of function least"; "buildings must be designed on the assumptions that, in the long run, the brief is wrong."[18] Liberated from conventions of architectural authorship and functionalism, the designer alone "cannot determine what an indeterminate building will look like," Weeks

FIGURE 4.12. Northwick Park Hospital, growing end.

asserted.[19] On Northwick Park Hospital's exterior the concrete mullions are thus spaced with apparent irregularity, not as usual to interior functional layouts or the architect's ideal proportions. Instead, the building's appearance derived from the structural loading conditions of engineers' calculations, which produce unexpected visual rhythms. Hence the architect disavows sole responsibility for design, instead enfranchising other agents. Indeterminacy at Northwick Park Hospital welcomes contingency. "Each elevation was a surprise and delight to us," rejoiced Weeks.[20]

Nevertheless, Weeks recognized the traditional aesthetic requirement for enduring identity, "a comprehensible building," he explained.[21] This was provided at Northwick Park Hospital by its internal circulation system. Branching glass-walled corridors connect the individual blocks, most clearly visible in the center of the complex (see fig. 4.11). The projected site plan shows the ensemble's full build-out, linked by "principal circulation routes." "The street system is firm," explained Weeks, "visible and identifiable everywhere," allowing the whole "to grow with order and to change with calm."[22] "The primacy of the communication network" maintains Northwick Park Hospital's coherent identity, according to Weeks.[23]

A resilient net as a model thus replaces the open-plan factory-shed antidote to obsolescence. Emphasizing communication, Northwick Park Hospital's design reflects postwar fascination with information technology. Not coincidentally, the project was included in a 1968 London Institute of Contemporary Art exhibition titled Cybernetic Serendipity.[24] But a communications net was perhaps too abstract a figure to provide memorable architectural identity. Weeks used another analogy to characterize Northwick Park Hospital as a whole: "a series of villages designed as [...] an urbanistic form."[25] The street provides both permanence and adaptability, and the town rather than the factory shed becomes the archetype for designing against obsolescence, a more flexible fix in shape and image.

Megastructures

The blurred distinction between architecture and urbanism as an effect of confronting obsolescence, which Weeks intuited, also characterized the influential megastructure type of architecture in the 1960s. These were typically constructions of great size and modular extensibility raised high above the ground. The earliest megastructural visions resemble Yona Friedman's 1957–58 scheme for a "Spatial Town" (see fig. 3.7). This was an urban district imagined on pylons set fifty feet above Paris, a multilevel, open superstructure fillable by lightweight, expendable enclosures that, as Friedman explained, "can be written off in a short period of time."[26] Such utopian megastructures, like those also of Constant Nieuwenhuys, embraced the liberating promise of obsolescence. "Every element would be left undetermined, mobile and flexible," proclaimed Constant (as he was known), to let people "play their lives in a variety of surroundings."[27]

In Japan, megastructures became reality, if more prosaic than Constant's dream. Kenzo Tange, with whom many of the Metabolists worked, produced the Yamanashi Press and Broadcasting Center (1961–64), which features soaring, solid service towers between which are slung less permanent-looking studio, workshop, and office units (fig. 4.13). The whole appears rearrangeable and extendable. Horizontal units could be added or taken away and vertical

FIGURE 4.13. Yamanashi Press and Broadcasting Center, Kofu (Japan), Kenzo Tange, 1961–64.

towers added. The Broadcasting Center is in effect a built fragment of mega-structural urbanism. Existing cities were seen to be obsolescing chaotically, constraining efficiency and freedom. The megastructure rationalizes this process. "A kind of man-made Nature," Tange explained, is "a system on the basis of which the future can develop freely."[28]

The megastructure's defining feature was its structural distinction between the permanent infrastructural frame and smaller-scale, shorter life-span components for private purposes—"the frame-and-capsule concept," as Reyner Banham defined it in his chronicle of the megastructure's ubiquity across the globe in the 1960s.[29] A crucial design question thus lay in the relationship between permanent and impermanent parts. How would these asynchronous temporalities, the mismatch between fast- and slow-changing elements, which were endemic to the modern built environment, be composed together in the management of obsolescence? One impulse was toward harmony. A triangular stability in the shape of an A-frame was first tried out by Tange, in collaboration with Massachusetts Institute of Technology students, in a

1959–60 studio project for Boston Harbor (fig. 4.14). Short-life residential units hang from the edge of the huge, fixed pyramidal transport and service A-shaped frame. Obsolescence is thus held in abeyance between the expendable and the permanent, a utopian "order in freedom and freedom in order," as Tange said.[30] This megastructure looming offshore rejects the existing city, thus reflecting the contemporary outlook of urban obsolescence then being imposed in those same years upon Boston's West End neighborhood, within sight of MIT's campus, where Tange and his students worked.

To some, however, the rigidity of Tange's megastructural frame seemed unrealistic (as the factory shed had to proponents of indeterminacy). His fellow Japanese architect Fumihiko Maki asked, what "if the megaform becomes rapidly obsolete"? That is, what if transportation methods change faster than residential habits? Then what becomes of the long-life frame? "It will be a great weight about the neck of urban society," Maki surmised.[31] To account for the unpredictability of obsolescence, the inherent inability to predict what

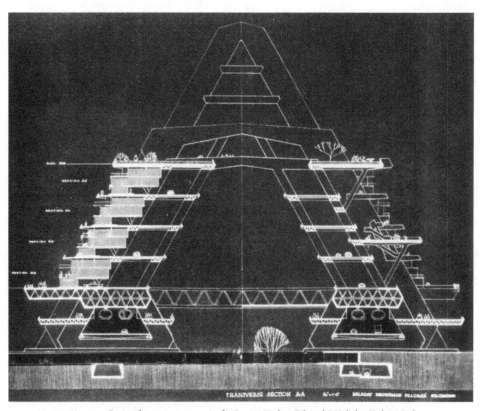

FIGURE 4.14. Project for a new community for Boston Harbor, Edward P. Haladay, Ted A. Niederman, George J. Pillorge, and Gus Solomons, Jr., for Kenzo Tange MIT design studio, 1959–60.

FIGURE 4.15. Project for Shinjuku redevelopment (Tokyo), Fumihiko Maki and Masato Otaka, 1960.

will become devalued and superseded first, Maki instead proposed a more fluid alternative, something he called "group form." In Maki's Shinjuku area Redevelopment Project for Tokyo (1960), a mixed-use complex straddling existing railroad tracks, Maki envisioned a design that could lose and gain its major and not just minor parts while still maintaining "visual consistency," like the large-scale flared "petals" of the Entertainment Square (fig. 4.15).[32]

A similar desire to loosen up the rigid megastructure informed the design of the Berlin Free University (1963–73) by the trio of George Candilis, Alexis Josic, and Shadrach Woods. The Berlin Free University's megastructure is a low-slung web of fixed corridors infilled with classrooms, courtyards, and common areas. On the exterior, the university's modular facade steps down with the fall of the earth, like a layer of ground cover in sympathy with existing conditions, unlike the aloof, archetypal megastructure (fig. 4.16).

FIGURE 4.16. Free University, Berlin, Candilis, Josic & Woods, 1963–73.

The Berlin Free University recognizes its site as a condition to which architecture must adapt as it grapples with change. Similarly, Maki's Shinjuku project acknowledges its locale (see fig. 4.15). A fragment of old Tokyo peeks through near Entertainment Square, in the lower right-hand corner of the model, a jumble of older structures beneath the level of the new podium. Shinjuku reproaches judgment of the existing city as *wholly* obsolete. "There is nothing less urbane, nothing less productive of cosmopolitan mixture, than raw renewal," wrote Maki.[33] This approach sows the seeds of a more nuanced approach to urban change, instead of the dominant paradigm of the cleared tabula rasa, exemplified by the case of Boston's West End.

The basic megastructural insight about differential change thus produced a spectrum of design fixes, from pyramidal harmony to flowing informality, from monumental aloofness to an incipient contextualism, all addressed to the broad question of how to give obsolescence its proper accommodation, form and image in architecture. The megastructure accepted a greater degree of formal mutability than the factory shed and picked up the implication of Weeks's indeterminacy that, under pressure of obsolescence, architecture had to be designed more like a changeful city than a static building. The mega-structure envisions in design a universe enduring through changing, simul-taneously and paradoxically progressing and recurring, a constant cycling of expandable short-life capsules within a more or less stable frame. The aes-thetic principles of the megastructure at the macro level grapple with the question of how to compose a changeful whole.

At the micro level the megastructure's crucial design question lay in fash-ioning the *joints* between components, where the building adapts for change. The Metabolist Kisho Kurokawa in fact made joinery detail his expressive focus. His Takara Beautilion pavilion for the 1970 Osaka World Expo, for example, exaggerated the size of open joints to indicate the possibility of ex-pansion (fig. 4.17). Obsolescence is actively welcomed; the form will shift as the future unfolds. Kurokawa was concerned, too, with the internal junction between differentially obsolescing elements. For his famed Nakagin Capsule

FIGURE 4.17. Takara Beautilion, Osaka, Kisho Kurokawa, 1970.

Tower (1970–72) (fig. 4.18), built to accommodate businessmen in Tokyo's central Ginza district, Kurokawa carefully diagrammed how the short-life steel housing capsules could be bolted and unbolted, pinned and unpinned to the long-life concrete service core (fig. 4.19). This, critically, is where the megastructure becomes operable, regenerating itself against obsolescence. The joinery detail is the design expression of the crucial spatial transition between permanence and impermanence that is central to the megastructural fix for obsolescence. Architecture thus becomes a product of technical mastery and visual communication. While megastructures could be found worldwide addressing the challenge of obsolescence, this particular design response, focused upon the joint, might be seen as especially Japanese through its abstraction of traditional wooden carpentry detail.

Much more difficult to image than the spatial aspects of differential obsolescence is the *temporal* moment of obsolescence, that instant in time when

FIGURE 4.18. Nakagin Capsule Tower, construction view, Tokyo, Kisho Kurokawa, 1970–72.

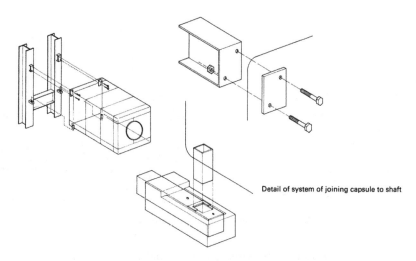

Detail of system of joining capsule to shaft

FIGURE 4.19. Nakagin Capsule Tower, joint detail.

the built environment loses its purpose and worth, becomes useless and valueless. What might that temporality of obsolescence look like? Could it, too, like the spatial joint, have an image fixed in architecture?

Imaging Limits

Few architects investigated obsolescence in the 1960s more tenaciously than Peter Cook, of the British group Archigram. Cook's extended series of drawings for an imagined megastructural Plug-In City (1962–66) was widely publicized in a 1964 Sunday *Times* color supplement (fig. 4.20). Obsolescence was an accepted fact of modern life, exalted by Cook and his compatriots in Archigram, which hailed expendability as a "direct expression of a freedom to choose."[34] For Archigram obsolescence not only would happen, it should happen, freeing people to choose and re-choose the best and latest modes of human living and invention.

Cook's Plug-In City abstracts the existing obsolescing built environment into its constituent parts, visually conceptualizing urban conditions as a "hierarchy of relative permanence."[35] In Cook's drawn schema, long-life transportation infrastructure provides the base. Medium-life shops, residences, and offices occupy the middle zone. Mobile boom cranes on top hoist about the component parts—from "3-year obsolescence" living modules to twenty-year towers, and the forty-year frame itself. Cook's drawings test how these

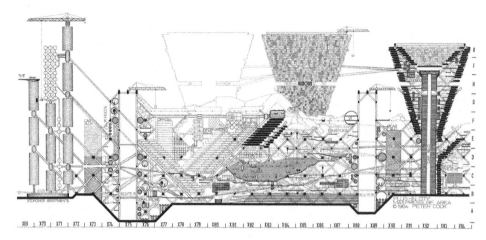

FIGURE 4.20. Plug-In City, section, max pressure area, Peter Cook, 1964.

elements might be recomposed more rationally and expressively in a total urban form. As the architectural historian Simon Sadler has written, "Plug-In wanted to make the kinesis and transformation of the modern city legible."[36]

If the Plug-In City models urbanism generally under obsolescence, then Cook's particular Plug-In University Node represents the architect's most focused experiment to imagine in architecture the *moment* of obsolescence. As part of his investigation, Cook produced a sixteen-frame stop-motion analysis of the Plug-In University's construction and adaptation (fig. 4.21). Initially, pylons and decks compose the basic "Brain Silo" unit. These are then subdivided into classrooms and multiplied into larger nodes. Then, in frame 12, architecture goes blank. This is the crucial moment of obsolescence, when the university as "Brain Silo" becomes "'Broadcasting' Centre," impelled, Cook's texts tells us, by a vaguely defined "trend [. . .] towards dispersal of study into home, workpoint, fun centre, etc." One function suddenly supersedes another. But architectural imaging fails; there is only text. Then architecture resumes in frame 13. The older form of the university, defined by teaching rooms, is replaced by inflatable housing bubbles, even as the underlying Plug-In lattice persists, notes the final box.

Cook and Archigram embraced obsolescence in architecture for its liberating potential, the agency it offered individuals to choose and change their habitations and habits. But as Cook explored obsolescence deeply in design, he came up against a limit. His Plug-In University Node experiment reveals that architecture is unable to represent obsolescence itself. Crucially, architectural imaging fails in frame 12. Architecture cannot visualize obsolescence's moment of devaluation and dysfunction. The process comes from outside the frame and remains elusive. And so, if architecture cannot represent the forces of obsolescence that act upon it, cannot fix an image of these abstract elements, then, we might ask, what of architecture's other more practical fixes for obsolescence being worked out in the 1960s—all the scientific analyses and formal solutions, all the architectures of obsolescence, from the factory shed to the megastructure to indeterminate design? Their concreteness in fact contradicts the abstractness of the problem of obsolescence, which arises

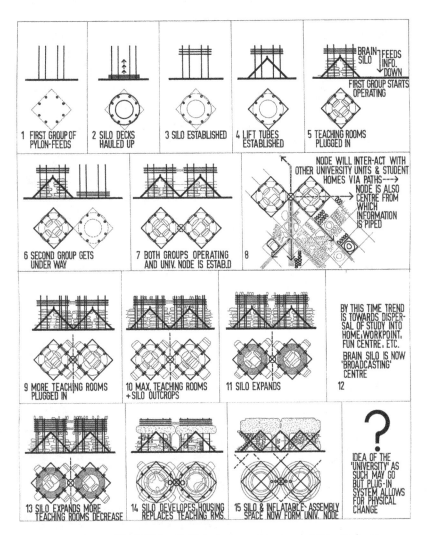

FIGURE 4.21. Plug-In University Node, sequence of development, Peter Cook, 1965.

from external factors of value and contingency. Could a tangible solution ever fully address an intangible problem? The Plug-In University Node experiment uncovered this paradox, this limit to architecture's fix of obsolescence.

The limits of architecture's fixes for obsolescence are touched upon, too, in the work of the English architect Cedric Price. Few embraced obsolescence's promise more wholeheartedly than Price, who believed fervently not only that obsolescence would happen but also that it should happen. From the early 1960s Price extolled the virtues of "an expendable aesthetic [. . .] planned obsolescence is the order within such a discipline."[37] Price was an influential visionary who built little. But when he did construct, as at London's Inter-Action community cultural center (1975–77), Price went so far as to provide directions for dismantlement, so as to give users "a real opportunity to change their minds."[38] Price was also the rare architect with membership in the National Institute of Demolition Contractors, formalizing his affiliation with expendability.[39]

The first of Price's projects to put his obsolescence convictions into practice was the design for the unbuilt Fun Palace (1962–67), a populist entertainment and cultural complex sited in industrial East London (fig. 4.22). In composition, it was a stripped-down megastructure of service towers and gantry cranes that would sling about the structure temporary enclosures and platforms for self-exploration in art, science, and therapy. "A laboratory of pleasure," Price's collaborator, the theater director Joan Littlewood, called it.[40] Price himself characterized the Fun Palace as a "short-life toy of dimensions and organizations."[41] Expendable and ephemeral, the Fun Palace, in Price's

LEA RIVER SITE

FIGURE 4.22. Project for Fun Palace: perspective for the Lea River site, London, Cedric Price, 1961–65.

rendering, glows apart from its workaday surroundings, thriving on its own transience and anticipated obsolescence, freed from architects' total control. "Nothing is to last for more than ten years, some things not even ten days," Littlewood declared, "no concrete stadia [. . .] no municipal geranium beds or fixed teak benches."[42] The Fun Palace embraces the promise of obsolescence, its gifts of freedom and users' agency, its break from the past and openness to the future. This contrasts with ossified industrial civilization (the nearby cooling towers and factory sheds) and normative culture that entombs rather than empowers people ("geranium beds" and "teak benches").

Simultaneously, Price was elaborating an even grander project for a postindustrial educational network he called the Potteries Thinkbelt, sited in his native West Midlands, formerly a center of national pottery production. The Potteries Thinkbelt was the Fun Palace on a regional scale: interchangeable, expendable parts, transported over miles of underused rail lines, for an ever-evolving program of higher education and self-improvement. Price said, "What I am talking about in the Thinkbelt [is] the capacity for activities to change as a result of thoughts changing. And the resulting architecture can last as long as these thoughts are current." The concept, explained Price's assistant Stephen Mullin, "offered the opportunity to avoid the rapid and inevitable obsolescence of fixed structures as they fail to respond to educational demands."[43]

A pair of images Price produced for the Potteries Thinkbelt reveals the project's profound engagement with the implications of obsolescence. At its western edge near Madeley village an abandoned rail siding is pictured renewed as a bustling node of the network, architect's lines drawn upon a photograph of the derelict site (fig. 4.23). A new traveling gantry crane, surmounted by a second boom crane, lifts prefabricated classroom modules from rows of railcars into a low-rise teaching zone beneath high-rise residences. It is an ambiguous image in terms of its temporality. Is the architecture in a state of assembly or disassembly? Is the landscape disappearing beneath infrastructure? Or is the tree in the foreground taking back the site? Indeed, we seem to have a representation of the process of obsolescence itself: simultaneous demolition and construction, an insubstantial present, permanently impermanent. The image of the Madeley Transfer Area in effect updates the idea of the ruin as architecture's figure of change (see fig. 1.1). Now architecture is not intertwined with nature but stands apart as a second nature, an alternative terrain. Development is no longer defined by history, along with nature, but is a product of technological progress, which disposes of buildings not in generations or centuries but in years or decades. Price even produced a detailed chart of the Potteries Thinkbelt components' use cycles and life spans, with

FIGURE 4.23. Project for Potteries Thinkbelt: perspective sketch of Madeley Transfer Area, Stafford-shire (England), Cedric Price, 1966.

most elements projected to last from five to twenty-five years. Rapid expend-ability overtakes slow adaptation. Moreover, fragmented remains no longer point back to a lost original, as in the ruinscape, or forward to some future completion. The principles of obsolescence dispose of precedent and deny the possibility of finish. The Potteries Thinkbelt is about process, not product: endless supersession, expendability, and replacement.

Yet even within this radically different conception of architectural time and form, one heroic fixture remains: the thick-inked cranes in the center where the diagonal lines converge. Cranes, as instruments and symbols of continuous transformation, feature prominently in the architectures of ob-solescence: in Henry Ford's factories, atop Buckminster Fuller's 4D Tower, at the peaks of Peter Cook's Plug-In City. Louis Kahn once wrote of the crane as "merely the extension of the arm like a hammer," a prosthesis for the ar-chitect's vitality.[44] And so, even as Price disclaims much conventional archi-tectural ideology, he still employs the crane as a singular agent of production in the Potteries Thinkbelt drama—an intact survivor from the magnificent industrial age, redolent of shipyards and factories. In other words, the past persists in Price's postindustrial, obsolescing future.

Sympathy for the obsolete infuses Price's imagery, too, for the Pottery Thinkbelt's Hanley Housing Area, sited north of Stoke-on-Trent, for which he also drew upon a photograph of a decayed site (fig. 4.24). At Hanley, across the bridge from the viewer, a new parking lot sits atop housing modules sunk into an abandoned old mining pit. Other new, flexible, prefabricated residential units cling to the base of looming, monstrous slag heaps. Gone, however, is the Madeley Transfer Area's pastoral bustle. In the spectral Hanley Housing Area, the most substantial structure is not of the architect's devising. Rather, it is an ancient, abandoned shed in the foreground that draws the eye and guards the bridge. Beneath Hanley's unnatural mounds, all seems deathly quiet upon a bare and littered ground. The distance traveled, from the Fun Palace's aloofness to the Hanley Housing Area's somber submission to its obsolete surroundings—the detritus of industrial civilization—speaks to a profound recognition about the age of obsolescence. Here the consequence of headlong expendability will be a world laid to waste, unlike the traditional ruinscape, where antiquity inspires the imagination. Instead, in the new cosmos governed by expendability, Price seems to discover that the undead waste of the past will come to haunt rather than vivify the promise of the future.

Plural architectures of obsolescence thus flourished in the 1960s: factory sheds and megastructures, indeterminate and interstitial hospitals, Japanese Metabolism and British Archigram, the explorations of Cook and Price. The architectural engagements of the decade promised fixes for many of obsolescence's tensions and contradictions: how to accommodate transience within permanence, to plan for ambiguity, to conjoin differential temporalities, to balance freedom and efficiency, to accept indeterminacy. All these plural architectures of obsolescence accepted accelerating change and supersession as facts of modern life, differing only in degree over how much obsolescence's effect on architecture should be welcomed and exploited rather than mitigated and contained.

The plural architectures of obsolescence also varied in terms of national contexts: American pragmatism and monumentality, home of system-built schools, Mies, and Kahn; Japanese openness to modern mutability, leavened

FIGURE 4.24. Project for Potteries Thinkbelt: photomontage of Hanley housing site 7, Staffordshire (England), Cedric Price, between 1963 and 1966.

by traditions of craft joinery; British empiricism and consumerism, deeply engaged both in research and expendability. Britain gave perhaps the fullest welcome to obsolescence, using architectural obsolescence to imagine release from hidebound, crumbling tradition. In England, birthplace of the Industrial Revolution, the infrastructure was also the first to fall to ruin in the postwar period, creating an opportunity for the poetry of Price. Yet it was precisely and paradoxically in this fullest embrace of obsolescence that limits began to be sensed. Cook's Plug-In University exposed an unresolved contradiction between the tangible fix and an intangible event. And Price revealed the obsolete remnant.

As efficiency progresses, so do mountains of waste. Garbage is modernity's "shadow world," writes the sociologist John Scanlan, the leftover of innovation and consumption, novelty and fashion.[45] Price's engagement explored rather than condemned this contradiction. His love of obsolescence uncovered its remnant, and for this, too, there is affection—the crane, the mounds, the derelict shed. Yet the beholder remains estranged from the desolate landscape of the Hanley Housing Area, distanced by the bridge, with little to grasp onto in the thinly drawn future. The imagined prospect appears no closer than the obsolete past. "The future is but the obsolete in reverse," Vladimir Nabokov wrote in his 1952 science-fiction short story "Lance." This time-twisting phrase names the future as distant and as ungraspable, as "'out of date'" as is the past, Nabokov insists. No matter in how much detail we try to envision what comes next, as in the Plug-In City and the Potteries Thinkbelt, the future's reality remains ungraspable. The future is as alien to the present as is the obsolete past, "a strangeness no amount of research can foresee," as Nabokov writes.[46] Temporal estrangement is the condition of Price's Hanley Housing Area image, too, its full consciousness of the consequences of obsolescence. The past is a wasteland, the future the same. Architecture's embrace of obsolescence touches a limit. Struggling with obsolescence was not Price's burden alone. At the same time in the 1960s that much of architecture operated under the paradigm's sway, believing in obsolescence's inevitability, others without and within architecture were openly critiquing obsolescence's logic and exploring ways to engineer its reversal. Architects and others soon became keenly aware of the problems of obsolescence and responded to these limits through design and other means.

Reversing Obsolescence

At the same time in the 1960s that many architects accepted obsolescence and even embraced its promise, others recoiled from obsolescence's consequences and implications. They rejected its apparent inevitability, its fast-changing world of megastructures, factory sheds, and indeterminacy. Yet both groups, or rather tendencies, whether they accepted or rejected it, believed that obsolescence had become the dominant paradigm of change in the built environment. The tension between these two impulses was present from the beginning of the decade. In January 1960 the leading American journal *Architectural Forum* declared, "Much of the urban product of the earlier industrial revolution is hopelessly obsolete and not worth saving." Yet there was unease, too. The same editorial called for "restoring harmonious continuity" and "subtle renewal programs."[1] In the 1960s skeptics of the obsolescence paradigm sought alternate means of conceptualizing and managing change: not transience but permanence, not expendability but adaptability, not supersession but continuity—in other words, the reversal of obsolescence. This chapter asks: What critiques of obsolescence were offered during this period? What alternatives pursued? What were the contest's results?

Critiquing Obsolescence

Americans, who since the 1920s had lived longest with the idea of obsolescence, began to openly question its verities around 1960. In 1959 the economist W. Paul Strassman published an article in the *Journal of Economic History* disputing the veracity of Joseph Schumpeter's "legend of Creative Destruction," as Strassman deemed it. Strassman argued that creative destruction was "not an apt description of the way dominant production methods succeeded one another in the U.S. from 1850 to 1914," as Schumpeter had claimed in his famous 1942 analysis of capitalism. Rather, the contrarian Strassman insisted, "the old and new, or two competing innovations, grew side by side for decades."[2] If, as the evidence suggested, creative destruction was historically false, then, implicitly, obsolescence, as a governing paradigm for conceptualizing and managing change into the future, ought to be reconsidered. In the event, Strassman failed to dent Schumpeter's reputation; creative destruction remains a ubiquitous trope, a convenient simplification of capitalism's complexities. But Strassman's critique does bespeak a moment when obsolescence began to lose its grip.

In 1959, again, *Harvard Business Review* surveyed corporate executives regarding "a barrage of criticism about one of [business's] characteristic processes, planned obsolescence." Perhaps surprisingly, the Harvard poll found, a majority of American business leaders agreed that "too large a part of our present economy is based upon superficial product obsolescence, inducing people to buy new models before their old models are worn out." Engineering and construction executives were especially troubled, perhaps reflecting values of solidity and permanence for their product.[3] In the heart of American capitalism, obsolescence was not the virtue it had once been perceived to be.

Cultural critiques of obsolescence also swelled in the early 1960s. The journalist Vance Packard's best-selling book *The Waste Makers* (1960) skewered the "throwaway spirit" of American consumer life. Packard satirized a "Cornucopia City" of the future, as he called it, where "all buildings will be made of special papier-mâché [. . .] houses can be torn down and rebuilt every spring and fall at housecleaning time."[4] Other popular writers, such as John Kenneth Galbraith, David Riesman, C. Wright Mills, and William H. Whyte, excoriated the passivity and waste of a society based upon "Progress through Planned Obsolescence" (a Packard chapter title). People were seen to be at the mercy of manipulative marketing methods, discarding still-useful objects, wasting their resources and the earth's. Skepticism of the obsolescence paradigm transcended the American setting and was found as well in postwar Europe's technocratic consumer societies. In literature, the Swiss architect-turned-writer Max Frisch twisted the objectivist certainties of the obsolescence paradigm into a horrific tragedy in his famed 1957 novel *Homo Faber*. The hyperrationalist protagonist declares, "As a technologist I am used to reckoning with the formulas of probability," before contingent chance and accident, his worldview's opposites, lead him inadvertently into a deadly love affair with his own daughter.[5] In science fiction, the Englishman J. G. Ballard envisioned dystopian, obsolescing world-cities, every cubic foot commoditized, the whole mess rotting from the inside out.[6]

Attacks upon the logic of obsolescence also resonated with the decade's antiestablishment leanings. Students for a Democratic Society's Port Huron Statement of 1962 explicitly disparaged "'planned obsolescence' as a permanent feature of business strategy."[7] The iconic Volkswagen Beetle was marketed in the United States as immune to superficial styling: "We do not believe in planned obsolescence. We don't change a car for the sake of change."[8] Expendable, mass-produced objects and environments, the essence of Fordist material culture, embodied a crisis of authenticity. Postwar life seemed to lack core values. Modern suburbs epitomized this apparent emptiness: cookie-cutter housing, overconsumption, alienation. In contrast, older urban centers once deemed obsolete came to be revalued.

In circles of professional expertise, American social scientists began to critique the paradigm of urban obsolescence. The sociologist Herbert Gans argued, for example, that Boston's West End was "not really a slum," that "obsolescence per se is not harmful: the judgment merely a reflection of middle-class standards."[9] The psychologists Marc Fried and Peggy Gleicher documented both the traumas of relocation for those displaced by urban renewal projects and the positive experiences those people had had in the so-called obsolete neighborhoods. Vivid street life and kinship networks trumped bureaucrats' measurements of architectural and environmental performance. Eschewing obsolescence's "loose, shifting temporary world," the MIT urban planner Kevin Lynch in 1958 called for a "happy place for human existence [. . .] emotional and perceptual continuity in the midst of flux."[10] The critique of urban obsolescence received its widest amplification in the author and activist Jane Jacobs's famed book *The Death and Life of Great American Cities* (1961). An architectural journalist, Jacobs, who lived in New York's Greenwich Village, became a fierce public antagonist to the city planner Robert Moses's grand urban renewal schemes, favoring instead the "organized complexity" and "common, ordinary things" of her neighborhood's street and social lives, as she wrote in a plain yet passionate style.[11] Studying the city deductively rather than through orthodox planning theory, Jacobs observed "ingenious adaptations of old quarters to new uses" and concluded that "lively, diverse, intense cities contain the seeds of their own regeneration."[12] Adaptation, in other words, was the key to successful urbanity, rather than obsolescence. "There is nothing economically or socially inevitable about [. . .] the decay of old cities," Jacobs declared. "Cities need old buildings." Furthermore, "Time makes certain structures obsolete for some enterprises, and they become available for others."[13] Jacobs's commonsensical approach and rhetoric, along with her public activism, lent her persona an air of saintliness, as many have noted, while her ideas, translated into numerous languages worldwide, inspired a generation's critique of top-down planning in favor of populist feeling for the prewar city's environs and communities.[14]

Some in the architectural community echoed these sentiments. The American architectural historian William Jordy, in a 1960 essay entitled "Humanism in Contemporary Thought," derided the "worship of obsolescence" that produced "slickness, shininess, thinness in our buildings."[15] The *Architectural Forum* editor Peter Blake's *God's Own Junkyard: The Planned Deterioration of American Landscape* (1964) blamed the "uglification" of America on the 1954 tax code's accelerated depreciation rate (introduced not because property was deteriorating or obsolescing faster, but to encourage development with quicker write-offs): "All of a sudden an owner was rewarded for selling out fast!"[16] Blake also attacked obsolescence's presumption of expendability, citing above all the infamous demolition of New York's monumental Pennsylvania Station, built in the first decade of the twentieth century and deemed already in 1950 an "economic waste" by its railroad company owner.[17] Penn Station's destruction, begun in 1963, inspired the American poet George Zabriskie's general lament: "We live in a time of planning our obsolescence, or tearing down / the walls about our ears: the manufacture of ruins which look / bombed-out is profitable and quick."[18] Zabriskie's poem was published in an important 1966 volume, *With Heritage So Rich*, sponsored by the United States Conference of Mayors, which argued for stronger preservationist policies. Many cities around the world had their own Penn Stations at this time. In Britain, a 1955 special issue of *Architectural Review* entitled "Outrage" had fulminated against heritage loss. But this didn't stop the demolition in 1961–62 of London's famed nineteenth-century Euston Station and its renowned gateway portico, which thereafter became a British preservationist touchstone. The late 1950s and 1960s seem internationally to have been an age of "historicide." "We eat the past," observed the poet Hans Magnus Enzensberger about the erasure of German memory, including the recent Nazi past.[19] The obsolescence paradigm in the 1960s was coming under attack on numerous fronts, from the American business community on economic and scholarly grounds to the culture at large in a critique of Western consumer society and its historical amnesias.

Preservationism

Alongside the multiple protests against obsolescence arose a series of positive strategies for its reversal. Historic preservation, which revalues the obsolete, advanced intensively in the 1960s. Before the mid-twentieth century, preservationism and obsolescence had coexisted more or less peaceably. It is hardly coincidental that the first great theorist of architectural obsolescence, Reginald P. Bolton, was also an active preservationist in his Upper Manhattan neighborhood. The industrialist Henry Ford abandoned successive obsolescent factories in 1910s Detroit, then painstakingly collected youthful architectural memories for his "Greenfield Village." John D. Rockefeller, Jr., sponsored Colonial Williamsburg. As the historian David Lowenthal has noted, "The world's greatest technocrats married genius for annihilation with instincts to preserve."[20] Preservationism and obsolescence were in fact two sides of the same modernizing coin. Both rationalized change in elite interests. Preservation provided built ideals of elite resilience in the midst of wholesale change. Protecting isolated urban treasures, like New York's City Hall, reinforced elite collective memory by ensuring "stability and continuity with a noble past," explains the historian Randall Mason.[21] Likewise, in Charleston, South Carolina, which pioneered whole-district preservation zoning in the 1930s, the professional middle-class women who led the crusade did so in their own privileged white interests, "protecting places with strong ancestral associations," the historian Robert Weyeneth writes.[22] Historians recognize that early preservationism was not opposed to but rather functioned as "an integral *part* of modernity," Mason asserts.[23] Salvaging an ancient cathedral, castle, manse, or civic monument—preservationism's purview since its mid-nineteenth-century origins—saves "a piece of our national life," explained a German art historian in 1905, securing top-down values.[24] The rest was made available for redevelopment. The Charleston preservationists let the poor and black rest of the city succumb to modernization and wholesale slum clearance.

But from around 1960 preservationism evolved in the face of obsolescence's depredations, especially toward the recent past. Previously, baroque seventeenth-century architecture in Europe could seem too new to preserve; monuments valued for their age were expected to "reveal the passage of *a considerable period of time*" (emphasis added), wrote the German art theorist Alois Riegl in 1928.[25] But now, around 1960, a building could be just a few decades old to elicit preservationist sentiment. Britain's Victorian Society was founded in 1958, its American branch in 1966. Supporters rallied against the demolitions of London's Covent Garden, Gropius's Bauhaus in Dessau, Louis Sullivan's Garrick Theater in Chicago, and New York's Penn Station (fig. 5.1). Sympathy emerged, too, for the machine age's everyday environs, its colliers and cottages. The German artists Bernd and Hilla Becher photographed Europe's fading industrial infrastructure, made obsolescent by economic development and policies of the postwar common market (fig. 5.2). "I felt it more or less my duty," Bernd explained, "to capture the plants threatened by destruction before they disappeared completely."[26]

Beginning in the early 1960s preservation protocols evolved accordingly. The 1964 international Venice Charter encompassed "modest works" and "setting," following recent Dutch and French legislation.[27] In Europe, the "urban conservation movement" sought to preserve whole historic city centers, in part to spur tourism. In Britain, buildings just thirty years old qualified for historic listing in 1970. Penn Station's death throes helped birth New York's Landmark Preservation Commission in the mid-1960s. America's first academic program in preservation was established at Columbia University in 1964.

Preservationism also became more populist. Working-class communities in Japan and West Germany fused architectural and social agendas to resist gentrification. In the United Kingdom, membership in preservation groups soared to three hundred thousand by 1977. German activism numbered in the millions. In Italy, the Bolognese Communist Party rallied to the slogan "Preservation Is Revolution." Even in politically moderate America, citizens believed that half of the nation's listed buildings had already been demolished.[28] This was the "Heroic Period of Conservation," the British historian and activist Alan Powers has written.[29] The new preservationism posed a formidable

FIGURE 5.1. Demonstrators, including writer Jane Jacobs (*third from right, with glasses*) and architect Philip Johnson (*far right*), protest Pennsylvania Station's demolition, New York, 1962. Photo by Walter Daran / Hulton Archive / Getty Images

FIGURE 5.2. Water towers, Bernd and Hilla Becher, 1967–80. © Bernd and Hilla Becher; Image copyright © The Metropolitan Museum of Art. Image source: Art Resource, NY

challenge to obsolescence. It reacted to what it perceived as obsolescence's extremes and pressed at its weak points. If an individual monument was worth saving, then why not its setting? Was architecture's worth entirely quantifiable by expert measurement? What about the intangible values of emotion and memory? If ancient, elite objects increased in value over time, then why not more recent and popular ones?

Vernacularism

Just as preservationism was engaging with the recent and the popular, so, too, were discourses on the vernacular finding varied outlets. Bernard Rudofsky's well known 1964 Museum of Modern Art exhibit on vernacular architecture, "Architecture without Architects," presented for reevaluation a broad range of seemingly obsolete environs, from hill towns to grass huts, which, Rudofsky argued, existed outside the economy of obsolescence, "the pursuit of profit and progress."[30] By contrast, "vernacular architecture does not go through fashion cycles. It is nearly immutable, indeed, unimprovable."[31] The structures Rudofsky featured were not, in his mind, outmoded and archaic, as the obsolescence paradigm would have them, superseded by progress. Rather, the vernacular represented the timeless virtues of good architecture and provided lessons for the contemporary world. Advocates of vernacular architecture promoted "a system of form-making which is a direct reflection of the process of life," the architecture professors William Zuk and Roger H. Clark wrote in 1970.[32] Nomads' tents, for example, seemed to represent more authentic adaptation to a world of flux, closer to nature and need than obsolescence's commercialized transience. The *Whole Earth Catalog*, first published in 1968, invited readers to be their own carpenters. The "process of repair," not replacement, should be the ruling principle of change, preached the Berkeley-based architect Christopher Alexander; "it simply lies there stretched out in time."[33] The elasticity of vernacularism countered the brittle temporality of obsolescence.

Vernacularism put value back in the ostensibly obsolete. So, too, did salvage architecture, which became a fashionable if marginal tactic in the 1960s. Discarded wood, metal, glass bottles, and automobile parts were recycled by youthful builders of the Drop-City commune, Colorado (1965); the Heineken Summer House, Netherlands (1965); Prickly Mountain, Vermont (1966); and the early 1970s desert projects of the architect Michael Reynolds (fig. 5.3). Reuse of the expendable reversed the logic of obsolescence and protested the profligacy of consumer society, aiming "to integrate waste into the cycle of use," explained the urban planner Kevin Lynch in 1972.[34]

Adaptive Reuse

How did architects respond to these critiques of the logic of obsolescence? At the moment in the 1960s when many accepted and even embraced obsolescence, others adopted tactics of resistance. The design technique most widely employed to revalue seemingly obsolete architecture was adaptive reuse. In the 1930s, to stem the "ravages of obsolescence," real estate experts had recommended updating appearances and equipment, an economical option during periods of financial crisis (the 1970s would be a similar moment).[35] Remodeling like this, however, had its limits. If an original function was no longer profitable, then only a new function would do. After World War II, accelerating urban deindustrialization left vast acres of empty factories, mills,

FIGURE 5.3. Salvage architecture, New Mexico, Mike Reynolds, 1979.

and warehouses. New uses began trickling in around 1960. St. Louis's Gaslight Square and San Francisco's Ghirardelli Square were pioneer developments, converted to shops and restaurants. New York artists, like Andy Warhol in 1964, colonized industrial loft districts for cheap studio space, relishing the patina and grit of the obsolescing environment as they found it. Retail, small business, and residential use followed. The pace of "adaptive reuse" accelerated in the 1970s; the term was coined early in the decade when the first books were published on the subject. By 1978 a third of American architects' income, it was estimated, came from rehab work.[36] Adaptive reuse offered the satisfactions of salvage, discovering treasures and finding ways to reuse them. "Obsolete buildings are fun to convert," enthused the *Whole Earth Catalogue* founder Stewart Brand.[37]

Recent modern architecture's lack of texture and history spurred the revaluation of urban shells and neighborhoods that wore their age visibly. Adaptive reuse brought the past's castoffs into a present made more temporally varied. The obsolete was made protean. An aesthetics of adaptive reuse emerged. Cavernous volumes were stripped down to bare brick, wood, and iron. Bright new modern partitions, glass enclosures, and ductwork were inserted (fig. 5.4). Adaptive reuse's emblematic motif, the exposed brick wall,

FIGURE 5.4. Detroit Cornice and Slate Building rehabilitation, Detroit, William Kessler, 1974.

offers an alternate temporality to obsolescence. The surface of Boston's 1970s rehabilitated Quincy Market, for example, is a malleable palimpsest, an incomplete erasure of the past, still susceptible to change (fig. 5.5). Old repairs, pipes, and fills index incremental evolution. This is soft change versus the traumas of sudden obsolescence.

On an urban scale, adaptive reuse largely meant gentrification, an elevation in an area's socioeconomic status, with older uses and residents replaced even as the buildings remained. Preservation and rehabilitation in Philadelphia's Society Hill area from the late 1950s pioneered the process. A London sociologist, Ruth Glass, coined the term "gentrification" in 1964. In a dynamic repeated across the developed world, thousands of West German poor and elderly lost their turn-of-the-century flats in the 1970s to a gentrifying middle class seeking "new spatial referents in its search for history and identity," writes the historian Rudy Koshar.[38] Revitalized inner urban areas offered mobile middle-class agents of change, generally seeking individualized achievement, an opportunity to inhabit what was perceived to be a more authentic, rooted site of social community and material tradition, than, for example, the modern suburb. "The scent of a single weathered threshold or the touch of a single tile": the architectural historian Mark Crinson quotes the philosopher

Walter Benjamin to characterize this desire for urban memory.[39] Moreover, gentrification was not purely a capitalist phenomenon. In late-1960s East Berlin, the state abandoned the mass demolition of prewar tenements in favor of rehabilitation in order to husband its resources and respond to preservationism. No longer was demolition the knee-jerk response to older urban fabrics, as it had been, in practice and in theory, for some decades. "Obsolescence became obsolete," writes the architectural historian Florian Urban about the situation in Germany and Eastern Europe generally.[40]

It should be noted that adaptive reuse reversed obsolescence's architectural logic, but not its social effects. Governments after the mid-1960s spent less on urban redevelopment because of straitened economies and political resistance. Now private capital took the lead. Mortgage and development finance flowed in, and capitalism generated profits in new ways. The Western

FIGURE 5.5. Quincy Market rehabilitation, Boston, Benjamin Thompson, 1976.

gentrified city reopens for investment, following the urban renewal agenda, but now with preservationism coopted. Under adaptive reuse, past investments no longer needed to be destroyed "in order to open up fresh room for accumulation," as the geographer David Harvey would have it.[41] The existing environment could be salvaged and reused, society and architects discovered. Meanwhile, working-class renters, industry, and small landlords disappeared. In the gentrified city, the fabric remains but the community is cleared out. Gentrification renders, in effect, the previous inhabitants obsolete, devalued in their worth to the contemporary city, to be replaced by higher-value settlers. The desire, even the fetish, for a seemingly more authentic habitation came at the cost of just those people and uses that had made the place seem "real." Gentrification is in effect the neutron bomb of urban renewal: buildings intact, people gone.

Concrete Brutalism

But what of new design? How did architects propose to counter obsolescence's omnipresence? Already during the war years leading modernists, like the historian Sigfried Giedion, appealed for "monuments [. . .] intended to outlive the period which originated them."[42] The impulse was a response both to the upheavals of the conflict and the desire for an architecture not just about technology but community and its endurance. This call for renewed permanence in architecture seemed answered by the archaic monumentality of Le Corbusier's famed *béton brut* (bare concrete) masterpiece, the Unité d'Habitation housing block in Marseilles of 1947–52 (fig. 5.6). Here an open frame invited flexibly configured apartment units. Yet these were held permanently in place, embodying Le Corbusier's deep preference for certitude and fixity in architecture, his appeals for "a sure and permanent home." As early as the 1930s Le Corbusier had been retreating from a streamlined, evanescent-looking machine aesthetic in favor of a vernacular palette of weathered brick and masonry. His feelings for eternity, always present in his idealization of geometry and order, now found visible expression in roughened architectural materiality. The postwar Unité's richly textured surface in Marseilles compared to "the well-weathered Doric columns" of Greek antiquity, wrote Reyner Banham; "few buildings in the world had such a hold on the imagination of younger architects."[43] The Unité spawned iterations worldwide, a veritable concrete brutalist vernacular from the 1950s through the 1970s, from the work of Denys Lasdun in Britain to that of Lina Bo Bardi in Brazil. Ponderous poured-in-place concrete monoliths scorned flexibility and expendability, daring obsolescence to do its worst. The commentator Sibyl Moholy-Nagy

FIGURE 5.6. Unité d'Habitation, Marseilles, Le Corbusier, 1947–52.

baldly declared one typical and well-known brutalist monument, Paul Rudolph's Temple Street parking garage in New Haven, Connecticut (1959–63),
to be "Rudolph's refutation of the artificial-obsolescence theory held by planners of disposable cities" (fig. 5.7).[44]

   More complexly, Rudolph's Art and Architecture Building at Yale University (1958–64) reflects the period's tension between accepting and resisting
obsolescence (fig. 5.8). Working with obsolescence, the broadly glazed, open
loft interiors were designed to be "manipulated in such a way as to change
the spaces as desired,"[45] explained Rudolph, and the geometrically irregular
plan was meant to "grow logically, i.e. the building is open ended,"[46] extendable toward the north (as eventually occurred in the 2000s)—a reasoned acceptance of obsolescence's deformations. On the other hand, the major tone
of Yale's Art and Architecture Building is permanence and fixity, expressed
by the rugged towers in Rudolph's distinctive corduroy-concrete ribbing,

revealing the chance variety of exposed aggregate. Entering between these shadowed projections into cavelike stair halls embedded with old architectural fragments is an architectural experience of deep, archaic mystery. The concrete brutalism of the Art and Architecture Building thus reverses obsolescence in several ways. It privileges permanence over transience, cocooning the open loft spaces within immutable concrete. It salvages the past. And while displaying precise rationality in its glazed boxes and grooved walls, it also revalues contingency and emotion in its textures and chiaroscuro. In its complexity, Rudolph's Art and Architecture Building replies to what lies across the street: the industrial loft box of Louis Kahn's Yale University Art Gallery (1951–53), embodying the conventional factory-shed solution to obsolescence of open floor plates and movable partitions. Almost immediately upon completion, Rudolph's Art and Architecture Building fell prey to criticism of its overbearing scale and abrasive surfaces, and it may even have been purposely set ablaze in 1969 as a protest against its perceived authoritarianism.

FIGURE 5.7. Temple Street Garage, New Haven, Paul Rudolph, 1959–63.

FIGURE 5.8. Yale University Art and Architecture Building, New Haven, Paul Rudolph, 1958–64.

More recently, however, the building has been lovingly restored; it is now a revered landmark. This historical trajectory of Rudolph's Art and Architecture Building subverts yet another of obsolescence's logics: that architectural value inevitably decreases over time.

Postmodernism

Among architects in the early 1960s seeking a return to permanent forms and values in the face of obsolescence was the Italian Aldo Rossi. Born in 1931 in Milan, Rossi, typically for his generation, reacted against the simplistic functionalism of established postwar modernism, with its focus on the fast-changing present, its evanescent needs and technologies. Instead of seeking inspiration for design in an analysis of function, Rossi came to believe that architectural creation was best inspired by past forms. In 1966 he published

FIGURE 5.9. San Cataldo Cemetery, Modena (Italy), Aldo Rossi, begun 1971.

his landmark theoretical book, *The Architecture of the City*, which recognized in Europe's ancient cities the persistence of counterexamples to modern transience and obsolescence, what Rossi called "primary elements." He cited, for example, the medieval Palazzo della Ragione, which had endured in Padua for the centuries, filled in with new uses, adapted, rebuilt, and subdivided, but still maintaining a coherent architectural image.[47] Rossi strove to generate in his own new architectural designs comparable "urban artifacts" of "meaningful permanences."[48] A 1964 Parma theater project offers an accretion of spaces in an iconic half-circle shape. Similarly, Rossi's San Cataldo cemetery in Modena (begun in 1971) displays an ethereal ensemble of urban palace forms, stripped of ornament and seemingly vacant, like a ruin (fig. 5.9). The architect explains, "I've always thought of architecture primarily as a monument and relatively indifferent to secondary functions."[49] In our context, architecture indifferent to function, as Rossi proposes, is architecture immune to obsolescence. It can neither be deformed nor devalued by changeful use; the Parma theater's strong shape persists regardless, and the Modena cemetery's ghostly ruins embody eternity, heedless of obsolescence.

As with Rossi, the trope of the ruin became the American Louis Kahn's retort to obsolescence. Kahn had been trained in the classical tradition at

FIGURE 5.10. Salk Institute, Meeting House project, La Jolla (California), Louis Kahn, 1960–62.

the University of Pennsylvania in the 1920s by Paul Cret, designer of the classical Federal Reserve Bank building, but, like many of his generation, Kahn turned to a relatively functionalist modernism that seemed more relevant in the 1930s and 1940s. In the 1950s Kahn designed open-plan, flexible, factory shed–type buildings that looked like abstract modernist boxes, in the dominant style of the time. But around 1960, reacting like Rossi to simplistic functionalism, and having digested his own formative experience in Italy as a scholar-in-residence in Rome a decade previously, which resonated with his earlier classical education, Kahn began conceiving his buildings differently and more monumentally, as wrapped ruins. Thin screen walls punctured by large openings encircle interior volumes, like an early iteration of his famed Salk Institute complex in La Jolla, California (fig. 5.10). Kahn designed in this manner for the rest of his career—for example, the monumental public buildings in Dhaka, Bangladesh. Here between the exterior walls and interior structures lie open galleries of no specific purpose, what Kahn called "an offering, and [does] not designate what it is to be used for" (fig. 5.11).[50] Unlike Mies's open space, embodying the factory shed's endless accommodation to changing function, Kahn's "offering" is superfluous to programmed purpose, representing what Kahn believes to be architecture's essence *beyond* use:

FIGURE 5.11. Suhrawardy Hospital, Dhaka (Bangladesh), Louis Kahn, 1962–83.

brick arches, central plans, and Roman permanence. Kahn explained about his wrapped ruins, "As time passes, when it is [a] ruin, the spirit of its making comes back."[51] Or again, "A building that has become a ruin is again free of the bondage of use."[52] Kahn's "wrapped ruins" appear to have achieved this transcendence. The "offering" space between ruin screen and core passes beyond present use, thus embodying, for Kahn, architecture's essence as pure symbolic form. With Kahn, what we get is the consolation of obsolescence, the pledge that loss of functionality will not devalue but rather redeem architecture. This is obsolescence's metaphysical reversal.

Kahn and Rossi are two of the founding figures of architectural postmodernism. Both rejected modernism's negation of history to bring back the imagery and character of traditional architecture, separating form from function to recuperate the past's imagery and transcend obsolescence. Each wrapped his buildings in archetypal, symbolic imagery structurally detached from interior, programmatic space. Similarly revaluing the past in a postmodernist vein, other younger American architects drew from the different

wellspring of American vernacular architecture, rather than from Kahn and
Rossi's deep Mediterranean history. One of these was Charles Moore, who
had been a student of Kahn's. Moore focused upon a more homespun, domestic modernism, working on the West Coast in the early 1960s and adapting the sloping shapes, raw wood, and picturesque layout of early northern
California barns, sheds, and settlements for the composition of his iconic
Sea Ranch condominiums (1964–65) overlooking the Pacific Ocean. "We ar-
ranged them by taking hints from the huts and industrial architecture of the
last century that can be seen all over California," Moore explained.[53] This vein
of postmodernism revalued the common, everyday vernacular architecture
of the generation or two previous, which was otherwise considered obsolete,
outdated, and old-fashioned, practically and symbolically, in modern postwar
consumer society.

Robert Venturi and Denise Scott Brown also revalued the American vernacular, but with more of an emphasis on the commercial strip. Unlike the
usual vernacular champions, who favored the premodern or at least precon-
temporary, Venturi and Scott Brown discovered richness, authenticity, and inspiration in the present world's newest creations. "Honky-tonk elements [. . .]
are here to stay," Venturi declared in his 1966 book, *Complexity and Contradiction in Architecture.*[54] In his own work, Venturi plastered a large billboard
sign and television antenna onto the Philadelphia Guild House apartment
house for the elderly of 1960–63 and deployed vernacular brown brick and
double-hung windows to create a familiar-looking urban apartment block
"to house elderly people who want to remain in their old neighborhood."[55]
This was an implicit rebuke of radical urban renewal, like Boston's West End,
which was taking place at the same time and both destroyed buildings and
displaced communities. Venturi rejected the obsolescence paradigm's rapid
expendability: "architecture's rate of change, typically and naturally, should be
more evolutionary than revolutionary."[56] Out of Venturi and Scott Brown's revaluation of what exists, especially the commercial vernacular, which seemed
transient, vulgar, and obsolescent to others, they derived their influential
late-1960s postmodernist theory of "architecture as shelter with symbols on
it"—the "decorated shed" idea.[57] In this formulation, programmatic function
(the generic shed) and messaging form (symbolic facade) are separate. This
is analogous to Kahn's wrapped-ruin archetype and Rossi's rehabilitation of
classical imagery, but less monumental and serious. Not only is obsolescent
vernacular symbolism revalued, but obsolescence seems neutered as an existential threat. If a building outlives its present use, just stick in a new function
and put up a new sign—it's not that big a deal. The perils of obsolescence are
much less dramatic than in the factory-shed, megastructure, expendable, or

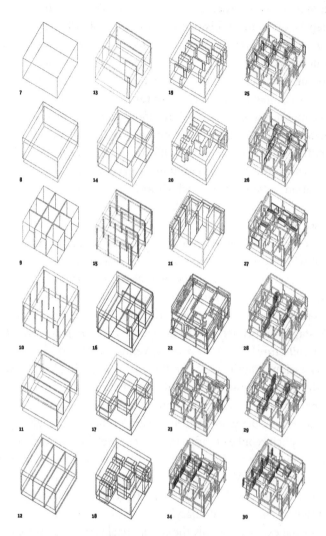

FIGURE 5.12. House II, transformational drawings, Hardwick (Vermont), Peter Eisenman, 1969–70.

indeterminate design responses, where only a radical rethinking of architectural form seemed capable of absorbing obsolescence's menace or promise.

Alienating form from function also undergirds the very different-looking but contemporaneous experiments of the architects John Hejduk and Peter Eisenman (which set the stage for the later movement called deconstructivism). In their schemes, point, line, plane, and volume would "generate principles of form and space," advancing "the evolution of form itself" (fig. 5.12).[58] Little consideration is given to use. Architecture here aims neither to fulfill nor to represent functional purpose, but rather to play with its own abstract elements. Eisenman justified what he called "post-functionalism" as architecture's avant-garde calling, paralleling modern art's abandonment of figuration in favor of abstraction. To get beyond the dominant paradigm of obsolescence, Eisenman took to disregarding function altogether as a generator of form. Eisenman thus rejected Louis Sullivan's late-nineteenth-century modernist credo, "form ever follows function," which had implicitly subjected architectural form to the power of obsolescence. In an age in which function refuses to stand still, form is always threatened with destruction. Yet form that forsakes function as its vivifying force, from Rossi to Eisenman, cuts the knot. Obsolescence loses its power to destroy.

Turning the Tide

Preservationism, vernacularism, salvage architecture, adaptive reuse, concrete brutalism, postmodernism, even deconstructivism: these diverse countertactics to obsolescence emerged in the 1960s. All sought to reverse obsolescence's logic by revaluing the past and emotion, by revealing obsolescence's waste, by refusing obsolescence's inevitability, by questioning functionalism itself. On the other side were the multiple architectures of obsolescence, more accepting of its inevitability and gifts: factory-shed solutions, interstitialism, megastructures, indeterminate, and expendable architecture, as well as academic research, and pop-culture enthusiasm for the phenomenon. But both these blocs, for and against obsolescence, believed in it and implicitly recognized its dominance. All acknowledged obsolescence's ubiquity as the way change was happening in modern life and the built environment. Moreover, the two factions were more or less evenly matched across the decade. The contest might have gone either way, with or against obsolescence, accepting mutability or privileging permanence. Passion and imagination were equally intense in the 1960s.

But by the mid-1970s the tide had turned. The architectures of obsolescence went into abeyance, in part as a consequence of larger societal changes that were responding critically to modernization. Obsolescence had been a largely top-down paradigm, invented and practiced by industry leaders and professional experts. But its consequences were starting to be resisted from the bottom up, as embodied in the anguished responses to the demolition of Boston's West End and so many other large-scale renewal projects. The unhappy outcome of these initiatives, in social costs and often unloved modern architectural results, alienated the public trust in experts' management of change. Not just in the built environment, but in the natural environment too, modernization was having unintended and frightful consequences. In the early 1960s Rachel Carson's environmental exposé, *Silent Spring*, inaugurated an era of doubt about the beneficence of industrial modernity, showing that efforts to improve the environment chemically had just the opposite effect, poisoning it. Even the unquestioned technological triumph of the U.S. space missions had the paradoxical effect, in the cultural milieu of the mid-1960s, of underscoring human precariousness as much as mastery. Newly pictured from orbit as a lonely "blue marble," the earth seemed fragile and finite—not a terrain for infinite consumption and expendability, as obsolescence would have it. Indeed, obsolescence's profligacy, its cavalier consumption and discarding of resources, offended a growing environmental sensibility percolating from below, first in the hippie counterculture, then throughout society. By 1972 a famous report by leading development scientists, *The Limits to Growth*, would call for slowing rates of industrial obsolescence as a key to "global equilibrium [. . .] the less resource depletion and pollution there will be."[59] In this context obsolescence lost its hold over the cultural imaginary, certainly as a process that should happen, and even as a process that would happen. So many people were calling into question its logic and ethics, trying to find alternate ways to conceive and manage change.

The undercutting of obsolescence in the cultural realm across the 1960s received a decisive politicoeconomic charge in the decade's last years and the early ones of the next. Capitalists in the developed West were struggling in the 1960s to maintain profits, constrained by workers' high pay demands, in the Fordist context, while at the same time having to compete with new, low-wage industrial competitors in Asia, notably from a revived postwar Japan, as well as Hong Kong and Taiwan. Meanwhile, Western business felt profits further squeezed by corporate taxes paying for welfare-state spending and social services, while at the same time being constrained, as they saw it, by government labor and financial regulations. Then came the oil shocks of 1973–74, which cast a pall over worldwide economic activity. Businesses already operating on low profit margins contracted, unemployment and inflation surged, and government tax revenues plummeted.

The economic crises of the early 1970s put paid to the obsolescence paradigm, which had depended upon visions of unlimited growth and consumption. The public and private investment that had sustained built-environment replacement collapsed. The developed world in the early 1970s slipped into recession. The open-ended future that obsolescence presumed seemed increasingly unrealistic. "Over the country depression lay like a fog," wrote the novelist Margaret Drabble about 1970s Britain.[60] "Mistrusted for its betrayals, the future became attenuated, eclipsed, forsaken," writes the historian

David Lowenthal.[61] Out of the ashes new economic paradigms materialized. Fordist mass production, with sales churned by workers' high wages, stylistic obsolescence, and fast expendability, no longer seemed tenable. Employers fought back, driving down wages to reestablish profits and inaugurating the decades-long stagnation in middle-class incomes that persists to this day. At the same time, Fordist standardized mass production, which had come to embody cultural conformity, consumerism, and inauthenticity, and so was not selling as well, came to be replaced by new visions of market segmentation and specialization—commodities made for *your* taste and aspirations. These could now be more profitably and flexibly produced offshore as globalized capital, increasingly freeing itself from state regulation, exploited manufacturing opportunities in Asia and other low-cost labor markets. Capitalism was evolving in response to crisis, ushering in what is now seen as a post-Fordist era of neoliberalism.

Also in the specifically architectural realm at this time, the tide could be seen explicitly turning against the proponents of obsolescence. Reyner Banham, a champion of architectural evanescence since the 1950s, in 1970 found himself under attack by youthful critics at a prominent design conference in Aspen, Colorado. "I could suddenly feel all these changes running together in a spasm of bad vibrations that shook the conference," Banham recalled. "We got ourselves together again, but an epoch had ended."[62] Banham soon pronounced the great megastructural solution to obsolescence to be itself obsolete: overly controlling, too long in construction, and "doomed, given the normal ten-year cycle of style and taste in the present century." Banham marked the end with Thamesmead New Town, outside London, begun in 1967—a monstrously monotonous run of concrete housing units, "the ultimate tombstone of the institutionalized and run-down concept of megastructure."[63] Few megastructures were ever realized, and fewer and fewer proposed: Paul Rudolph's 1970 Lower Manhattan Expressway project, a long A-frame of apartments above a multilane highway, was one of the last, unbuilt visions.

As a design response that accepted and even welcomed obsolescence, factory-shed solutions fared little better than the megastructure. This was evidenced in post-occupancy evaluation of Ezra Ehrenkrantz's famed California School Construction Systems Development buildings of the 1960s, when in 1972 evaluators went back to see how the buildings actually worked. Not well, it turned out. The demountable walls, designed to be movable, proved to be poor sound insulators in open classrooms. Just as damning, few occupants even knew that the walls moved or that the heating and air conditioning outlets shifted.[64] Aesthetically, the factory-shed design made all buildings look industrial, inciting user dismay. In other words, the factory-shed solution to obsolescence expressed too bluntly its industrial origins, but did not make its adaptability legible enough to users. In the event, educators returned to structured learning in fixed spaces, making the design's signature flexibility itself obsolete.

Obsolescence's logic of discard lost its allure among even avowed modernists. Already in 1962, Philip Johnson, an early promoter of Mies and the European International Style, was picketing against Penn Station's demolition (see fig. 5.1). The British archmodernists Alison and Peter Smithson in 1968 memorialized the recent loss of London's great rail terminal as the "Euston Murder."[65] At the level of the architectural establishment in the early 1970s, the British profession adopted long life as a guiding principle. The president of the Royal Institute of British Architects, Alex Gordon, declared, "There is nothing more disturbing in visual, functional, and social terms, and nothing more disturbing to amenity, than an accelerating rate of functional obsolescence and the rebuilding that follows it."[66]

History and memory emerged as valued sources of invention in architectural theory. "Accept and delight in the past for its disruptive, its poetic, role in the present," urged the British editor Theo Crosby in 1973.[67] That same year the English theorist and historian Colin Rowe advocated "collage" urban design, "paying attention to the leftovers of the world."[68] The Italian novelist Italo Calvino's *Invisible Cities*, published in English in 1974, became a touchstone of the lyrical architectural imaginary, "a zodiac of the mind's phantasms" (22). A world of melting architectural forms, color, desire, and dreams is envisioned in the wonderful drawn fantasies of Raimund Abraham, and also of Rem Koolhaas's *Delirious New York* (1978), on the cover of which two skyscrapers lie side by side in bed. Obsolescence's rationalism no longer held undisputed sway in the thinking of the Western architectural profession.

Preservation, too, was winning more battles. Important new legislation in 1974–75 established preservation districts in Japan, controlled demolitions in Britain, and strengthened historic listings in East Germany.[69] The official European Architectural Heritage Year of 1975 was celebrated en masse in forty-five cities across the continent. In the United States, a highly symbolic moment came when the Tax Reform Act of 1976 provided for the first time "tax incentives to encourage the preservation of historic structures" and disallowed deductions for the demolition of such buildings.[70] In a country where social policy often runs through the tax code, this was a significant triumph of preservationist ideology. Sixty years after architectural obsolescence had first been recognized in the U.S. tax code, the Tax Reform Act of 1976 could be said to mark in America the end of the era of obsolescence's dominance.

At its inception, the invention of architectural obsolescence had solved key contradictions of modernization. For early twentieth-century real estate businessmen, it overcame the problem of how to think systematically about properties that were visibly sound and young in years but were underperforming from a capitalist perspective. Obsolescence rationalized rapid demolition, reinvestment, and rebuilding, making sense of an otherwise senseless waste of resources. In mid-century, planners around the world turned the idea of obsolescence to social purposes. The concept's use justified urban renewal in economistic, seemingly apolitical terms, eliciting broad consent and neutering opposition. Culturally, obsolescence made sense of an unnervingly transient built environment, now made emblematic of beneficent progress. Yet there were internal contradictions to the paradigm. What to do with stubborn remnants and emotion, the desire for permanence, the intangible and the immeasurable, much less capitalism's penchant for ceaseless change, including its own? How would the logic of obsolescence account for these? The reversals of obsolescence exploited these contradictions, using them to transcend its outlook. But the outcome was not predetermined. Agency and contingency played their parts. The will of individuals, like the urban critic Jane Jacobs, and movements, like preservationism, were instrumental. Unanticipated crises that foreclosed obsolescence's limitless future—the Vietnam War, the oil embargo—were factors that helped tip the scales. The obsolescence paradigm's contradictions were always there to be cracked open, but it took historical circumstance and individual agency for these to be exploited, pushing the worldview beyond workability.

Sustainability

By the mid-1970s in architectural culture, the option of exuberant, liberating expendability had been largely eclipsed by careful conservation, the techniques of preservationism and vernacularism, postmodernism, and even concrete brutalism, all emerging across the 1960s. Collectively, we might gather all these plural countertactics to obsolescence under the heading of sustainability, to define a paradigm different from obsolescence for comprehending and managing architectural change, which seeks to maintain rather than expend existing resources, human-made and natural, thus reversing the logic of obsolescence.

One particular technique from that era has become so dominant as to now be synonymous with the general category of sustainability: ecological architecture. On the fringes of architecture in the 1960s and 1970s, rough-hewn, low-tech buildings, often of salvaged materials, were part of a countercultural, back-to-the-land movement. Environmental consciousness, however,

FIGURE 5.13. Federal Environment Agency, aerial view, Dessau (Germany), Sauerbruch Hutton, 1997–2005.

was more generally on the rise. The natural world was cast as frail, finite, and embattled. Earth Day was first marked in the 1970, closely followed by the U.S. Clean Air and Water Acts. The late-1960s Apollo mission photographs dramatized the fact that "from space, we see a small and fragile ball," as an oft-quoted United Nations environmental report later put it, a literal world-view that helped to internationalize environmentalism. This quotation is from the landmark 1987 document *Our Common Future*, which called for systemic economic, political, and administrative reforms to counter headlong resource depletion with a new "process of change [. . .] made consistent with future as well as present needs."[71]

In architecture, consciousness grew of the built environment's role in excessive energy consumption, carbon emissions, global warming, and material wastefulness. The term "sustainability" started to appear in architectural discourse in the mid-1980s, linked to landscape architecture and then urban planning before being connected to architectural design specifically. The term sustainability named an impulse that had been gathering force since the 1960s. The architect and theorist Sim Van der Ryn, for example, wrote about sustainable communities first in terms of overall economic, physical, and ecological development that minimized harm to the environment, and then in

ENERGIEAUSWEIS
für Nichtwohngebäude

Erstellt am: 20.02.2006

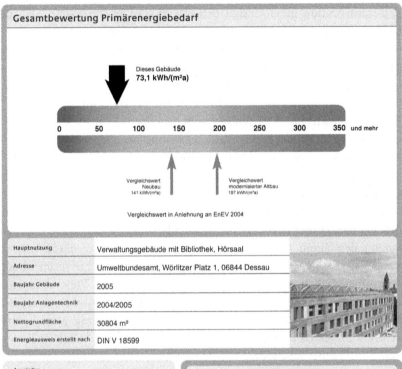

Gesamtbewertung Primärenergiebedarf

Dieses Gebäude
73,1 kWh/(m²a)

| 0 | 50 | 100 | 150 | 200 | 250 | 300 | 350 und mehr |

Vergleichswert
Neubau
141 kWh/(m²a)

Vergleichswert
modernisierter Altbau
197 kWh/(m²a)

Vergleichswert in Anlehnung an EnEV 2004

Hauptnutzung	Verwaltungsgebäude mit Bibliothek, Hörsaal
Adresse	Umweltbundesamt, Wörlitzer Platz 1, 06844 Dessau
Baujahr Gebäude	2005
Baujahr Anlagentechnik	2004/2005
Nettogrundfläche	30804 m²
Energieausweis erstellt nach	DIN V 18599

Aussteller

IEMB
Salzufer 14
10587 Berlin

Unterschrift Aussteller

Verteilung Energiebedarf

Energiebedarf [kWh/(m²a)]

Nutzenergie	48
Endenergie "Normverbrauch"	59
Primärenergie "Gesamtenergie-effizienz"	73

| 0 | 10 | 20 | 30 | 40 | 50 | 60 | 70 | 80 | 90 |

Heizung | Warmwasser | Beleuchtung | Lüftung | Kühlung

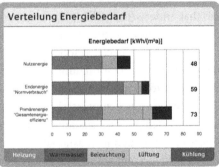

FIGURE 5.14. Federal Environment Agency, Dessau (Germany), "Energy Performance."

terms of architecture itself, of how these objectives for resource conservation could be applied at the scale of individual buildings.[72] The U.S. Green Building Council, founded in 1993, widely markets its LEED (Leadership in Energy and Environmental Design) certifications for resource efficiency. Similar standards and checklists exist globally.

Demonstration green-design projects ensued in Europe and North America. Germany's Federal Environment Agency building in Dessau (Sauerbruch Hutton, 1997–2005) is a high-tech system of energy efficiency under glass, built of renewable materials on reclaimed industrial land (fig. 5.13). Alternative energy provide a fifth of the power, from rooftop photovoltaic systems and solar collectors to landfill methane gas and a subterranean geothermal heat exchanger. Charts and graphs quantify architecture's energy performance (fig. 5.14). In a general sustainable tone—valuing what exists—the Dessau design also rests lightly on the ground, incorporates an old train station, and is color coded in its facade's glass panels to its surroundings: green facing a park, red facing factory buildings, orange facing residential blocks.

Today, the age of obsolescence appears to have been superseded by that of sustainability. Disuse has been met by impulses for adaptation and revaluation, not demolition. Deference to what exists underwrites contextualist and postmodern design. Developed nations have ceased erasing their historic built environments wholesale, sustaining them with webs of laws. Preservationism is spreading globally under UNESCO's "World Heritage" rubric, established in 1972, now numbering nearly a thousand sites and growing. Monuments are being preserved by and for humanity as a whole under UNESCO's supranational aegis, transcending individual nation-states' identities and protocols that underwrote earlier preservationism. Likewise, green design takes on universal qualities, representing the architectural wing of what the scientist Freeman Dyson has called today's "worldwide secular religion" of environmentalism.[73] Respect for nature's autonomy, combined with strict sumptuary discipline and an intergenerational outlook, produces an ethics the reverse of obsolescence's quick supersession and expendability. Against obsolescence's accelerated temporality, sustainability promotes the long view. The 1987 U.N. report famously defined sustainable development as that which "meets the needs of the present without compromising the ability of future generations to meet their own needs."[74] In other words, what obsolescence was for the mid-twentieth-century architectural imagination—that is, the dominant worldview for comprehending and managing change—sustainability has become for the twenty-first. And yet there are still roles that obsolescence plays today, and lessons in obsolescence's architectural history for understanding the past and imagining the future.

6

Sustainability and Beyond

The age of obsolescence did not produce its imagined future. Obsolescence as a dominant worldview for comprehending architectural change now appears to have been an anomaly. In historical perspective, its faith in quick-change innovation and technology seems an interregnum between traditional views of longevity and duration, illustrated in Piranesi's ruin views (see fig. 1.1), and the current regime of sustainability, which is also rooted in continuity with history and nature (see fig. 5.13). Notwithstanding all those in mid-century who believed obsolescence to be eternal—architectural life spans forever shortening—in the developed world we now largely presume the opposite. Long life instead is the aspirational ideal. Anticipated ephemerality is limited to specific structures, such as Olympic venues or biodegradable building experiments. No one thinks, as so many did a half century ago, that nearly every structure in the built environment would or should fade within a generation. What, then, is to be learned from the history of obsolescence? What lessons does it have for our understandings of twentieth-century architecture and history? What meanings from the history of obsolescence can be applied to efforts at sustainability today?

Seen through the lens of obsolescence, disparate tendencies in twentieth-century architecture come into related focus, from the canonical modernisms of Mies, Le Corbusier, the Metabolists, and Cedric Price to the mainstream establishment productions of schools, offices, and hospitals. Importantly, the architectural history of obsolescence narrated here transcends these divides. It teaches the value of intradisciplinarity, relating ordinarily separated practices in architecture: avant-garde and establishment, historic preservation and real estate, urban planning and postmodernism. All engaged with obsolescence, producing multiple architectures of obsolescence, from factory-shed flexibility to megastructures to experiments in expendability. There were multiple responses to obsolescence, too, in different national contexts from capitalist real estate speculators in the 1920s in the United States to the British welfare state to Japanese interest in postwar regeneration and the focus of Eastern European communists upon ideological rather than economic obsolescence. The architectural history of obsolescence thus reveals national architectural differences defined not by style but by politics, economy, and culture. Additional investigations might further pluralize obsolescence and its multiple architectures, and deepen understanding of architecture's interactions with politics, economy, and society across the world.[1]

Coming to Terms with Capitalism

One class of lessons emerges concerning architecture's relation to history, particularly that of capitalism. The historian Eric Hobsbawm asked a momentous question: "How is it, then, that humans and societies structured to resist dynamic development come to terms with a mode of production whose essence is endless and unpredictable dynamic development[?]"[2] Architectural history might have answers.

A century ago the inventors of architectural obsolescence rationalized the risks and apparent chaos of capitalist redevelopment through principles of competition and measurable performance, supersession and expendability. Hazard was tamed, contingency made manageable, even profitable. Subsequently, the paradigm of architectural obsolescence was expanded to the urban and social realms, theorized in response to the Great Depression then implemented by postwar planners on a metropolitan scale. Widespread publicity and application of the idea of architectural obsolescence arguably helped acculturate people to processes of "endless and unpredictable dynamic development," as Hobsbawm characterized capitalism, made more or less livable in everyday experience. Amid fast-paced architectural developments, which might otherwise have seemed inexplicable, the discourses of obsolescence provided a name and a logic for this visceral experience of everyday change. The reassuring rationale of obsolescence also implicitly explained and justified capitalist dynamism itself, as much a naturalized background part of life as the changeful buildings around us. The obsolescent built environment was a site of both depredation and mediation: the place to "come to terms" with new modes of change.

For their part, architects were slow to address obsolescence's implications. But after 1960 many sought to manage, in design, Hobsbawm's contradiction between dynamism and constancy, to find ways to live with ceaseless change. Tactics from factory-shed monumentality to megastructures' differential obsolescence to indeterminacy's open-endedness sought to accommodate change and stasis all at once—to accept obsolescence and a lack of determinate finish, to allow both order and identity to be in flux. These were architectural ways, pragmatic and lyrical, to reconcile with ceaseless change. "It requires poetic imagination to portray a world in which both, the fast and slow group, have their complementary place," writes a sociologist of time, Helga Nowotny.[3]

At the same moment, architects and others concerned with the built environment discovered that all that was solid did not necessarily melt into air. There were survivals and attachments that would have to be accounted for. Revaluation of the obsolete, by preservationism, vernacularism, and postmodernism, exposed a crucial contradiction in the capitalist logic of creative destruction. The past persists as unpredictably as the future unfolds. What we find emerging in the 1960s, and blossoming subsequently, is capitalism's capacity to manage the contradictions of its own development, to take what it had made obsolete—the industrial-age built environment—and exploit its revaluation through processes of adaptive reuse, gentrification, and historic preservation. The conundrum of capitalist "deadwood" is overcome. Rather than discarding expensive investments, capitalism found value in supporting new meanings to recommoditize them.

Manfredo Tafuri, the great theorist of architecture's relation to capitalism, somewhat missed the mark writing around 1970 of a pop art–inspired design aesthetic, which he illustrated with the peaks of New York's art deco skyscrapers, writing that this "reutilizing the residues and castoffs of [technological] production [. . .] takes its place in the rear guard."[4] Tafuri, wedded to a tragic narrative of avant-garde modernism's uselessness to capitalism, claimed that this "game" of recycled imagery covered up but did not seriously address the development of capitalist urbanism, as had avant-garde architecture previously. He missed an emerging story. A rearguard aesthetic, stylistically, could stand in capitalism's vanguard, ideologically, precisely by reutilizing and revaluing residues and castoffs. The architectural history of obsolescence suggests the limits of seeing creative destruction as capitalism's unaltering paradigm of change. Critics as perceptive as the geographer David Harvey remain wedded to creative destruction as "just as central in daily life as it ever was."[5] The "only" means "to open up fresh room for accumulation" is "to have to destroy [the existing physical landscape]," Harvey has asserted.[6] But the eclipse of obsolescence by sustainability suggests otherwise. Creative destruction, like obsolescence, appears as an historical conceptualization, not as something eternal. There may be ways to think about capitalism other than as unceasing change and creative destruction.

The architectural history of obsolescence illustrates the flexibility of capitalism, its capacity to absorb critique and evolve from its own contradictions, to exploit the built environment one way and then the other: obsolescence, then sustainability. There may not be one essential mode of change in capitalism. If capitalism is reconceived as something more complicated than ceaseless change—encompassing also retention, recycling, and reuse—then we have a different theoretical picture and critical footing. Justifications for radical change under the banner of capitalist logic, for example, would no longer have the force of history. Capitalism represented as sometime conservator of what exists changes its economic, social, and environmental dynamics.

Finally, like capitalism, as the critic Fredric Jameson writes, obsolescence might be judged both "positively *and* negatively all at once [. . .] as catastrophe and progress all together [. . .] at one and the same time the best thing [. . .] and the worst."[7] The paradigm possessed undoubtedly authoritarian, destructive aspects: experts' tools ended up as weapons against whole communities. Yet obsolescence also enjoyed progressive dimensions, striking at the status quo without remorse, clearing the way for new physical environments and more socially just distribution of resources—air, open space, and housing. Architecturally, the belief in obsolescence produced innovative design worldwide and replaced dim tenement districts with modern, landscaped spaciousness. Left alone, these neighborhoods would not have remained unchanged. Boston's retained North End and South End neighborhoods, unlike the demolished West End, were spared the wrecking ball but have been gentrified nevertheless. Rising housing costs eventually expel working-class residents as effectively as does urban renewal. Obsolescence, understood as an historical force, as Jameson writes about capitalism, represents "the framework, and the precondition for the achievement of some new and more comprehensive" mode—in our case, sustainability.[8] Obsolescence was the phase passed through, for better *and* for worse, on the way to a new worldview for comprehending and managing change in the built environment.

Obsolescence Endures

Seeing obsolescence and sustainability in sequence points to obsolescence's part in the genealogy, the prehistory of sustainability. But the relation between the two is as much filial as agonistic. There are numerous similarities between the architectures and ideologies of the two paradigms that might lead to reconsideration of sustainability, understood here as not just as green design but as other tactics, too, for conserving existing resources, natural and human-made, including preservationism and vernacularism. Adaptive reuse, for example, is a variation on the megastructure. In both, new components inserted into long-life frames accommodate change (see figs. 4.19 and 5.4). Obsolescence and preservation are also mutually intertwined. Obsolescence's traumas are assuaged by preservation, while preservation feeds off fears of obsolescence. Both define the past as broken off from the present. They need each other to survive. As the historian David Lowenthal writes, "To expunge the obsolete and restore it as heritage are, like disease and its treatment, conjoint and even symbiotic."[9] Sustainability also feeds off fears from the age of obsolescence that human progress will waste the world. This is intimated in Cedric Price's Potteries Thinkbelt slagheap imagery (see fig. 4.24). But now anxiety is enlarged beyond the built environment to the earth as a whole. Ecological architecture conceives of a world of finite resources and at-risk nature. So urgent does the situation appear that any human expropriation may be proscribed. Such is the goal of net-zero building, in which no external energy resources are consumed. Against obsolescence's expendability, perceived as a threat to everything, sustainability ideally seeks to conserve it all.

Both obsolescence and sustainability also present simplified models of change that attempt to discipline time and idealize its shape. Obsolescence proposes quickened linear supersession and expendability. Sustainability offers slow adaptability and circular conservation—emblematized by the universal recycling symbol of three chasing arrows (devised for the first Earth Day in 1970). An eternal return recasts obsolescence's linear, open future. Yet aspects of each appear in the other's temporality. Cyclicality governs obsolescence's recurrent pattern of innovation and expendability. Sustainability presumes a forward motion in time, toward reuse or technical advance. Obsolescence and ecological architecture mirror each other, too, in their dependence upon measurable performance. Today's tables of building energy use echo the data-mania of earlier obsolescence charts (see figs. 1.3 and 5.14). In both approaches, architectural worth is reduced to expert numbers. And capitalism, which sired obsolescence a century ago, generates profits today from sustainability's technophilia. Economic prosperity is pinned to green innovation in U.S. politicians' frequent promotion of the alternative energy industry.[10] Yet what will happen to today's green building when future innovation renders its performance substandard? How sustainable will its obsolescence be? In other words, we have not overcome the other side of the argument in the 1960s— belief in the promise of obsolescence—as much as a triumphalist narrative of sustainability might have it. Our time remains, as lived experience always does, polytemporal, in the sociologist Bruno Latour's phrasing. "The past is not surpassed but revisited, repeated, surrounded, protected, recombined, reinterpreted and reshuffled."[11] Obsolescence endures, even if not as a dominant worldview.

Today, obsolescence coexists with sustainability, though it is subordinate. The view is still heard that "if a building becomes redundant for the business it was originally built for it should be knocked down and replaced," as the head of the British Arts Council declared in the mid-1990s.[12] "You know, our Arizona stadium will be torn down in 30 years because it will be useless," prophesies Peter Eisenman about a 2006 structure of his.[13] The U.S. federal tax code adheres to depreciation figures established eight decades ago: forty years for nonresidential property. Several building types seem especially susceptible to obsolescence today. In America's older inner suburban towns, Main Street preservation cohabits with ruthless domestic teardowns. Small but serviceable postwar homes on valuable land are replaced by large new residences featuring supersized kitchen-family rooms. These are both more lucrative for developers' profit margins and more compatible with the informal eating and gathering practices of contemporary life. In places like historic Lexington, Massachusetts, every new housing start begins with a demolition, Cape Cods for McMansions—the selective obsolescence of postwar suburbia.[14] American convention centers and casinos have notably short lives, too, replaced by larger, up-to-date profit centers. And every U.S. concrete sports stadium, vintage 1970, has been exchanged in the past generation for a quirkier, more historical-looking model, with lucrative luxury boxes (even as some of these become obsolete, like Atlanta's 1997 Turner Field, anticipated to be demolished in 2017 with the team's move to the suburbs).[15]

Like the older stadiums, postwar public buildings around the world, especially of the concrete brutalist variety, suffer obsolescence, even if more aesthetic than functional. Northwick Park Hospital's streaked gray blocks have been compared stylistically to a "Russian nuclear reactor" by hospital staff.[16] Owners of Tokyo's Nakagin Capsule Tower have sought its replacement for a decade, citing insufficient land coverage, changing lifestyles, and excessive rehabilitation costs—though preservationists resist the building's demolition. The megastructure's capsule units were never swapped out as planned. Today the Nakagin Capsule Tower stands forlorn among later urban additions, no longer heroic, just out-of-time (fig. 6.1).

In China, capitalist modernization today sweeps away the past, echoing the American trajectory a century ago. "In both countries, older inner-city

FIGURE 6.1. Nakagin Capsule Tower, Tokyo, photographed 2013.

neighborhoods were viewed as obsolete,"[17] write the urban experts Yan Zhang and Ke Fang. But the parallels extend only so far. The Chinese state steers development as much as the market does. Beijing is more like the top-down, nineteenth-century remaking of Paris than the capitalist free-for-all of Chicago. And the centralized urban form in China is hardly considered obsolete, outperformed by suburbs, as it was perceived to be in mid-twentieth-century America. "In China today, the city reigns supreme," declares the urban planner and historian Thomas Campanella.[18] And even as Chinese cities undergo radical redevelopment, tactics of sustainability temper obsolescence. Shanghai effaces its working-class, alley-and-courtyard *lilong* housing precincts, but plans historic preservation and ecodistricts. Surviving tenements cluster beneath tower blocks alongside adaptive reuse and postmodern contextualism in gentrifying neighborhoods (fig. 6.2). The city's most popular tourist site is the reconstructed, high-end, *lilong*-style shopping district of Xintiandi. In

China, a rich polytemporality exists in dynamic tension between modernization and conservation, obsolescence and sustainability.

Meanwhile, in the urban Western world, tens of thousands of obsolete dwellings have been razed on both sides of the Atlantic in the past generation—in the former East Germany, for instance, and in the city of Detroit alone some 161,000.[19] Urban obsolescence persists. But it is not perceived as an existential crisis as it was in the mid-twentieth century. Artists and tourists now seek aesthetic and historical meaning in the postindustrial detritus of shrinking cities, discovering "admiration for its peculiar beauty," explains the pioneering photographer Camilo J. Vergara of his *American Ruins* project, "symbols of what led this nation into the twentieth-century" (fig. 6.3).[20] Critics discern here nostalgia "for the ruins of modernity," observes the philosopher Andreas Huyssen. "The mammoth has changed from aggressor to victim and now earns our wistful affection," notes the architectural historian and theorist Robert Harbison.[21] Some have taken the critique further, calling the aesthetic "ruin porn," thinking of work like the coffee-table tome *The Ruins of Detroit*,

FIGURE 6.2. Shanghai, 2012, view from roof of 1933 Slaughterhouse.

FIGURE 6.3. Camilo José Vergara, *Remains of an Old Montgomery Ward Warehouse, West Side of Detroit*, 1996.

by Yves Marchand and Romain Meffre (2010).[22] Lush pictures of abandonment empty obsolescence of its menace.

Contemporary Design

In architecture, too, obsolescence has lost its edge. Once it energized discourse and design; now it is a minor chord. Architects remain interested in transience and flexibility, but their attention lacks the urgency that infused the last century. Technical solutions are occasionally offered to manage building life, like Designing for Disassembly (DfD), by two architects of the firm Llewelyn Davies Yeang.[23] Half a century ago this practice's founding principals, Richard Llewelyn Davies and John Weeks, wrestled strenuously with the theoretical, aesthetic, and practical implications of obsolescence, producing the idea of indeterminate architecture, a kind of "open work" in building resonating with contemporary artistic and cultural trends. Subsequently, the issue of obsolescence became more narrowly conceived. As a 1985 study concluded, "The question of hospital obsolescence is always a question of economic obsolescence."[24] Gone are the broader cultural, technological, organizational, social, and philosophical facets supplementing the economic, which heightened the sense of excitement and urgency around obsolescence in the 1960s.

Only occasionally does contemporary architecture grant creative significance to obsolescence. Rem Koolhaas is a rare exception. Trained in late-1960s London, Koolhaas retains that moment's romance with obsolescence, particularly his admiration for Cedric Price. "He was a sceptic torturing a conservative discipline," Koolhass proclaims about his generation's great teacher of expendability.[25] (From the same era, the architect Richard Rogers supported the 1990s demolition of his 1960s Reliance Controls Factory. "The older I get the less I like about old buildings.")[26] In design, Koolhaas explores issues of architectural transience and life spans, generating, for example, a well-publicized though unrealized plan of Paris's La Défense district (1991), which "declared that every building in this entire zone that is less than twenty-five years [old] has to be destroyed, because it is worthless."[27] The La Défense project's insistence on expendability was more a theoretical than a realistic proposition, but it demonstrated Koolhaas's creative engagement with obsolescence at the contemporary urban scale. In practice, Koolhaas now expresses his understanding of obsolescence in smaller-scale work, as in the provisional-looking ceiling of his Illinois Institute of Technology campus center (1997–2003) (fig. 6.4).

Obsolescence's capacity to drive innovation is constrained, Koolhaas argues, by the contemporary mania for preservation. "A huge section of our world (about 12 percent) is now off-limits," Koolhaas claims, with a number pulled more or less out of thin air for rhetorical effect. In response to this constraint, the architect proposes an international Convention Concerning the Demolition of World Cultural Junk (satirizing UNESCO's 1972 Convention on World Heritage) "to liberate oversaturated urban territory through the demolition of junk."[28] Koolhaas's energy derives, in effect, from refighting the battles of the 1960s between obsolescence and preservation. But now the roles are reversed. Emotion, hyperbole, and provocation are Koolhaas's weapons, and they are aimed at preservation, which arguably demonstrates obsolescence's present subordinate position.

Obsolescence has been voided as an agent of creativity. Instead, risk and uncertainty are neutralized, not only by the tactics of sustainability but also in the aesthetics of today's "supermodernism," a term deployed by the Dutch architecture critic Hans Ibelings. Taut glass boxes around the world by architects like Toyo Ito, Herzog & de Meuron, Jean Nouvel, and others convey an image of absolute and total finish (fig. 6.5). The skins of these buildings completely wrap the structures, symbolizing, in Ibelings's view, a monolithic timelessness. The flux of a networked world is naturalized as a shimmering,

FIGURE 6.4. McCormick Tribune Campus Center, Illinois Institute of Technology, Chicago, Rem Koolhaas, 1997–2003.

flickering, visual effect upon reflective surfaces, the critic argues. The symbolic effect is an image of architecture as "a safe container, a flexible shell."[29] The aesthetic difference from the factory shed is that the earlier type visually emphasized its skeletal steel structure, which was open to dynamic penetration, movement, and adaptation (see fig. 4.9), whereas the supermodern box, according to Ibelings, reads like an inviolable treasure chest whose hermetic perfection transcends the flux of the world. Obsolescence is neutered as a critical risk factor of mutability in modern life, these jewel boxes suggest, obsolescence's power to move design negated.

Lessons of Obsolescence

Still, the history of obsolescence has lessons to teach architecture about time. Attend to the temporality of function, it suggests. This goes beyond architecture's usual temporal dimensions of historical association (looking like the past), natural mutability (changing like nature), or procession through space

FIGURE 6.5. Prada Boutique, Tokyo, Herzog & de Meuron, 2003.

(movement in time). The temporality of use is remote to most architects and architectural historians, who mainly focus on the period of creation. At least since the Renaissance, the architect's ideal role has been to sire architecture: to beget a building by design, husband it through construction, then move on to further acts of procreation. "You know, I have designed buildings that I have never been to," the renowned architect Frank Gehry proclaims, "because the people I worked with weren't there at the end, so I didn't go see them."[30] In this culture, the designing architect is neither encouraged nor paid to nurture a building through its useful existence. But the theme of obsolescence teaches that the life of buildings matters and implicitly makes this a high priority.

Taking obsolescence seriously teaches the value not just of sustenance but of transcendence, too. Expendability educates us to ends. Buildings are not forever. They never were and have been less so under capitalism. Yet the pendulum may have swung too far, from discarding to hoarding the past. We need to face buildings' mortality as we face our own, the authors of the book *Buildings Must Die* have argued, so "that death and waste can play their parts in architectural creativity."[31] Obsolescence teaches letting go of the past—for worse and for better. Obsolescence might also tutor us to relinquish the future, too. Why do we grip posterity so tightly in preservation laws? Is this striving for immortality? Why not allow the future its own, different choices? Perhaps we should let historic landmark listings expire, so that our descendants can decide for themselves if something be worth keeping. Acknowledging obsolescence can teach trust in the future.

The history of obsolescence demonstrates the value, in a vibrant architectural culture, of the simultaneous impulses both for extreme transformation and resistance to it. This was the characteristic struggle of the 1960s, when the cultural dominance of obsolescence was under the most intense pressure. The promise of obsolescence proceeded side by side with the equally passionate rejection of its logic. The moment faced up to obsolescence's, and modernity's, duality of liberation and oppression. Revolutions in modern life both emancipate *and* grind upon humanity, the art historian T. J. Clark has written in his account of modern art; the "experience of modernity is precisely the experience of the *two* states, the two tonalities, at the same time."[32] The 1960s experienced obsolescence in just this modernist manner, as liberation *and* constraint: the promise of obsolescence *and* the consolation of sustainability.

Today the impulses stand imbalanced. Sustainability is in the ascendant, obsolescence eclipsed in architectural culture. "The current moment has almost no idea how to negotiate the coexistence of radical change and radical stasis that is our future," writes Koolhaas.[33] The past is made a precious jewel. The contemporary most often bows delicately to the old, afraid to touch it, cleaned up and revered, as with many recent insertions into the historical fabric. In Hong Kong at the 2011 Asia Society Center building by Tod Williams Billie Tsien Architects, a new steel-columned walkway runs parallel at a respectful distance from the restored masonry wall of an old explosives magazine berm (fig. 6.6). Less refined but more instructive is the temporality of a renovated factory building in Zlín, Czech Republic (fig. 6.7).[34] Here, a century ago, the shoe manufacturer Tomáš Baťa imagined twenty-year building life spans. But in 2006 the frame of Building No. 23 was refurbished for a Business Innovation Center by Pavel Mudřík and Pavel Míček. The building has also been augmented with projecting bronze bays. But, more significant, something has been deducted from the architecture. To lighten the structure, broad voids appear in the upper floors, shrinking the historical frame. The past is visibly released. Baťa's intention—a limited-life architecture—is

FIGURE 6.6. Asia Society Hong Kong Center, Hong Kong, Tod Williams Billie Tsien, 2011.

honored unconsciously. Building No. 23 embodies preservation, growth, *and* attrition all at once, treating the past flexibly, not reverentially.

Undetermined History

The architectural history of obsolescence teaches us about polytemporality. We live in an age of both obsolescence *and* sustainability, past and present all at once. Yet polytemporality is not a full theory of time. It is a static snapshot describing a single moment's complexity that implicitly suggests a process of cumulative change rather than rupture, the past continuing into the present. But this does not account for *how* change happens, which is history's big question. Under what circumstances, by what mechanism, does one moment become another? The architectural history of obsolescence might have lessons to teach here, too.

The account in this book suggests a model of change of one cultural dominant succeeding another: obsolescence, then sustainability. The changeovers are based in part upon the working through of deep structural problems, when the stresses within a conceptual framework can no longer be accommodated and a new mode is invented that resolves these tensions, yet leads to others. Philosophers of science have written about such paradigm shifts (e.g., from Newtonian to Einsteinian physics). "Accumulated awareness of seeming inconsistencies gradually leads to observational and conceptual recognition of paradigm breakdown. [. . .] Eventually a recognition emerges that paradigm change is inevitable," writes Erich von Dietze about Thomas Kuhn's famous 1962 account of scientific paradigm shifts.[35] Regarding the evolution of the built environment, a century ago the inventors of the idea of architectural obsolescence used the concept to overcome the seeming irrationality of capitalist real estate development. Rapid disinvestment and reinvestment now made sense and profit. The protagonists of sustainability, in turn, exploited obsolescence's own contradictions to engineer that paradigm's reversal, revaluing its waste and accounting for suppressed feeling.

But the historical progress was never predetermined. Rather, it proceeded

FIGURE 6.7. Building 23 rehabilitation, Zlín (Czech Republic), Pavel Mudřík and Pavel Míček, 2006.

through agency and circumstance, misintention and misunderstanding, as much as through structural logic. It took Earle Shultz's leadership of NABOM during the 1920s, in the circumstance of the new U.S. federal income tax, to publicize the idea of architectural obsolescence, which became a broad American cultural myth that extended well beyond NABOM's limited intentions. Later, in the 1960s, British obsolescence researchers misunderstood U.S. tax code building life-span numbers as scientific evidence to advance analyses of obsolescence. At the same time, the unexpectedly persuasive critique of urban obsolescence by such people as Jane Jacobs drove a wedge into the dominant paradigm, cracking it open in concert with historical circumstances, like the 1970s oil crisis, that disfavored the paradigm.

History could have gone differently, we must believe. Without the U.S. tax code and NABOM, would the idea of obsolescence have taken such hold of architectural imaginations? Architectural obsolescence need not have become a dominant worldview; modernism was advancing without it. Le Corbusier and Gropius both believed in traditional, final, formal solutions, not the endless mutability of obsolescence, as we have seen in chapter 3—the former plumping for "a sure and permanent home," the latter decrying "transient novelties."[36] Likewise, sustainability need not have superseded obsolescence. The sides appeared balanced in the 1960s: Reyner Banham and Cedric Price as persuasive as Jane Jacobs and preservationism. But even as the critics of obsolescence pushed at the paradigm's contradictions—what to do with its remainders? how to account for unquantifiable values?—external crises brought to the fore obsolescence's top-down, resource-greedy nature, leading to its eclipse. Loss of faith in technocracy, a hallmark of 1960s counterculture and unrest, was followed by the 1970s oil crisis and recession, which put paid to dreams of endless abundance and expendability. By the time prosperity resumed in the 1980s, sustainability as we have broadly defined it, the desire to conserve rather than expend existing resources, occupied the heights in guises from postmodernism to ecologism.

The architectural history of obsolescence is *"undetermined history,"* in the phrase of the historian Joan Scott.[37] By that Scott means a succession of events that are not predestined, tending toward a single present reality, but rather are contingent, matters of accident and agency, as much as underlying structure, logic, and teleology. Such history writing, in Scott's formulation, serves the purpose of critique, revealing historical and present constructs that might seem natural and inevitable (such as obsolescence in its time and sustainability now) to be in fact "an interpretation of reality rather than reality itself [. . .] a set of options that prevailed by ruling out others."[38] The ultimate objective of such history writing, which emphasizes past contests and contingencies, is to open the current moment itself to change, so that the future may be openly imagined as proceeding in alternative, as yet unglimpsed directions, not just continuing a naturalized present. History from this perspective appears as unpredictable as obsolescence itself. Radical change may or may not happen. The future unfolds in excess of our fondest projections. Above all, the architectural history of obsolescence teaches that narratives of change are themselves changeable creations. Obsolescence and sustainability are both historically invented, possess exploitable contradictions, and can be historically reversed. What might lead to sustainability's supersession? What are its contradictions?

Contradictions of Sustainability

To begin to understand the possibilities for sustainability's supersession, as it once eclipsed obsolescence, let us look first at environmentalism's ideology as it was recognized in the late 1960s. Its service to capitalism, declared the young French radical intellectual group Utopie in 1970, was to "transfer the ugly reality of social relations to an idealized model of marvelous nature." Raising the alarm on environmental crisis serves "to unify a disintegrating society," declared Utopie's leader, the philosopher Jean Baudrillard; "nothing better than a touch of ecology and catastrophe to unite the social classes. [. . .] Social relations with their conflicts and history are completely rejected in favor of nature."[39] Fifty years later the analysis still rings true.

If obsolescence was the ideology of change for mid-twentieth-century capitalism, then, arguably, sustainability performs the same function for current-day capitalism. Neoliberalism, as it is often called, seeks unfettered free trade, capital mobility, and modes of transnational production unrestrained by state regulation and local workers' rights. It idealizes a supranational global economy that is decentered and deterritorialized (for example, many companies in the American high-tech sector have headquarters on the West Coast and factories in Asia). Thus, in terms of social space, sustainability echoes and reinforces capitalism's current and increasing inequalities. The expert and affluent in their green enclaves win the profits and call the tune for the poor elsewhere, who bear the waste and do with less. "Eco-apartheid," the critic Andrew Ross labels this global geography of inequality.[40] And Jane Jacobs's nostalgia for small-town neighborhood community fueled the elite-class gentrification of inner cities, which expelled working-class inhabitants without recourse to state amelioration. Jacobs, a fierce libertarian critic of urban obsolescence, believed individual free choice, not government policy, underpinned cities' vitality. The market decides who can afford to live where and at what price. No big plans ought to interfere with things as they occur and exist, what Jacobs liked to call the "real."

It may be going too far to declare that "sustainability culture is inherent to the logic of late capitalism," as does the philosopher Adrian Parr.[41] But the symbiosis is evident. Both sustainability and neoliberalism manage risk with great operational sophistication. The challenges of financialized neoliberal capitalism are mediated through complex new technologies and techniques, from computerized trading to credit default swaps. Likewise, sustainability depends upon machine and managerial innovations to equilibrate change: green engines and preservation protocols. At the same time, sustainability is promoted as an economic growth machine to support capitalist accumulation. Ecobranding proves effective marketing. Sustainability's technophilia fuels corporate profits. Technology and administration are architectural sustainability's foci, not politics, transferring onto nature and away from the social. Not coincidentally, the neoliberal deregulation of capital flows and accumulation accompanies sustainability's hyperregulation of environments both built and natural. The latter, arguably, diverts attention from the former.

As much as sustainability promises a new, brighter future, can it ever break the current order? Sustainability advocates might excoriate capitalist exploitation of the environment and seek dramatic changes in consumption patterns, but its ethic is continuity and conservation. It is a privilege of the wealthy, who can afford to curb their consumption in the name of environmental salvation and to revalue obsolete objects as salvaged treasure. Unlike obsolescence, sustainability denies the promise of radical change. As the architect Ellen Grimes asserts, sustainability is an "inherently conservative term."[42] Sustainability suffers from an inherent contradiction: to change *and* to preserve the world. Its highest ideal is utopian equilibrium, in which all is stable harmony.

But could there ever be such a thing as sustainable capitalism, harmonious equilibrium for a system of ceaseless change and development, always thriving on the production, consumption, and reinvestment in the new? Can sustainability deliver the growth upon which capitalism thrives? This is the conundrum the sociologist Wolfgang Sachs identifies between sustainable development's "crisis of nature" and "crisis of justice." The first demands "self-limitation." The second insists upon "individual liberty."[43] Can you have it both ways—austerity and social justice? Can one demand less for the world, when there are already so many with so little? This seems to point to a contradiction between sustainability and capitalism. Is sustainability's regime of restrained consumption compatible with capitalism's drive for ceaseless growth and change? Can sustainability deliver both justice and freedom when its ethic is limitation and preservation? Or is sustainability merely an ideology of conservation, its practice in architecture potentially as profligate as obsolescence? Witness the supertall skyscrapers trumpeting LEED certification projected for Jakarta, Mumbai, and Shanghai. Might, in fact, sustainability be nothing more than neoliberal capitalism's updated opiate of the masses, a diverting faith? In other words, sustainability, no less than obsolescence, is ideological. Productive for design, to be sure, firing architects' imaginations as obsolescence once did, but nevertheless rife with illusion and contradiction.

Beyond sustainability's complex relationship to contemporary capitalism what are some of the paradigm's contradictions that might someday lead to its eclipse? First there are sustainability's attitudes toward nature and technology. Sustainability holds two opposed thoughts in mind about nature: that it is both fragile *and* destructive. Our least intervention will lead to catastrophe. Proposed solutions proffered by experts to environmental crises, such as climate change, are equally contradictory. More technology, such as complex energy recycling systems, is called upon to solve problems produced by technology (e.g., the reckless energy consumption of air conditioning). In effect, more modernization will redress the problems of prior modernization, what the sociologist Ulrich Beck calls "reflexive modernization."[44] In a related tension, game-changing innovation will, paradoxically, serve a paradigm of measured change. On the one hand, industry and architects constantly propose breakthrough technology to increase building performance. On the other hand, advocates of sustainability promote slow (if any) growth in consumption and settlement patterns. Moreover, proponents of a fundamentalist sustainability, like the well-known William McDonough, believe nature can be administered without touching its integrity: "Everything that is received from the earth can be freely given back without causing harm to any living system."[45] The worldview of sustainability ultimately presumes nature's knowability. Humans measure, predict, and order the natural course.

As sustainability becomes increasingly technical—focused upon performance measurements, engineering innovation, and LEED scorecards—it tends to lose touch with its more political and emotional origins and tactics. In the 1960s affection for older urban environments overturned obsolescence's rationalistic logic and impelled activism for the environment and obsolete architecture. The ideal of justice, prominent in other fields, like political science's conceptions of sustainability, is presently marginal in architecture, requiring special pleading, overshadowed by a predominantly technical discourse.[46] Longevity may be better ensured by feeling than engineering. A "friends of . . ." organization nurtures attachment through the generations. "In architecture, love conquers and endures," once noted the architectural historian Vincent Scully.[47]

Another tension is that sustainability's rationalism includes equal measures of religiosity. "Environmentalism, as a religion of hope and respect for nature, is here to stay,"[48] writes the scientist Freeman Dyson. Photovoltaics symbolize for consumers, manufacturers, and activists a pious commitment to environmental sensitivity, regardless of how much energy they might actually produce. Similarly, the Yale University architecture professor Michelle Addington argues that tight building envelopes' supposedly superior thermal insulating performance actually "has no basis in physics."[49] In the historical arc of architectural moralism, sustainability returns to transcendent, nonhuman sources. Twentieth-century modernism purported to operate on behalf of architecture's human inhabitants and functions. Sustainability's ethical commitment, on the other hand, is to the conservation of natural systems, an echo of premodernism's belief in the divine mathematical harmonies. And the faith's universalism contradicts its avowed localism. The same ethics and standards are applied worldwide transcending local difference and resistances, in the name, ironically, of place saving.

Optimistically, too, sustainability seeks to fix the world around it. The German Federal Environment Agency headquarters in Dessau not only conserves resources, its design is locked into its present surroundings (see fig. 5.13). Green glass panels face parkland, red ones look toward a brick-built factory, orange ones are turned to residential neighbors. Architecture repairs the environment and represents it as fixed, each nearby feature permanently in place. Future change is unimaginable. The world will always be as it currently is, contextualist design presumes. And contradictory consequences are unaccounted. The majority of cars in the agency's parking lot, shortly after completion, came from Berlin, sixty miles away, because employees preferred to live in the capital rather than the provincial city where the organization was sited for political reasons. Architecture's good intentions for sustainability are canceled out. A lesson from the age of obsolescence has yet to be absorbed. Contingency confounds easy architectural fixes.

Beyond Sustainability

These then are some of the contradictions of sustainability: between nature and technique, reason and faith, stasis and change, limitation and justice. Like the contradictions of capitalist development a hundred years ago, and those of obsolescence fifty, these may lead beyond sustainability to a new worldview for comprehending and managing change in the built environment. Today we may await sustainability's passing as a dominant paradigm, the cracking open of its contradictions, a glimpse of a postsustainable future, subsumed within a different worldview, as did our forebears a half century ago in reversing obsolescence.

Yet the future's path is difficult to discern, as obscure to us as sustainability would have been to the most prescient observers a half century ago. What agents with what agendas, and what circumstances with what resonances, might challenge sustainability, as Shultz and the federal tax code did a century earlier to the worldview of architectural permanence? What features of sustainability will survive into future frameworks, as quantitative measurements of architectural value and performance have persisted from obsolescence to sustainability? How much of sustainability's historical contribution will be passed down, its concern for the future, its respect for the autonomy of nature and the conservation of resources?

A contemporary byword related to sustainability that may eventually impact architecture is "resilience." Emerging in the 1970s in relation to ecologies, such as forests, and then applied to human social systems, resilience has more recently been taken up by urban planning in the wake of serial disasters, from Hurricane Katrina and the September 11 attacks to the housing bubble and global recession. A 2006 handbook defines resilience as "the capacity of a system to absorb disturbance; to undergo change and still retain essentially the same, function, structure, and feedbacks."[50] Resilience thinking thus conceptualizes change in terms of never-ending catastrophe, against which the resilient system must be designed with adaptability and diversity. Like sustainability, resilience presumes a fragile world, increasingly so, buffeted by hazard and risk. Different than sustainability, resilience thinking does not seek efficient, optimized control of an equilibrium state, but rather emphasizes redundancy and expects disaster, a series of constant crises throwing systems out of balance.[51] Resilience thinking thus incorporates dramatic change much more than does sustainability. In this it perhaps approximates the earlier obsolescence paradigm in its acceptance or at least acknowledgment of radical change—though with resilience change is catastrophic, not beneficent. Resilience possesses a particular political economy, too, as the urban researcher Michael Quinn Dudley has pointed out, which "requires an interventionist state" to anticipate and manage the constant disturbance; in this way, resilience provides a kind of retort to neoliberalism's denigration of the public sector.[52] For architecture, it remains to be seen how much resilience thinking can be scaled down from the systems level to the built object. But resilience, as a way to conceptualize change in architecture and design, may represent a hybrid of obsolescence and sustainability—incorporating the former's acceptance of radical contingent change within the latter's framework of systems crisis management.

Still the future is insusceptible to divination. Posterity will be as strange to us as the past. This is what Nabokov meant when he wrote, "The future is but the obsolete in reverse." No amount of imagination or analysis can pierce the fog of contingency veiling what will come. But we may deduce, from the history outlined here, that the cracks in sustainability, when they appear, will run along the fault lines sketched above. Ultimately, the outcome of a struggle to unseat a dominant paradigm is not preordained. Sustainability may persist. Capitalism certainly has survived, adapting to critique and crises. Yet worldviews *do* change, architectural history teaches us. Obsolescence waxed, then waned. Obsolescence preceded sustainability, and something else may come after sustainability, an as yet unformed, unnamed worldview for comprehending and managing change in the built environment. History does not proceed along a rigid path; accident and agency, along with the evolution of internal contradictions, helped invent obsolescence and then sustainability. The best and final lesson of the history of obsolescence for sustainability and beyond may be as simple and important as this: we must regard the future as just as malleable, contingent, and unpredictable as obsolescence itself.

Notes

Introduction

1. Sarah Bradford Landau and Carl W. Condit, *Rise of the New York Skyscraper, 1865–1913* (New Haven, CT: Yale University Press, 1996), 249–52.

2. *New York Times*, 10 and 30 April 1910.

3. "Architectural Autopsies," *Buildings and Building Management*, 14 March 1927, 46–48; Landau and Condit, *New York Skyscraper*; Neil Harris, *Building Lives: Constructing Rites and Passages* (New Haven, CT: Yale University Press, 1999), 137–39; Nathan Silver, *Lost New York* (Boston: Houghton Mifflin, 2000); *Atlanta Constitution*, 5 February 1911; Earle Shultz, *The Effect of Obsolescence on the Useful and Profitable Life of Office Buildings* (Chicago: National Association of Building Owners and Managers, 1922), 215.

4. "New Skyscraper for Old," *Scientific American*, 21 May 1910, 414.

5. Cecil C. Evers, *The Commercial Problem in Buildings* (New York: Record & Guide, 1914), 58.

6. James Marston Fitch, *Historic Preservation: Curatorial Management of the Built World* (New York: McGraw-Hill, 1982), 31.

7. Marvin Trachtenberg, *Building-in-Time: From Giotto to Alberti and Modern Oblivion* (New Haven, CT: Yale University Press, 2010), x, xxii. See also Kevin Lynch, *What Time Is This Place?* (Cambridge, MA: MIT Press, 1972); George Kubler, *The Shape of Time: Remarks on the History of Things* (New Haven, CT: Yale University Press, 1962); Harris, *Building Lives*; Edward Hollis, *The Secret Lives of Buildings: From the Ruins of the Parthenon to the Vegas Strip in Thirteen Stories* (London: Portobello, 2009).

8. Robert Kronenburg, *Flexible: Architecture That Responds to Change* (London: Peter King, 2007); Anastasia Karandinou, *No Matter: Theories and Practices of the Ephemeral in Architecture* (Farnham: Ashgate, 2013); Stephen Cairns and Jane M. Jacobs, *Buildings Must Die: A Perverse View of Architecture* (Cambridge, MA: MIT Press, 2014). See also Fred Scott, *On Altering Architecture* (London: Routledge, 2008); Stewart Brand, *How Buildings Learn: What Happens After They're Built* (New York: Penguin, 1994); Neil Levine, "The Architecture of the Unfinished and the Example of Louis Kahn," in *Fragments: Architecture and the Unfinished: Essays Presented to Robin Middleton*, ed. Barry Bergdoll and Werner Oechslin (London: Thames & Hudson, 2006); Mohsen Mostafavi and David Leatherbarrow, *On Weathering: The Life of Buildings in Time* (Cambridge, MA: MIT Press, 1993); Robert Bevan, *The Destruction of Memory: Architec-*

ture at War (London: Reaktion, 2006); Donald Kunze, David Bertolini, and Simone Brott, eds., *Architecture Post Mortem: The Diastolic Architecture of Decline, Dystopia, and Death* (Farnham: Ashgate, 2013).

9. John Scanlan, *On Garbage* (London: Reaktion, 2005), 35. See also Giles Slade, *Made to Break: Technology and Obsolescence in America* (Cambridge, MA: Harvard University Press, 2006); Bärbel Tischleder and Sarah Wasserman, eds., *Cultures of Obsolescence: History, Materiality, and the Digital Age* (New York: Palgrave Macmillan, 2015); Gillian Pye with Simone Schroth, eds., *Trash Culture: Objects and Obsolescence in Cultural Perspective* (Oxford: Peter Lang, 2010); Nigel Whiteley, "Toward a Throw-Away Culture: Consumerism, 'Style Obsolescence' and Cultural Theory in the 1950s and 1960s," *Oxford Art Journal* 10, no. 2 (1987): 3–27.

10. Jeff Byles, *Rubble: Unearthing the History of Demolition* (New York: Harmony, 2005), chronicles American building losses, but without connection to larger economic and architectural issues. Harris, *Building Lives*, includes a brief section on American interwar depreciation laws and short building life-span myths. Stephen Cairns and Jane M. Jacobs, *Buildings Must Die: A Perverse View of Architecture* (Cambridge, MA: MIT Press, 2014), has a chapter on obsolescence that is more theoretical than historical. The architectural historian Florian Urban has revealed postwar communist planners' deployment of the idea of obsolescence, but not the concept's broader design implications, nor its specifically capitalist ramifications. Florian Urban, "From Periodical Obsolescence to Eternal Preservation," *Future Anterior* 3, no. 1 (Summer 2006): 24–35; Florian Urban, *Neo-Historical East Berlin: Architecture and Urban Design in the German Democratic Republic, 1970–1990* (Farnham: Ashgate, 2009).

11. Robert M. Fogelson, *Downtown: Its Rise and Fall, 1880–1950* (New Haven, CT: Yale University Press, 2001); Max Page, *The Creative Destruction of Manhattan, 1900–1940* (Chicago: University of Chicago Press, 1999).

12. Alison Isenberg, *Downtown America: A History of the Place and the People Who Made It* (Chicago: University of Chicago Press, 2004), 193. See also Robert A. Beauregard, *Voices of Decline: The Postwar Fate of U.S. Cities*, 2nd ed. (New York: Routledge, 2003); Jon C. Teaford, *The Rough Road to Renaissance: Urban Revitalization in America, 1940–1985* (Baltimore, MD: Johns Hopkins University Press, 1990); Douglas W. Rae, *City: Urbanism and Its End* (New Haven, CT: Yale University Press, 2003).

13. Thomas W. Hanchett, "U.S. Tax Policy and the Shopping-Center Boom of the 1950s and 1960s," *American Historical Review* 101, no. 4 (October 1996): 1082–1110.

14. Page, *Creative Destruction*, 5.

15. Marshall Berman, *All That Is Solid Melts into Air: The Experience of Modernity* (New York: Simon & Schuster, 1982), 332.

16. Fredric Jameson, *The Cultural Turn: Selected Writings on the Postmodern, 1983–1998* (London: Verso, 1998), 164; Jameson, "Postmodernism, or the Cultural Logic of Late Capitalism," *New Left Review* 1, no. 146 (July–August 1984): 53–92. In a similar vein see also Reinhold Martin, "Financial Imaginaries: Toward a Philosophy of the City," *Grey Room* 42 (Winter 2011): 60–79.

17. David Harvey, *The Urban Experience* (Baltimore, MD: Johns Hopkins University Press, 1989), 83. See also Richard Walker, "A Theory of Suburbanization: Capitalism and the Construction of Urban Space in the Unites States," in *Urbanization and Urban Planning in Capitalist Society*, ed. Michael Dear and Allen J. Scott (New York: Methuen, 1981), 406.

18. Manfredo Tafuri, *Architecture and Utopia: Design and Capitalist Development* (Cambridge, MA: MIT Press, 1976), 135.

19. Karl Marx and Friedrich Engels, *Manifesto of the Communist Party* (1848), quoted in Ulrich Beck, "The Reinvention of Politics: Towards a Theory of Reflexive Modernization," in

Reflexive Modernization: Politics, Tradition, and Aesthetics in the Modern Social Order (Stanford, CA: Stanford University Press, 1994), 2. Beck explicitly translates *veralten* as "obsolete," as opposed to Samuel Moore's nineteenth-century translation as "antiquated."

20. Eric Hobsbawm, "Interview: World Distemper," *New Left Review* 61 (January–February 2010): 150.

21. Peter Cowan, "Studies in the Growth, Change and Ageing of Buildings," *Transactions of the Bartlett Society* 1 (1962–63): 72.

22. David Edgerton, *The Shock of the Old: Technology and Global History since 1900* (New York: Oxford University Press, 2007), 206.

23. Reyner Banham, "Vehicles of Desire," *Art*, 1 September 1955, 3; reprinted in Reyner Banham, *A Critic Writes: Essays by Reyner Banham* (Berkeley and Los Angeles: University of California Press, 1996).

24. George Nelson, "Obsolescence," *Industrial Design* 3 (December 1956): 88.

25. Louis Sullivan, "The Tall Building Artistically Considered," in *Kindergarten Chats and Other Writings* (1896; New York: Dover, 1979), 208.

26. Rudy Koshar, *Germany's Transient Pasts: Preservation and National Memory in the Twentieth Century* (Chapel Hill: University of North Carolina Press, 1998), 290.

Chapter One

1. Daniel M. Abramson, *Building the Bank of England: Money, Architecture, Society, 1694–1942* (New Haven, CT: Yale University Press, 2005), 193–96.

2. Leon Battista Alberti, *On the Art of Building in Ten Books*, trans. Joseph Rykwert, Neil Leach, and Robert Tavernor (Cambridge, MA: MIT Press, 1988), book 6, chapter 2, p. 156.

3. David B. Brownlee, "The First High Victorians: British Architectural Theory in the 1840s," *Architectura* 15 (1985): 33–36.

4. John Ruskin, *The Seven Lamps of Architecture* (1849; New York: Farrar, Straus & Giroux, 1988), 187.

5. Mariana Griswold van Rensselaer, "Recent Architecture in America. III. Commercial Buildings," *Century Illustrated Magazine*, August 1884, 511.

6. Quoted in David Harvey, *Paris: Capital of Modernity* (New York: Routledge, 2003), 261.

7. Nathaniel Hawthorne, *The House of the Seven Gables* (1851; New York: Heritage Press, 1935), 405, 237. Also Walt Whitman, "Tear Down and Build Over Again," *American Review* 11 (November 1845): 538.

8. Hawthorne, *House of the Seven Gables*, 397.

9. Victor Hugo, *Notre-Dame of Paris*, trans. John Sturrock (1831; Harmondsworth: Penguin, 1978), 195.

10. David Harvey, *The Urban Experience* (Baltimore, MD: Johns Hopkins University Press, 1989), 174. See also Gerhard Dohrn-van Rossum, *History of the Hour: Clocks and Modern Temporal Orders*, trans. Thomas Dunlap (Chicago: University of Chicago Press, 1996); John Bender and David E. Wellbery, eds., *Chronotypes: The Construction of Time* (Stanford, CA: Stanford University Press, 1991).

11. Richard K. Fleischman and Thomas N. Tyson, "Cost Accounting during the Industrial Revolution: The Present State of Historical Knowledge," *Economic History Review* 46, no. 3 (August 1993): 512. Also Alfred D. Chandler, Jr., *The Visible Hand: The Managerial Revolution in American Business* (Cambridge, MA: Belknap, 1977).

12. Fleischman and Tyson, "Cost Accounting," 514.

13. Karl Marx, *Capital: A Critique of Political Economy* vol. 1, trans. Samuel Moore and Edward Aveling, ed. Frederick Engels (Chicago: Charles H. Kerr, 1906), 442. Also Florian Urban, *Neo-Historical East Berlin: Architecture and Urban Design in the German Democratic Republic, 1970–1990* (Farnham: Ashgate, 2009), 37.

14. Joseph B. Hall, *Depreciation of Office Buildings: Its Relation to the Income Tax* (Chicago: National Association of Building Owners and Managers, 1925), 3. "Obsolescence, on the other hand, connotes much more sudden and uncertain displacements or losses of value," explained a speaker at the 1922 national convention of American commercial building owners and managers, "We think of it as resulting in destruction of values due not to physical useless, but rather decreased worth predicated on comparison of the greater efficiency of new devices over older ones." Joseph J. Klein, "Depreciation and Obsolescence," *Proceedings of the Annual Convention of the National Association of Building Owners and Managers* (1922), 240. See also Earl A. Saliers, *Principles of Depreciation*, and Roy B. Kester, *Accounting Theory and Practice*, quoted in H. J. Burton, ed., *Valuations and Depreciations of City Buildings* ([Chicago]: National Association of Building Owners and Managers, [1919]), 69, 77.

15. Frank Eugene Kidder, *The Architect's and Builder's Pocket-Book*, 12th ed. (New York: John Wiley, 1895), 702.

16. Earle Shultz and Walter Simmons, *Offices in the Sky* (Indianapolis, IN: Bobbs & Merrill, 1959), 147.

17. Henry James, *The American Scene* (1907; New York: Penguin, 1994), 420.

18. Cecil C. Evers, *The Commercial Problem in Buildings* (New York: Record & Guide, 1914), v, 58. See also Richard Hurd, *Principles of City Land Values* (New York: Record & Guide, 1903).

19. Randall Mason, *The Once and Future New York: Historic Preservation and the Modern City* (Minneapolis: University of Minnesota Press, 2009), 15.

20. Reginald Pelham Bolton, *Building for Profit: Principles Governing the Economic Improvement of Real Estate* (New York: De Vinne, 1911), 68, 73, 53.

21. Ibid., 75.

22. Ibid., 71.

23. Ibid., 76.

24. Ibid., 65.

25. Ibid., 68.

26. Ibid., 36, 39, 72.

27. See, e.g., Evers, *Commercial Problems*, 235; Saliers, *Principles of Depreciation* (1915), quoted in Burton, *Valuations and Depreciations*, 69; Klein, "Depreciation and Obsolescence," 240; Stanley L. McMichael, and Robert F. Bingham, *City Growth and Values* (Cleveland, OH: Stanley McMichael, 1923), 279; Frederick Morrison Babcock, *The Appraisal of Real Estate* (New York: Macmillan, 1924), 228–9; Hall, *Depreciation of Office Buildings*, 3.

28. Hall, *Depreciation of Office Buildings*, 4.

29. Quoted from *United States Cartridge Co. v. United States* (1932), in U.S. Department of the Treasury, Bureau of Internal Revenue, *Bulletin "F" (Revised 1942): Income Tax Depreciation and Obsolescence Estimated Useful Lives and Depreciation Rates* (Washington, DC: Government Printing Office, 1942), 1.

30. Peter Smith, "Tax Depreciation," in *Strategic Management of Built Facilities*, ed. Craig Langston and Rima Lauge-Kristensen (Oxford: Butterworth-Heinemann, 2002), 160. See also W. Elliot Brownlee, *Federal Taxation in America: A Short History*, 2nd ed. (Cambridge: Cambridge University Press, and Washington, DC: Woodrow Wilson Center Press, 2004); Richard J.

Joseph, *The Origins of the American Income Tax: The Revenue Act of 1894 and Its Aftermath* (Syracuse, NY: Syracuse University Press, 2004); John D. Buenker, *The Income Tax and the Progressive Era* (New York: Garland, 1985).

31. Letter from David O. Gates to S. W. Scofield, 31 August 1917, reprinted in Burton, *Valuations and Depreciations*, 2.

32. Shultz and Simmons, *Offices in the Sky*, 90.

33. Ibid., 105.

34. Marc A. Weiss, *The Rise of the Community Builders: The American Real Estate Industry and Urban Land Planning* (New York: Columbia University Press, 1987), 29. See also Robert H. Wiebe, *Businessmen and Reform: A Study of the Progressive Movement* (Cambridge, MA: Harvard University Press, 1962).

35. Quoted in Shultz and Simmons, *Offices in the Sky*, 74.

36. "Report by Committee on Depreciation and Obsolescence," *Proceedings of the 8th Annual Convention of the National Association of Building Owners and Managers* (1915), 209.

37. Shultz and Simmons, *Offices in the Sky*, especially 117–21; and also for Shultz: "Our Town," *Chicago Tribune*, 24 January 1952; Obituary, *Chicago Tribune*, 7 December 1968.

38. Earle Shultz, "The Obsolescence Questionnaire," *Bulletin of the National Association of Building Owners and Managers* 62 (January 1922): 131.

39. Earle Shultz, *The Effect of Obsolescence on the Useful and Profitable Life of Office Buildings* (Chicago: National Association of Building Owners and Managers, 1922), 203.

40. Ibid., 218, 216.

41. Ibid., 205.

42. Ibid., 220.

43. National Association of Building Owners and Managers, *Office Building Obsolescence: A Study of the W.C.T.U. Temple, Chicago* (Chicago: NABOM, 1927), 4–5.

44. John Roberts, "Obsolescence in the Marshall Field Wholesale Building," *Bulletin of the National Association of Building Owners and Managers* 150 (September 1930): 43. See also Deborah Fulton Rau, "The Making of the Merchandise Mart, 1927–1931: Air Rights and the Plan of Chicago," in *Chicago Architecture and Design, 1923–1993*, ed. John Zukowsky (Munich: Prestel Verlag, 1993), 108ff.

45. Paul E. Holcombe, "Depreciation and Obsolescence in the Tacoma Building," *Bulletin of the National Association of Building Owners and Managers* 137 (June 1929): 20.

46. Ibid., 29.

47. Ibid., 32.

48. National Association of Building Owners and Managers, *Office Building Obsolescence*, 18.

49. Ibid., 14.

50. Joseph Mann, "Report of Counsel," *Proceedings of the National Association of Building Owners and Managers* (1931), 465.

51. "Ask for More Equitable Obsolescence Allowance," *Bulletin of the National Association of Building Owners and Managers* 153 (December 1930): 108.

52. Carl W. Condit, *Chicago, 1910–29: Building, Planning, and Urban Technology* (Chicago: University of Chicago Press, 1973), 302; Daniel Bluestone, "Chicago's Mecca Flat Blues," in *Giving Preservation a History: Histories of Historic Preservation in the United States*, ed. Max Page and Randall Mason (New York: Routledge, 2004), 214ff.; Carol Willis, *Form Follows Finance: Skyscrapers and Skylines in New York and Chicago* (New York: Princeton Architectural Press, 1995): 109ff.

53. Homer Hoyt, *One Hundred Years of Land Values in Chicago: The Relationship of the Growth of Chicago to the Rise in Its Land Values* (Chicago: University of Chicago Press, 1933), 335–36. See also "Ask for More Equitable Obsolescence Allowance," 107.

54. Roderick D. McKenzie, "The Ecological Approach to the Study of the Human Community," in Robert E. Park, Ernest W. Burgess, and Roderick D. McKenzie, *The City* (1925; Chicago: University of Chicago Press, 1967), 75; Ernest W. Burgess, "The Growth of the City: An Introduction to a Research Project," in Park, Burgess, and McKenzie, *The City.*

55. See Milton Horace Westhagen, "A Theory of the Obsolescence of Buildings: Its Relation to Public Finance, Education, and Other Services of the Community, with Special Reference to Chicago" (Ph.D. diss., Northwestern University, 1946).

56. Jennifer S. Light, *The Nature of Cities: Ecological Visions and the American Urban Professions, 1920–1960* (Baltimore, MD: Johns Hopkins University Press, 2009), 4, also 180 n. 10.

57. U.S. Department of the Treasury, Bureau of Internal Revenue, *Bulletin "F" (Revised January 1931). Income Tax. Depreciation and Obsolescence. Revenue Act of 1928* (Washington, DC: U.S. Government Printing Office, 1931); U.S. Department of the Treasury, Bureau of Internal Revenue, *Depreciation Studies: Preliminary Report, January 1931* (Washington, DC: Government Printing Office, 1931).

58. Mann, "Report of Counsel," 465; U.S. Department of the Treasury, Bureau of Internal Revenue, *Depreciation Studies,* 2.

59. Burton, *Valuations and Depreciations,* 4.

60. "Obsolescence Report Widely Distributed," *Bulletin of the National Association of Building Owners and Managers* 66 (20 September 1922), 15. See also ProQuest Historical Newspapers and America's Historical Newspapers.

61. *New York Times,* 18 January 1931, Real Estate section, 20; "Obsolescence of Modern Skyscrapers," *Architect and Engineer* 104, no. 1 (January 1931): 125–27; "An Object Lesson in Obsolescence," *Literary Digest* 101, 29 June 1929, 55–56; K. Burke, "Waste—The Future of Prosperity," *New Republic,* 16 July 1930, 228–31.

62. Mary Ethel Jameson, "Obsolescence in Buildings: A Selected List of References," in *Selected Readings in Real Estate Appraisal,* ed. A. N. Lockwood et al. ([January 1935] Chicago: American Institute of Real Estate Appraisers, 1953); Burke, "Waste—The Future of Prosperity."

63. John E. Burton, "Building Obsolescence and the Assessor," *Journal of Land and Public Utility Economics* 9 (May 1933): 109–20; Charles F. Abbott, "Obsolescence and the Passing of High-Pressure Salesmanship," in *A Philosophy of Production: A Symposium,* ed. J. George Frederick (New York: Business Bourse, 1930), 165; "Future of Buildings Discussed," *Los Angeles Times,* 29 December 1929, E4; J. C. Knapp, "Obsolescence Insurance," *Architectural Forum* 58 (May 1933): 440ff. (expanded version in *Architecture* [January 1935]: 15–16); Knud Lönberg-Holm, "Time Zoning as a Preventive of Blighted Areas," *Architectural Record* 74 (November 1933): 340–41.

64. *New York Times,* 29 November 1931, Real Estate section, 2.

65. W. C. Clark, "Obsolescence," in *Property Management: Proceedings and Reports of the Property Management. Annals of Real Estate Practice,* vol. 5 (Chicago: National Association of Real Estate Boards, 1925), 143.

66. *Atlanta Constitution,* 5 February 1911; Moritz Kahn, "Industrial and Commercial Buildings: Their Probable Life, Obsolescence and Depreciation," *Buildings and Building Management,* 26 April 1926, 40. See also "Architectural Autopsies," *Buildings and Building Management,* 14 March 1927, 46–48.

67. Jon C. Teaford, *The Rough Road to Renaissance: Urban Revitalization in America, 1940–1985* (Baltimore, MD: Johns Hopkins University Press, 1990), 20–21.

68. Graham Aldis, "Depression and Overbuilding in Chicago," *Skyscraper Management* 21 (June 1936): 17–19.

69. Thomas Tallmadge, *The Story of Architecture in America* (New York: Norton 1927), 185.

70. Quoted in Jeff Byles, *Rubble: Unearthing the History of Demolition* (New York: Harmony, 2005), 159.

71. John T. Flynn, "Whatever Goes Up," *Collier's*, 14 September 1929, 10. See also Byles, *Rubble;* Bernard L. Jim, "Ephemeral Containers: A Cultural and Technological History of Building Demolition, 1893–1993" (Ph.D. diss., Case Western Reserve University, 2006).

72. [E. B. White], "Destructionist," *New Yorker*, 23 March 1929, 13.

73. Flynn, "Whatever Goes Up," 10. See also Shultz and Simmons, *Offices in the Sky*, 205; Tallmadge, *Story of Architecture*, 185.

74. Lönberg-Holm, "Time Zoning"; Bernard London, *Ending the Depression through Planned Obsolescence* (New York, 1932), especially 6–7, 14; Giles Slade, *Made to Break: Technology and Obsolescence in America* (Cambridge, MA: Harvard University Press, 2006), 72–77.

75. Christine Frederick, *Selling Mrs. Consumer* (1929), quoted in Glenn Adamson, ed., *Industrial Strength Design: How Brooks Stevens Shaped Your World*, (Cambridge, MA: MIT Press, 2003), 4. See also Janice Williams Rutherford, *Selling Mrs. Consumer: Christine Frederick and the Rise of Household Efficiency* (Athens and London: University of Georgia Press, 2003), 150; Slade, *Made to Break*, 58–62; Susan Strasser, *Waste and Want: A Social History of Trash* (New York: Metropolitan Books, 1999).

76. "Research and Obsolescence," *Buildings and Building Management*, 4 July 1927, 66.

77. Quoted in Annabel Wharton, "Two Waldorf-Astorias: Spatial Economies as Totem and Fetish," *Art Bulletin* 85, no. 3 (September 2003): 533.

78. Clark, "Obsolescence," 153–54. See also Abbott, "Obsolescence," 156, 159.

79. Joseph Schumpeter, *Capitalism, Socialism, and Democracy*, 3rd ed. (New York: Harper & Brothers, 1950), 83–4. See also Thomas K. McCraw, *Prophet of Innovation: Joseph Schumpeter and Creative Destruction* (Cambridge, MA: Belknap Press of Harvard University Press, 2007), especially chapters 15 and 21.

80. Bolton, *Building for Profit*, 51.

81. Roy B. Kester, *Accounting Theory and Practice*, quoted in Burton, *Valuations and Depreciations*, 78.

82. Shultz, "Effect of Obsolescence," 220. See also London, *Ending the Depression*, 12.

83. George T. Mortimer, president, Equitable Office Building Corporation (New York), letter to H. J. Burton, in Burton, *Valuations and Depreciations*, 14. See also Klein, "Depreciation and Obsolescence," 242.

84. Albert W. Noonan, technical director, National Association of Assessing Officers, 1936, quoted in Walker, *Urban Blight and Slums*, 158; Clark, "Obsolescence," 162. See also Report of the Mayor's Advisory Commission, New York City, 1917, in Burton, *Valuations and Depreciations*, 113; Burton, "Building Obsolescence," 112; John Kesselring, "The Measure of Obsolescence in Buildings," *Municipal Finance* 9 (February 1936): 52; William T. Hogan, *Depreciation Policies and Resultant Problems* (New York: Fordham University Press, 1967), 36.

85. Shultz and Simmons, *Offices in the Sky*, 205.

86. Burton, "Building Obsolescence," 111.

87. Clarence Long, *Building Cycles and the Theory of Investment* (Princeton, NJ: Princeton University Press,1940), 165.

88. "Obsolescence in Buildings," *Journal of the American Institute of Architects* 10 (April 1922): 106.

89. Eugene B. Church, "Some Fallacies of Obsolescence: A Contribution to the Controversy," *Pencil Points* 13 (July 1932): 489.

90. Ibid., 487.

91. Ibid., 489.

92. Aldous Huxley, *Brave New World* (1932; New York: Harper, 1946), 58-62.

93. Evan Watkins, *Throwaways: Work Culture and Consumer Education* (Stanford, CA: Stanford University Press, 1993), 1.

94. David Harvey, "The Urban Process under Capitalism: A Framework for Analysis," in *The Urban Experience* (Baltimore, MD: Johns Hopkins University Press, 1989), 83.

95. Eric Hobsbawm, "Interview: World Distempers," *New Left Review* 61 (January–February 2010): 150.

96. Andrew Edgar and Peter Sedgwick, eds., *Cultural Theory: The Key Concepts* (New York: Routledge, 2002), 250.

97. Adela Adam Nevitt, *Housing, Taxation and Subsidies: A Study of Housing in the United Kingdom* (London: Nelson, 1966), 43. See also Michael Veseth, *Mountains of Debt: Crisis and Change in Renaissance Florence, Victorian Britain, and Postwar America* (New York: Oxford University Press, 1990); Hugh J. Ault and Brian J. Arnold, *Comparative Income Taxation: A Structural Analysis* (Boston: Kluwer Law International, 1997); Martin Daunton, *Just Taxes: The Politics of Taxation in Britain, 1914–1979* (Cambridge: Cambridge University Press, 2002); Roy G. Blakey and Gladys C. Blakey, *The Federal Income Tax* (London: Longmans, Green, 1940); Harrison Spaulding, *The Income Tax in Great Britain and the United States* (London: P. S. King, 1927); Sven Steinmo, *Taxation and Democracy: Swedish, British and American Approaches to Financing the Modern State* (New Haven, CT: Yale University Press, 1993).

Chapter Two

1. City Planning Board (Boston), *A General Plan for Boston: A Preliminary Report* (Boston: City Planning Board, 1951), 42–43.

2. Ibid., 42.

3. Ibid., 40.

4. Sandy Isenstadt, "The Visual Commodification of Landscape in the Real Estate Appraisal Industry, 1900–1992," *Business and Economic History* 28, no. 2 (Winter 1999): 61–69.

5. Federal Housing Administration, *Underwriting Manual* (Washington: U.S. Government Printing Office, 1938), paragraphs 935, 918. For the FHA's social policy, see Amy E. Hillier, "Redlining and the Homeowners' Loan Corporation," *Journal of Urban History* 29, no. 4 (2003): 394–420. For FHA commercial lending citing obsolescence, see Gabrielle Esperdy, *Modernizing Main Street: Architecture and Consumer Culture in the New Deal* (Chicago: University of Chicago Press, 2008), chapter 4.

6. Roderick D. McKenzie, "The Ecological Approach to the Study of the Human Community," in Robert E. Park, Ernest W. Burgess, and Roderick D. McKenzie, *The City* (Chicago: University of Chicago Press, 1967; first published 1925), 74–75; Ernest W. Burgess, "The Growth of the City: An Introduction to a Research Project," in ibid., 58–59.

7. "Obsolete Cities: A Challenge to Community Builders," *[Graphic] Survey* (1 October 1932), 438.

8. Carol Aronovici, "Let the Cities Perish," *[Graphic] Survey* 68, no. 13 (1 October 1932): 439.

9. Ibid., 439.

10. M. Christine Boyer, *Dreaming the Rational City: The Myth of American City Planning* (Cambridge, MA: MIT Press, 1983), 205ff.

11. Herrold, "Obsolescence in Cities," 73–75. See also the references cited in Mary Ethel Jameson, "Obsolescence in Buildings: A Selected List of References," in *Selected Readings in Real Estate Appraisal*, ed. A. N. Lockwood (Chicago: American Institute of Real Estate Appraisers, 1953); Westhagen, "A Theory of the Obsolescence of Buildings"; Robert A. Beauregard, *Voices of Decline: The Postwar Fate of U.S. Cities*, 2nd ed. (New York: Routledge, 2003); Robert M. Fogelson, *Downtown: Its Rise and Fall, 1880–1950* (New Haven, CT: Yale University Press, 2001), especially chapter 7, "Inventing Blight: Downtown and the Origins of Urban Redevelopment"; and Alison Isenberg, *Downtown America: A History of the Place and the People Who Made It* (Chicago: University of Chicago Press, 2004).

12. George Herrold, "Obsolescence in Cities," *Planners' Journal* 1, no. 4 (November–December 1935): 73. See also Homer Hoyt, *One Hundred Years of Land Values in Chicago: The Relationship of the Growth of Chicago to the Rise in Its Land Values* (Chicago: University of Chicago Press, 1933), 121–22; John Kesselring, "The Measure of Obsolescence in Buildings," *Municipal Finance* 9 (February 1936): 51–54.

13. Herrold, "Obsolescence in Cities," 73. See also Milton Horace Westhagen, "A Theory of the Obsolescence of Buildings; Its Relation to Public Finance, Education, and Other Services of the Community, with Special Reference to Chicago" (Ph.D. diss., Northwestern University, 1946), 25–26.

14. Quoted in Fogelson, *Downtown*, 331.

15. The Council for Research on Housing Construction, *Slum Clearance and Rehousing* (London: P. S. King, 1934), 17.

16. Mabel L. Walker, *Urban Blight and Slums: Economic and Legal Factors in Their Origin, Reclamation, and Prevention* (Cambridge, MA: Harvard University Press, 1938), 13.

17. Quoted in Thomas O'Connor, *Building a New Boston: Politics and Urban Renewal, 1950 to 1970* (Boston: Northeastern University Press, 1993), 131. For cancer and disease metaphors, see Fogelson, *Downtown*, 349, and "On Outwitting Obsolescence," *Pencil Points* (September 1944): 63; Harry D. Freeman and George H. Herrold, "Obsolescence in Cities: Concluding Discussion," *Planners' Journal* 2, no. 2 (March–April 1936): 49; Walter Gropius, *The New Architecture and the Bauhaus*, trans. P. Morton Shand (Cambridge, MA: MIT Press, 1965), 109.

18. Walker, *Urban Blight and Slums*, 6.

19. Marc A. Weiss, "The Origins and Legacy of Urban Renewal," in *Urban and Regional Planning in an Age of Austerity*, ed. Pierre Clavel, John Forester, and William W. Goldsmith (New York: Pergamon), 55–56.

20. Edith E. Wood, *Slums and Blighted Areas in the United States* (1938), quoted in José Luis Sert, *Can Our Cities Survive?* (Cambridge, MA: Harvard University Press, 1942), 16.

21. Herrold, "Obsolescence in Cities," 75.

22. Andrew M. Shanken, *194X: Architecture, Planning, and Consumer Culture on the American Home Front* (Minneapolis: University of Minnesota Press, 2009); Donald Albrecht, ed., *World War II and the American Dream: How Wartime Building Changed a Nation* (Washington: National Building Museum, 1995); Helen Meller, *Towns, Plans and Society in Modern Britain* (Cambridge: Cambridge University Press, 1997).

23. Walter Gropius and Martin Wagner, "Epilogue: The New City Pattern For the People and

By the People," in *The Problem of the Cities and Towns: Report of the Conference on Urbanism, Harvard University, March 5-6, 1942*, ed. Guy Greer [Cambridge, MA, 1942?], 101.

24. Mabel L. Walker, "The American City is Obsolescent," *Vital Speeches of the Day* 13, no. 22 (1 September 1947): 697.

25. Luther Gulick, "Five Challenges in Todays [*sic*] New Urban World," *American City* 71, no. 12 (December 1956): 149. See also American Institute of Planners, "Statement of Policy on Urban Redevelopment and Expansion," *Journal of the American Institute of Planners* 16, no. 2 (Spring 1950): 93-97.

26. Eugene Rabinowitch, "The Only Real Defense," *Bulletin of the Atomic Scientist* 7, no. 9 (September 1951): 242. See also Miles L. Colean, *Renewing Our Cities* (New York: Twentieth Century Fund, 1953), 33, 67; Murray Fraser with Joe Kerr, *Architecture and the "Special Relationship": The American Influence on Post-War British Architecture* (New York: Routledge, 2007), 145; Ludwig Hilberseimer, *The Nature of Cities* (Chicago: Paul Theobald, 1955), 281-84.

27. Anthony Vidler, "Air War and Architecture," in *Ruins of Modernity*, ed. Julia Hell and Andreas Schönle (Durham, NC: Duke University Press, 2010), 32.

28. Ford Foundation, *Metropolis*, 1963 reprint of 1959, 4.

29. George Sternlieb, "Are Cities Obsolete?" *Trans-Action* 7, no. 6 (April 1970): 86.

30. Jean Gottmann, *Megalopolis: The Urbanized Northeastern Seaboard of the United States* (New York: Twentieth Century Fund, 1961), 403-17; Wolf Von Eckardt, *The Challenge of Megalopolis* (New York: Macmillan, 1964); Bernard Weissbourd, "Are Cities Obsolete?," *Saturday Review*, 19 December 1964; Robert Moses, "Are Cities Dead?," *Atlantic Monthly*, January 1962. See also Samuel Jackson, "Are American Cities Obsolete?" *Vital Speeches* 36, no. 23 (15 September 1970): 706-10.

31. Colean, *Renewing Our Cities*, 6-7. See also, on the idea of a "fluid city," Walker, "The American City Is Obsolescent," 697, 99.

32. Frederick J. Adams and Edwin S. Burdell, "Obsolescence in Cities: Discussion," *Planners' Journal* 2, no. 1 (January-February 1936): 17.

33. Emphasis added. Kevin Lynch, "Environmental Adaptability," *Journal of the American Institute of Planning* 24, no. 1 (1958): 16.

34. Herbert J. Gans, *The Urban Villagers: Group and Class in the Life of Italian-Americans* (New York: Free Press, 1962), 11.

35. Frederick Johnstone Adams, "Rehousing vs. Rehabilitation," *Journal of the American Institute of Planners* 11, no. 3 (July-September 1945): 11; Adams and Burdell, "Obsolescence in Cities: Discussion," 16-19.

36. Adams, Howard & Greeley, Announcement of Partnership Formation, 1949 (Loeb Library, Harvard University).

37. Boston Housing Authority (Urban Redevelopment Division), *Declaration of Findings Relative to West End Land Assembly and Redevelopment Project* (1955), 14-16.

38. Boston Housing Authority (Urban Redevelopment Division), *West End Project Report: A Preliminary Redevelopment Study of the West End of Boston* (1953), 14.

39. Gans, *Urban Villagers*, 313.

40. Boston Housing Authority, *Declaration of Findings*, 11-12.

41. Boston Housing Authority, *West End Project Report*, 14.

42. Carl Feiss, "Outer Skins and Contact Environments," *A.I.A. Journal* 45 (June 1966): 61. See also *American Sociological Review* 11, no. 1 (1946): 124-5.

43. C.-E. A. Winslow, "Health and Housing," in Committee on the Hygiene of Hous-

ing, American Public Health Association, *Housing for Health* (Lancaster, PA: Science Press, 1941), 14.

44. Joel Schwartz, "Robert Moses and City Planning," in *Robert Moses and the Modern City: The Transformation of New York*, ed. Hilary Ballon and Kenneth T. Jackson (New York: Norton, 2007), 131.

45. Committee on the Hygiene of Housing, American Public Health Association, *An Appraisal Method for Measuring the Quality of Housing: A Yardstick for Health Officers, Housing Officials and Planners*, vol. 1 (New York: American Public Health Association, 1945), 2, 15.

46. Ibid., 14–15.

47. Ibid., 16.

48. Ibid., 16, 45.

49. Allan A. Twichell, "An Appraisal Method for Measuring the Quality of Housing," *American Sociological Review* 13, no. 3 (June 1948): 738.

50. Committee on the Hygiene of Housing, *An Appraisal Method*, 27.

51. Ibid., 50.

52. Allan A. Twichell and Anatole Solow, "A Technique for the Appraisal of Housing in Urban Problem Areas," *Planners' Journal* 8, no. 3 (July–September 1942): 28.

53. Quoted in Lawrence J. Vale, *From the Puritans to the Projects: Public Housing and Public Neighbors* (Cambridge, MA: Harvard University Press, 2000), 276.

54. Theodore M. Porter, *Trust in Numbers: The Pursuit of Objectivity in Science and Public Life* (Princeton, NJ: Princeton University Press, 1995), 8.

55. Quoted in Vale, *From the Puritans to the Projects*, 278.

56. Marc Fried and Peggy Gleicher, "Some Sources of Residential Satisfaction in an Urban Slum," *Journal of the American Institute of Planners* 27, no. 4 (November 1961): 312.

57. Gans, *Urban Villagers*, 310.

58. Walker, *Urban Blight and Slums*, 64–66, fig. 21; Walter Firey, *Land Use in Central Boston* (Cambridge, MA: Harvard University Press, 1947), table 8, p. 173. Also, Boston City Planning Board, *The People of Boston, Vol. I, Population Distribution* (1939); *General Plan for Boston*, 44; O'Connor, *Building a New Boston*, chap. 3; Gans, *Urban Villagers*, 285–86.

59. Isenberg, *Downtown America*, 193.

60. Jane Jacobs, interview with James Howard Kunstler, *Metropolis* (March 2001), accessed 7 July 2011, http://www.kunstler.com/mags_jacobs2.htm.

61. Johannes Fabian, *Time and the Other: How Anthropology Makes Its Object* (New York: Columbia University Press, 1983), 144ff. See also "technoideological coding" in Evan Watkins, *Throwaways: Work Culture and Consumer Education* (Stanford, CA: Stanford University Press, 1993); and Maria Paz Balibrea, "The Case for Obsolescence: Thinking Time and Space in Joaquim Jordà's *Numax presenta*," in *Barcelona: Visual Culture, Space and Power*, ed. Helena Buffery and Carlota Caulfield (Cardiff: University of Wales Press, 2012): 73–88.

62. *United States Statutes at Large, 1937*, vol. 50, part 1 (Washington, D.C.: United States Government Printing Office, 1937), chapter 896, p. 888.

63. *United States Statutes at Large, 1949*, vol. 63, part 1 (Washington, D.C.: United States Government Printing Office, 1950), chapter 338, section 2, 102, pp. 413–14.

64. Christine Frederick, *Selling Mrs. Consumer* (1929), quoted in *Industrial Strength Design: How Brooks Stevens Shaped Your World*, ed. Glenn Adamson (Cambridge, MA: MIT Press, 2003), 4.

65. George Nelson, "Obsolescence," *Industrial Design* 3 (December 1956): 88.

66. David Harvey, *Paris: Capital of Modernity* (New York: Routledge, 2003), 150.

67. Gans, *Urban Villagers*, 286, 113-14. See also O'Connor, *Building a New Boston*, 130.

68. Gans, *Urban Villagers*, chapter 13.

69. See notes 25, 28-30 above.

70. M. Allen Pond, *Public Health Report*, 10 May 1946, 667.

71. Louis Justement, *New Cities for Old: City Building in Terms of Space, Time, and Money* (New York: McGraw-Hill, 1946), 41.

72. Equity Residential, "The West End Apartments," promotional flyer, 2007; Thomas C. Palmer, Jr., "Once Supplanted by Charles River Park, the West End Returns," *Boston Globe*, 17 May 2007.

73. These included two historic buildings on Cambridge Street by well-known architects, the Harrison Gray Otis house (c. 1795), by Charles Bulfinch, and West Church (c. 1806), attributed to Asher Benjamin; on Blossom Street, the City of Boston Health Unit (originally West End House, 1930) and Blackstone Junior High School (originally the Winchell School, 1915); on Chambers Street, St. Joseph's Roman Catholic Church and rectory (c. 1900). Two tenement buildings also survived the eminent-domain process, at 25 North Anderson Street and 42 Lowell Street, still standing in 2015 as surreal fragments of a lost neighborhood. Boston Housing Authority, Urban Redevelopment Division, *Supporting Documentation to the Redevelopment Plan: West End Land Assembly and Redevelopment Plan* (1955), 1.

74. Hans Bernoulli, *Die Stadt und ihr Boden: Towns and the Land* (Zurich: Erlenbach, 1946), 9-10, 117.

75. Gavin Stamp, "The Art of Keeping One Jump Ahead: Conservation Societies in the Twentieth Century," in *Preserving the Past: The Rise of Heritage in Modern Britain*, ed. Michael Hunter (Stroud, Gloucestershire: Alan Sutton, 1996), 85; "Why Save," *Architects' Journal* 51, no. 162 (17-24 December 1975): 1288; Franklin Medhurst and J. Parry Lewis, Urban *Decay: An Analysis and a Policy* (London: Macmillan, 1969), 81; See also "Persistence of Obsolete Dwellings," *Town and Country Planning* 27, no. 2 (February 1959): 75; "Correspondence: Obsolete Buildings," *Town and Country Planning* (September-October 1959): 313-15; J. N. Jackson, "Housing Obsolescence in Manchester," *Architect and Building News*, 15 June 1960, 763ff.; Franklin Medhurst, "The Obsolete Center" [Manchester], *Architect and Building News*, 15 June 1960, 759-62; Frances Jones, "A Study in Obsolescence" [Liverpool], *Town Planning Review* 38, no. 3 (October 1967): 187-201.

76. T. T. Hewitson, "Prevention of Obsolescence in Buildings," *Report of Proceedings: Town and Country Planning Summer School; St. Andrew's University, 1954* (London: Town Planning Institute, n.d.), 29.

77. Nick Tiratsoo, Junichi Hasegawa, Tony Mason, and Takao Matsumura, *Urban Reconstruction in Britain and Japan, 1945-1955* (Luton: University of Luton Press, 2002), 10.

78. Florian Urban, "From Periodical Obsolescence to Eternal Preservation," *Future Anterior* 3, no. 1 (Summer 2006): 27; Florian Urban, "The Invention of the Historic City: Building the Past in East Berlin, 1970-1990" (Ph.D. diss., Massachusetts Institute of Technology, 2006), 79; Florian Urban, *Neo-Historical East Berlin: Architecture and Urban Design in the German Democratic Republic 1970-1990* (Farnham: Ashgate, 2009), 44.

79. See David Hamer, "Planning and Heritage: Towards Integration," in *Urban Planning in a Changing World: The Twentieth Century Experience*, ed. Robert Freestone (New York: Routledge, 2000).

80. George Manuel and Denis Hatfield, *District Six* (Cape Town: Longmans, 1967) and Deborah M. Hart, "Political Manipulation of Urban Space: The Razing of District Six, Cape Town,"

in *The Struggle for District Six: Past and Present*, ed. Shamil Jeppie and Crain Soudien (Cape Town: Buchu, 1990). For postwar urban redevelopment around the world, see Freestone, *Urban Planning in a Changing World*.

Chapter Three

1. Le Corbusier, *Towards a New Architecture*, trans. Frederick Etchells (1931; New York: Dover, 1986), 48, 263, 3, 138. Alternately, Le Corbusier, *Toward an Architecture*, trans. John Goodman (Los Angeles: Getty Research Institute, 2007), 118, 262, 87, 183.

2. Walter Gropius, *The New Architecture and the Bauhaus*, trans. P. Morton Shand (1936; Cambridge, MA: MIT Press, 1965), 54.

3. "Manifesto of Futurist Architecture," trans. Reyner Banham, *Journal of the Royal Institute of British Architects* 64 (February 1957): 139. The Italian is from Antonio Sant'Elia, "L'architettura futurista manifesto," *Lacerba*, 1 August 1914, 229.

4. Quoted in Esther Da Costa Meyer, *The Work of Antonio Sant'Elia: Retreat into the Future* (New Haven, CT: Yale University Press, 1995), 155.

5. Le Corbusier, *Towards a New Architecture*, 271. See also Antoine Picon, "Anxious Landscapes: From Ruin to Rust," *Grey Room* 1 (Fall 2000): 64–83.

6. Reyner Banham, *Theory and Design in the First Machine Age* (London: Architectural Press, 1960), 329.

7. Raymond Willoughby, "Building Tells the Story of Progress," *Nation's Business* 21, no. 6 (June 1933): 24. Also Lisa Schrenk, *Building a Century of Progress: The Architecture of Chicago's 1933–34 World's Fair* (Minneapolis: University of Minnesota Press, 2007).

8. Quoted in Joachim Krausse and Claude Lichstenstein, *Your Private Sky: R. Buckminster Fuller, The Art of Design Science* (Zurich: Lars Müller, 1999), 135.

9. Lindy Biggs, *The Rational Factory: Architecture, Technology and Work in America's Age of Mass Production* (Baltimore, MD: Johns Hopkins University Press, 1996), 6; Steven Watts, *The People's Tycoon: Henry Ford and the American Century* (New York: Knopf, 2005), 280–81.

10. Daniel M. Abramson, "Obsolescence and the Fate of Zlín," in *A Utopia of Modernity: Zlín*, ed. Katrin Klingan (Berlin: JOVIS, 2009), 165–67. See also Ladislava Horňáková, ed., *The Baťa Phenomenon: Zlín Architecture, 1910–1960* (Zlín : Regional Gallery of Fine Arts in Zlín, 2009); Eric Jenkins, "The Bata Shoe Company's Elevator-Office in Zlín," *Centropa* 7, no. 3 (2007): 253–65.

11. Bellerive-Plage, Lausanne (Switzerland), Marc Picard, 1936–37 (Allen Cunningham, ed., *Modern Movement Heritage* [New York: E & FN Spon, 1998], 6); Zonnestraal Sanatorium, Hilversum (Netherlands), Jan Duiker and Bernard Bijvoet, 1919–31 (Wessel De Jonge, "Zonnestraal Sanatorium, Hilversum [Jan Duiker]," in *Modern Movement Heritage*, 149ff.; also Theodore H. M. Prudon, *Preservation of Modern Architecture* [Hoboken, NJ: Wiley, 2008], 500–511). See also Sigfried Giedion on the amortization of houses, quoted in Hilde Heynen, "Transitoriness of Modern Architecture," in *Modern Movement Heritage*, 32.

12. "Schools," *Architects' Journal*, 4 November 1937, 708; Scott Williamson, "The Basis of Planning," *Architectural Association Journal* (November 1936): 186.

13. *Pencil Points* (September 1944): 66.

14. *House and Home*, May 1959, 136. Also, "Your Bathroom Will Be Obsolete after the War," *House Beautiful*, December 1942, 58ff.; "This House Won't Be Obsolete 10 Years from Now," *House Beautiful*, May 1949, 150ff.; "What Makes a 1940 Store Obsolete?" *Architectural Forum*

(July 1950): 62–63; James C. Downs, Jr., "Are Apartments Economically Obsolete?" *Architectural Forum* 94 (February 1951): 107ff.

15. Jack Quinan, *Frank Lloyd Wright's Larkin Building: Myth and Fact* (Chicago: University of Chicago Press, 2006), 128.

16. J. Gordon Lippincott, *Design for Business* (Chicago: P. Theobald, 1947),

17. Quoted in Glenn Adamson, ed., *Industrial Strength Design: How Brooks Stevens Shaped Your World* (Cambridge, MA: MIT Press, 2003), 4.

18. Paul Mazur, *The Standards We Raise* (1953), quoted in Ernest Black, "Planned Style Obsolescence" (B.A. thesis, Harvard University, 1962), 32.

19. Giles Slade, *Made to Break: Technology and Obsolescence in America* (Cambridge, MA: Harvard University Press, 2006), 28; Lizabeth Cohen, *A Consumers' Republic: The Politics of Mass Consumption in Postwar America* (New York: Knopf, 2003), 109. See also Victoria De Grazia, "Changing Consumption Regimes in Europe, 1930–1970: Comparative Perspectives on the Distribution Problem," in *Getting and Spending: European and American Consumer Societies in the Twentieth Century*, ed. Susan Strasser, Charles McGovern, and Matthias Judt (Cambridge: Cambridge University Press, 1998); Nigel Whiteley, "Toward a Throw-Away Culture: Consumerism, 'Style Obsolescence' and Cultural Theory in the 1950s and 1960s," *Oxford Art Journal* 10, no. 2 (1987): 3–27.

20. Quoted in Slade, *Made to Break*, 232.

21. George Nelson, "Obsolescence," *Industrial Design* 3 (December 1956): 81–88. Republished in 1957, 1965, and 1967, including in *Perspecta* 11 (1967): 170–76; and George Nelson, *Problems of Design* (New York: Whitney Museum, 1965).

22. Quoted in Timothy Mennel, "'Miracle House Hoop-La': Corporate Rhetoric and the Construction of the Postwar American House," *Journal of the Society of Architectural Historians* 64, no. 3 (September 2005): 340.

23. Alice T. Friedman, *American Glamour and the Evolution of Modern Architecture* (New Haven, CT: Yale University Press, 2010), 114.

24. Paolozzi quoted in David Robbins, ed., *The Independent Group: Postwar Britain and the Aesthetics of Plenty* (Cambridge, MA: MIT Press, 1990), 192.

25. Reyner Banham, "Vehicles of Desire," *Art*, 1 September 1955, 3; reprinted in Reyner Banham, *A Critic Writes: Essays by Reyner Banham* (Berkeley and Los Angeles: University of California Press, 1996).

26. Richard Llewelyn Davies, ed. (Nuffield Provincial Hospitals Trust), *Studies in the Function and Design of Hospitals* (London: Oxford University Press, 1955), 146.

27. Lancelot Law Whyte, ed., "Introduction," in *Aspects of Form: A Symposium on Form in Nature and Art* (London: Lund Humphries, 1951,) 2.

28. Richard Llewelyn Davies, "Endless Architecture," *Architectural Association Journal* 67 (November 1951): 107–8, 112.

29. Alison Smithson and Peter Smithson, "But Today We Collect Ads," *Ark* (November 1956), reprinted in Steven H. Madoff, ed., *Pop Art: A Critical History* (Berkeley and Los Angeles: University of California Press, 1997), 3–4; Alison Smithson and Peter Smithson, "The Aesthetics of Change," *Architects' Year Book* 8 (1957): 14–22; Alison Smithson and Peter Smithson, "Fix," *Architectural Review* 76 (December 1960): 437–39.

30. Peter Cook, ed., *Archigram*, rev. ed. (1972; New York: Princeton Architectural Press, 1999), 78. See also Warren Chalk, "Architecture as Consumer Product," *Perspecta* 11 (1967): 135–37.

31. Elain Harwood, "White Light/White Heat: Rebuilding England's Provincial Towns and Cities in the Sixties," in *The Sixties: Life: Style: Architecture (Twentieth Century Architecture 6)*, ed. Elain Harwood and Alan Powers (London: Twentieth Century Society, 2002), 59. See also Friedman, *American Glamour.*

32. Cedric Price, "Activity and Change," *Archigram* 2 (1962), n.p.; Cedric Price and Joan Littlewood, "The Fun Palace," *Drama Review: TDR* 12, no. 3 (Spring 1968): 129–30.

33. Alison Smithson and Peter Smithson, "Team 10 Primer" (1962), in *Theories and Manifestoes of Contemporary Architecture*, ed. Charles Jencks and Karl Kropf, 2nd ed. (Chichester: Wiley-Academy, 2006), 234.

34. Quoted in Ellen Perry, "Aesthetics and Technology of Preassembly," *Progressive Architecture* 45 (October 1964): 170–71.

35. Constant Nieuwenhuys, "New Babylon/An Urbanism of the Future," *Architectural Design* 34 (June 1964): 304–5.

36. Jean Aubert, "Becoming Outdated," and Jean Baudrillard, "The Ephemeral," in *Utopie: Texts and Projects, 1967–1978*, ed. Craig Buckley and Jean-Louis Violeau, trans. Jean-Marie Clarke (Cambridge, MA: MIT Press, 2011), 77.

37. Robert Venturi, Denise Scott Brown, and Steven Izenour, *Learning from Las Vegas: The Forgotten Symbolism of Architectural Form*, rev. ed. (1972; Cambridge, MA: MIT Press, 1977), 34, 87ff.

38. Noboru Kawazoe, "Material & Man," in Kiyonori Kikutake, Noboru Kawazoe, Masato Ohtaka, Fumihiko Maki, and Noriaki Kurokawa, *Metabolism: The Proposals for New Urbanism* (Tokyo: Bijutu Syuppan Sha, 1960), 48. See also Kisho Kurokawa, *Metabolism in Architecture* (Boulder, CO: Westview Press, 1977); Günter Nitschke, "Tokyo 1964," *Architectural Design* 34 (October 1964): 481–508; Cherie Wendelken, "Putting Metabolism Back in Place: The Making of a Radically Decontextualized Architecture," in *Anxious Modernisms: Experimentation in Postwar Architectural Culture*, ed. Sarah Williams Goldhagen and Réjean Legault (Cambridge, MA: MIT Press, 2000).

39. Manfredi Nicoletti, "Obsolescence," *Architectural Review* 143 (June 1968): 413–15.

40. Peter Cowan and Bev Nutt, "Obsolescence in the Built Environment," 4 reports (Joint Unit for Planning Research: University College, London, 1970); B. Nutt and D. Sears, "Functional Obsolescence in the Planned Environment." *Environment and Planning* 4 (1972): 13–29. See also John Weeks, "Planning for Growth and Change," *Architects' Journal*, 7 July 1960, 20–22; Peter Cowan, "Studies in Growth, Change and Ageing of Buildings," *Transactions of the Bartlett Society* 1 (1962–63): 53–84; John Weeks, "Indeterminate Architecture," *Transactions of the Bartlett Society* 2 (1963–64): 83–106; Richard Llewelyn Davies, "Hospitals and Community," *Architectural Association Journal* 79 (April 1964): 267–80; John Weeks, "Hospitals for the 1970s," *Royal Institute of British Architects Journal* 71 (December 1964): 507–16; Peter Cowan and Jill Nicholson, "Growth and Change in Hospitals," *Transactions of the Bartlett Society* 3 (1964–65): 63–79; Peter Cowan, "Depreciation, Obsolescence and Aging," *Architects' Journal*, 16 June 1965, 1395–1401; Peter Cowan, ed., *The Office: A Facet of Urban Growth* (New York: American Elsevier, 1969); John Weeks, "Multi-Strategy Buildings," *Architectural Design* 39 (October 1969): 536–40; John Weeks and Gordon Best, "Design Strategy for Flexible Health Sciences Facilities," *Health Services Research* 5 (Fall 1970): 263–84; John Weeks, "Hospitals," *Architectural Design* 43, no. 7 (1973): 436–63.

41. Cowan, "Studies in Growth, Change and Ageing," 72, 69. Graph also published in Cowan, "Depreciation, Obsolescence and Aging."

42. Cowan, "Studies in Growth, Change and Ageing," 66, 62.

43. "Designing against Obsolescence . . . Two Industrial Plants by Yamasaki," *Architectural Record* 131 (January 1962): 113–20; Walter McQuade, "Buildings for Books—Are They Obsolete?" *Architectural Forum* 120 (May 1964): 80–82; Robert Propst, *The Office: A Facility Based on Change* (Ann Arbor, MI: Herman Miller, 1968), 33; Weeks, "Indeterminate Architecture," 85.

44. Lyndon Johnson, "Domestic Health and Education Message," *Congressional Quarterly Almanac*, vol. 22 (Washington, DC: Congressional Quarterly Service, 1966), 1256. See also "Aid for Aging Hospitals," *Architectural Forum* 113 (October 1960); C. Ray Smith, "Can We Keep Hospitals from Dying?" *Progressive Architecture* 50 (February 1969): 122–27; William B. Foxhall, "A Systems-Analysis Approach to Hospital Design," *Architectural Record* 147 (March 1970): 112–15; Stephen Verderber and David J. Fine, *Healthcare Architecture in an Era of Radical Transformation* (New Haven, CT: Yale University Press, 2000).

45. Herbert McLaughlin, John Kibre, and Mort Raphael, "Remodeling and Expansion: Study Tells Which Areas Change Most Often and Why," *Modern Hospital* 120 (March 1973): 99.

46. George Rand and Chris Arnold, "Evaluation: A Look Back at the '60s [*sic*] Sexiest System," *AIA Journal* 68 (April 1979): 86. See also Ezra Ehrenkrantz, "SCSD—Better Schools for the Money," *AIA Journal* 42 (September 1964): 91–96; Christopher Arnold, "School Construction Systems Development," *Architectural Design* 37 (November 1967): 495–506.

47. William Zuk and Roger H. Clark, *Kinetic Architecture* (New York: Van Nostrand Reinhold, 1970), 134

48. Quoted in Ilfryn Price, "Facility Management as An Emerging Discipline," in *Workplace Strategies and Facilities Management*, ed. Rick Best, Craig Langston, and Gerard de Valence (Oxford: Butterworth-Heinemann, 2003), 38.

49. Building Performance Research Unit, School of Architecture, University of Strathclyde, *Building Performance*, ed. T. A. Markus (New York: Wiley, 1972), v, http://www.strath.ac.uk /architecture/department/history/, accessed 21 July 2014. Also Ilfryn Price, "Facility Management as an Emerging Discipline," 30–38; Stewart Brand, *How Buildings Learn: What Happens after They're Built* (New York: Penguin, 1994), 65–66; Hashim Sarkis, "The Paradoxical Promise of Flexibility," in *CASE: Le Corbusier's Venice Hospital and the Mat Building Revival*, ed. Hashim Sarkis (Munich: Prestel, 2001).

50. Zuk and Clark, *Kinetic Architecture*, 11.

51. Georges Candilis, Alexis Josic, and Shadrach Woods, "Recent Thoughts on Town Planning and Urban Design," *Architects' Year Book* 11 (1965): 183.

52. Illustrated in Neil Harris, *Building Lives: Constructing Rites and Passages* (New Haven, CT: Yale University Press, 1999), 157.

53. Banham, "A Clip-On Architecture," *Design Quarterly* 63 (1965): 5.

54. Avigail Sachs, "Marketing through Research: William Caudill and Caudill, Rowlett, Scott (CRS)," *Journal of Architecture* 13, no. 6 (2008): 742. See also Jonathan King and Philip Langdon, eds., *The CRS Team and the Business of Architecture* (College Station: Texas A & M University Press, 2002), 96–99; "Reports Published by Caudill Rowlett Scott Prior to the Current Investigation Series," in Caudill Rowlett Scott, *The Practice of the Caudill Rowlett Scott Firm* (Houston: Caudill Rowlett Scott, 1965).

55. Cowan, "Studies in Growth, Change and Ageing," 60; Weeks, "Indeterminate Architecture," 88–89; Llewelyn Davies, "Hospitals and Community," 274; Cowan, "Depreciation, Obsolescence and Aging," tables 1–3; B. Nutt and D. Sears, "Functional Obsolescence in the Planned Environment," Environment and Planning 4, no. 1 (1972): 28.

56. Banham, "1960—Stocktaking," in *A Critic Writes*, 59.

Chapter Four

1. Francis Duffy, *The Changing Workplace*, ed. Patrick Hannay (London: Phaidon, 1992), 74.

2. Ezra Ehrenkrantz, "SCSD—Better Schools for the Money," *AIA Journal* 42 (September 1964): 93.

3. Eberhard Zeidler, "McMaster Health Sciences Center. 1. Concept and Credo," *Canadian Architect* 17 (September 1972): 36.

4. Richard Rogers and Renzo Piano, quoted in "Centre National d'Art et de Culture, George Pompidou," *Domus* 566 (January 1977): 14; Piano quoted in Nathan Silver, *The Making of Beaubourg: A Building Biography of the Centre Pompidou, Paris* (Cambridge, MA: MIT Press, 1994), 180.

5. Mies (1958), quoted in Fritz Neumeyer, *The Artless Word: Mies van der Rohe on the Building Art*, trans. Mark Jarzombek (Cambridge, MA: MIT Press, 1991), 339.

6. Detlef Mertins, *Mies* (London: Phaidon, 2014), 445. See also pp. 388–399, 455–467.

7. Mies, quoted in Alice T. Friedman, *American Glamour and the Evolution of Modern Architecture* (New Haven, CT: Yale University Press, 2010), 64.

8. Richard Llewelyn Davies, "Hospitals and Community," *Architectural Association Journal* 79 (April 1964): 272.

9. John Weeks, "Multi-Strategy Buildings," *Architectural Design* 39 (October 1969): 538.

10. John Weeks, "Hospitals," *Architectural Design* 43, no. 7 (1973): 442.

11. John Weeks, "Hospitals for the 1970s," *Royal Institute of British Architects Journal* 71 (December 1964): 507.

12. John Weeks, "Indeterminate Architecture," *Transactions of the Bartlett Society* 2 (1963–64): 90.

13. John Weeks, "Planning for Growth and Change," *Architects' Journal* (7 July 1960): 20. For Northwick Park Hospital, see also Jonathan Hughes, "The Indeterminate Building," in Jonathan Hughes and Simon Sadler, eds., *Non-Plan: Essays on Freedom, Participation and Change in Modern Architecture and Urbanism* (Oxford: Architectural Press, 2000).

14. Peter Cowan and Jill Nicholson, "Growth and Change in Hospitals," *Transactions of the Bartlett Society* 3 (1964–65): 63–79.

15. Umberto Eco, *The Open Work*, trans. Anna Cancogni ([London]: Hutchinson Radius, 1989), 104, 83.

16. Alastair Grieve, *Constructed Abstract Art in England after the Second World War; A Neglected Avant-Garde* (New Haven, CT: Yale University Press, 2005), 14, 39–41, 88.

17. John Weeks, "Changing Spaces," *HD [Hospital Development]: The Journal for Healthcare Design & Development* 30 (July 1999): 15; Weeks, "Hospitals for the 1970s," 509.

18. Weeks, "Hospitals," 443.

19. Weeks, "Hospitals for the 1970s," 511.

20. Ibid., 516.

21. Weeks, "Planning for Growth and Change," 22.

22. Weeks, "Indeterminate Architecture," 96; Weeks, "Hospitals for the 1970s," 516.

23. Weeks, "Hospitals for the 1970s," 511.

24. Jasia Reichardt, ed., *Cybernetic Serendipity: The Computer and the Arts* (New York: Praeger, 1969): 69.

25. Weeks, "Hospitals for the 1970s," 510; John Weeks, "Changing Spaces: Northwick Park," *Hospital Development* 30 (July 1999): 15.

26. Yona Friedman (1960), quoted in *Exit Utopia: Architectural Provocations, 1956–76*, ed. Martin Van Schaik and Otakar Mácel (Munich: Prestel, 2005), 14.

27. Constant Nieuwenhuys, "New Babylon/An Urbanism of the Future," *Architectural Design* 34 (June 1964): 304–305.

28. Kenzo Tange, in Günter Nitschke, "Tokyo 1964," *Architectural Design* 34 (October 1964): 501.

29. Reyner Banham, *Megastructure: Urban Futures of the Recent Past* (New York: Harper & Row, 1976), 192.

30. Kenzo Tange, in *Architecture Culture, 1943–1968: A Documentary Anthology*, ed. Joan Ockman and Edward Eigen (New York: Rizzoli, 1993), 334.

31. Fumihiko Maki, *Investigations in Collective Form* (St. Louis: The School of Architecture, Washington University, 1964), 11.

32. Ibid., 11.

33. Ibid., 34.

34. Peter Cook, ed., *Archigram*, rev. ed. (New York: Princeton Architectural Press, 1999), 78.

35. Ibid., 41.

36. Simon Sadler, *Archigram: Architecture without Architecture* (Cambridge, MA: MIT Press, 2005), 17.

37. Cedric Price, "Activity and Change," *Archigram* 2 (1962): n.p.

38. "Inter-Action Centre," *Royal Institute of British Architects Journal* 84 (November 1977): 458.

39. Jeff Byles, *Rubble: Unearthing the History of Demolition* (New York: Harmony, 2005), 15.

40. Joan Littlewood, "Non-Program: A Laboratory of Fun," *Drama Review: TDR* 12, no. 3 (Spring 1968): 130.

41. Cedric Price, "The Fun Palace: Argument," *Drama Review: TDR* 12, no. 3 (Spring 1968): 129. See also Mary Louise Lobsinger, "Cybernetic Theory and the Architecture of Performance: Cedric Price's Fun Palace," in *Anxious Modernisms: Experimentation in Postwar Architectural Culture*, ed. Sarah Williams Goldhagen and Réjean Legault (Cambridge, MA: MIT Press, 2000).

42. Littlewood, "Non-Program," 131.

43. Price, in Samantha Hardingham and Kester Rattenbury, eds., *Supercrit #1: Cedric Price Potteries Thinkbelt* (Abingdon: Routledge, 2007), 119; Stephen Mullin, "Cedric Price: 1934–2003" (obituary), *Arq: Architectural Research Quarterly* 7, no. 2 (June 2003): 116. See also Stanley Mathews, *From Agit-Prop to Free Space: The Architecture of Cedric Price* (London: Black Dog, 2007).

44. Kahn, "Form and Design" (1960), in Vincent Scully, Jr., *Louis I. Kahn* (New York: Braziller, 1962), 120.

45. John Scanlan, *On Garbage* (London: Reaktion, 2005), 35.

46. Vladimir Nabokov, "Lance" (1952), in *Nabokov's Dozen* (N.p.: Lifetime Library, 1971), 202.

Chapter Five

1. Douglas Haskell, ed., "American Rebuilding," *Architectural Forum* 112 (January 1960): 85, 96, 146.

2. W. Paul. Strassman, "Creative Destruction and Partial Obsolescence," *Journal of Economic History* 29 (September 1959): 335, 345.

3. John B. Stewart, "Problems in Review: Planned Obsolescence," *Harvard Business Review* 37 (September–October 1959): 22, Exhibit I.

4. Vance Packard, *The Waste Makers* (New York: David McKay, 1960), 4.

5. Max Frisch, *Homo Faber*, trans. Michael Bullock (New York: Harcourt Brace Jovanovich, 1959), 19.

6. J. G. Ballard, "The Concentration City" (1957), "Chronopolis" (1960), and "Billenium" (1961), in J. G. Ballard, *The Complete Stories of J. G. Ballard* (New York: Norton, 2009). See also Daniel Horowitz, *The Anxieties of Affluence: Critiques of American Consumer Culture, 1939–1979* (Amherst: University of Massachusetts Press, 2004).

7. Quoted in Giles Slade, *Made to Break: Technology and Obsolescence in America* (Cambridge, MA: Harvard University Press, 2006), 163.

8. Quoted in Glenn Adamson, ed., *Industrial Strength Design: How Brooks Stevens Shaped Your World* (Cambridge, MA: MIT Press, 2003), 130.

9. Herbert J. Gans, *The Urban Villagers: Group and Class in the Life of Italian-Americans* (New York: Free Press, 1962), x, 310. See also Marc Fried and Peggy Gleicher, "Some Sources of Residential Satisfaction in an Urban Slum," *Journal of the American Institute of Planners* 27, no. 4 (November 1961): 305–15; Chester Hartman, "The Housing of Relocated Families," *Journal of the American Institute of Planners* 30 (November 1964): 266–86; Marc Fried, "Grieving for a Lost Home," in *The Urban Condition*, ed. Leonard J. Duhl (New York: Basic Books, 1963).

10. Kevin Lynch, "Environmental Adaptability," *Journal of the American Institute of Planning* 24, no. 1 (1958): 23–24.

11. Jane Jacobs, *The Death and Life of Great American Cities* (1961; New York: Vintage, 1992), 434, 4.

12. Ibid., 194, 448.

13. Ibid., 7, 187, 189.

14. See *Reconsidering Jane Jacobs*, ed. Max Page and Timothy Mennel (Chicago: Planners Press, 2011), as well as *Contemporary Perspectives on Jane Jacobs: Reassessing the Impacts of an Urban Visionary*, ed. Dirk Schubert (Farnham: Ashgate, 2014), and Alice Sparberg Alexiou, *Jane Jacobs: Urban Visionary* (New Brunswick, NJ: Rutgers University Press, 2006).

15. William H. Jordy, "Humanism in Contemporary Thought: Tough- and Tender-Minded," *Journal of Architectural Education* 15, no. 2 (Summer 1960): 6.

16. Peter Blake, *God's Own Junkyard: The Planned Deterioration of America's Landscape* (New York: Holt, Rinehart & Winston, 1964), 28.

17. Hilary Ballon, *New York's Pennsylvania Stations* (New York: Norton, 2002), 95.

18. George Zabriskie, "Images of Tradition," in United States Conference of Mayors (Special Committee on Historic Preservation), *With Heritage So Rich* (New York: Random House, 1966), 115.

19. Rudy Koshar, *Germany's Transient Pasts: Preservation and National Memory in the Twentieth Century* (Chapel Hill: University of North Carolina Press, 1998), 290, 292.

20. David Lowenthal, "The Heritage Crusade and Its Contradictions," in *Giving Preservation a History: Histories of Historic Preservation in the United States*, ed. Max Page and Randall Mason (New York: Routledge, 2004), 33.

21. Randall Mason, *The Once and Future New York: Historic Preservation and the Modern City* (Minneapolis: University of Minnesota Press, 2009), x. See also Max Page, *The Creative Destruction of Manhattan, 1900–1940* (Chicago: University of Chicago Press, 1999), 113ff; Page and Mason, eds., *Giving Preservation a History*.

22. Robert R. Weyeneth, "Ancestral Architecture: The Early Preservation Movement in Charleston," in Page and Mason, eds., *Giving Preservation a History*, 275. See also Stephanie Yuhl, *A Golden Haze of Memory: The Making of Historic Charleston* (Chapel Hill: University of North Carolina Press, 2005).

23. Mason, *Once and Future New York*, x.

24. Koshar, *Germany's Transient Pasts*, 42.

25. Alois Riegl, "The Modern Cult of Monuments: Its Character and Its Origin" (1928), trans. Kurt W. Forster and Diane Ghirardo, in *Oppositions Reader*, ed. K. Michael Hays (New York: Princeton Architectural Press, 1998), 624.

26. Quoted in Susanne Lange, *Bernd and Hilla Becher: Life and Work*, trans. Jeremy Gaines (Cambridge, MA: MIT Press, 2007), 187.

27. John Earl, *Building Conservation Philosophy*, 3rd ed. (Shaftesbury: Donhead, 2003), 161.

28. Koshar, *Germany's Transient Pasts*, 307; S. Andreae, "From Comprehensive Development to Conservation Areas," in *Preserving the Past: The Rise of Heritage in Modern Britain*, ed. Michael Hunter (Stroud: Alan Sutton, 1996); Norman Williams, Edmund H. Kellogg, and Frank B. Gilbert, *Readings in Historic Preservation: Why? What? How?* (New Brunswick, NJ: Center for Urban Policy Research, 1983), 34.

29. Alan Powers, "The Heroic Period of Conservation," *Twentieth Century Architecture* 7 (2004): 8–18.

30. Bernard Rudofsky, *Architecture without Architects: A Short Introduction to Non-Pedigreed Architecture* (Garden City: Doubleday, 1964), Preface, n.p.

31. Ibid., caption to fig. 1.

32. William Zuk and Roger H. Clark, *Kinetic Architecture* (New York: Van Nostrand Reinhold, 1970), 5.

33. Christopher Alexander, *The Timeless Way of Building* (New York: Oxford University Press, 1979), 479–80, 492.

34. Kevin Lynch, *What Time Is This Place?* (Cambridge, MA: MIT Press, 1972), 191. See also Martin Pawley, *Garbage Housing* (London: Architectural Press, 1975); Forrest Wilson, "Building with the Byproducts of Society," *AIA Journal* 68 (July 1979): 40–49.

35. John E. Burton, "Building Obsolescence and the Assessor," *Journal of Land and Public Utility Economics* 9 (May 1933): 120. See also Graham Aldis and F. P. Burt, "Modernizing Old Office Buildings," *Architectural Forum* 52 (June 1930): 867–71, and "Seventeen Examples of Successful Remodeling," *Architectural Forum* 58 (January 1933): 45ff.

36. Barbaralee Diamonstein, *Buildings Reborn: New Uses, Old Places* (New York: Harper & Row, 1978).

37. Stewart Brand, *How Buildings Learn: What Happens After They're Built* (New York: Penguin, 1994), 104.

38. Koshar, *Germany's Transient Pasts*, 317. See also M. Christine Boyer, *The City of Collective Memory: Its Historical Imagery and Architectural Entertainments* (Cambridge, MA: MIT Press, 1994); Briann Greenfield, "Marketing the Past: Historic Preservation in Providence, Rhode Island," in Page and Mason, eds., *Giving Preservation a History*, 163–84; Neil Smith, "Gentrification, the Frontier, and the Restructuring of Urban Space," in *Gentrification of the City*, ed. Neil Smith and Peter Williams (Boston: Allen & Unwin, 1986); Sharon Zukin, *Loft Living: Culture and Capital in Urban Change* (Baltimore, MD: Johns Hopkins University Press, 1982).

39. Mark Crinson, "Urban Memory—An Introduction," in *Urban Memory: History and Amnesia in the Modern City*, ed. M. Crinson (London: Routledge, 2005), xviii.

40. Florian Urban, *Neo-Historical East Berlin: Architecture and Urban Design in the German Democratic Republic, 1970–1990* (Farnham: Ashgate, 2009), 56.

41. David Harvey, *The Urban Experience* (Baltimore, MD: Johns Hopkins University Press, 1989), 83.

42. J. L. Sert, F. Léger, and S. Giedion, "Nine Points on Monumentality" (1943), in Sigfried Giedion, *Architecture, You, and Me* (Cambridge, MA: Harvard University Press, 1958), 48.

43. Reyner Banham, *The New Brutalism: Ethic or Aesthetic?* (New York: Reinhold, 1966), 16.

44. Paul Rudolph, *The Architecture of Paul Rudolph*, introduction by Sibyl Moholy-Nagy (New York: Praeger, 1970), 18. See also James S. Russell, "Obdurate by Design: The Difficult Cause of Willful Buildings That Demand Heroic Efforts to Preserve," *Architectural Record* 202 (September 2014): 48–50.

45. Rudolph (1964), in Paul Rudolph, *Writings on Architecture* (New Haven, CT: Yale University Press, 2008), 99.

46. Ibid., 98. See also Timothy M. Rohan, *The Architecture of Paul Rudolph* (New Haven, CT: Yale University Press, 2014), esp. 84–113.

47. Aldo Rossi, *The Architecture of the City* (Cambridge, MA: MIT Press, 1982), 22, 28–32. See also Hans Gerhard Hannesen, "Cara Architettura!," in *Aldo Rossi Architect* (London: Academy Editions, 1994).

48. Rossi, *The Architecture of the City*, 55, 59.

49. Aldo Rossi, *Buildings and Projects* (New York: Rizzoli, 1985), 48.

50. Kahn, in John W. Cook and Heinrich Klotz, *Conversations with Architects* (New York: Praeger, 1973), 204.

51. Ibid., 183. See also Neil Levine, *Modern Architecture: Representation and Reality* (New Haven, CT: Yale University Press, 2009), 245.

52. Kahn, quoted in Richard Padovan, *Towards Universality: Le Corbusier, Mies and De Stijl* (New York: Routledge, 2002), 212.

53. Yukio Futagawa and Charles Moore, "Dialogue with Charles Moore—On Sea Ranch," *GA Houses* 101 (2008): 53 (first published 1975). See also Donlyn Lyndon and Jim Alinder, *The Sea Ranch* (New York: Princeton Architectural Press, 2004), especially 40–42.

54. Robert Venturi, *Complexity and Contradiction in Architecture*, 2nd ed. (1966; New York: Museum of Modern Art, 1977), 44.

55. Ibid., 110.

56. Robert Venturi, *Iconography and Electronics upon a Generic Architecture: A View from the Drafting Room* (Cambridge, MA: MIT Press, 1996), 276.

57. Robert Venturi, Denise Scott Brown, and Steven Izenour, *Learning from Las Vegas* (Cambridge, MA: MIT Press, 1972), 90.

58. K. Michael Hays, ed., *Oppositions Reader* (New York: Princeton Architectural Press, 1998), 86, 12.

59. Donella Meadows, Dennis L. Meadows, Jorgen Randers, and William W. Behrens, *The Limits to Growth: A Report for the Club of Rome's Project on the Predicament of Mankind*, 2nd ed. (New York: Universe Books, 1974), 173.

60. Margaret Drabble, *The Ice Age* (New York: Knopf, 1977), 59.

61. David Lowenthal, "The Past of the Future: From the Foreign to the Undiscovered Country," in *Manifestos for History*, ed. Keith Jenkins, Sue Morgan, and Alun Munslow (New York: Routledge, 2007), 211.

62. Nigel Whiteley, *Reyner Banham: Historian of the Immediate Future* (Cambridge, MA: MIT Press, 2002), 264.

63. Reyner Banham, *Megastructure: Urban Futures of the Recent Past* (New York: Harper & Row, 1976), 184, 190.

64. Building Systems Information Clearinghouse, *Evaluation: Two Studies of SCSD Schools* (Menlo Park, CA: Educational Facilities Laboratories, 1972), Table II.

65. Alison Smithson and Peter Smithson, *The Euston Arch and the Growth of the London, Midland and Scottish Railway* (London: Thames & Hudson, 1968).

66. *RIBA Journal* 81, no. 1 (January 1974), 10.

67. Theo Crosby (1973), quoted in Alan Powers, "The Heroic Period of Conservation," *Twentieth-Century Architecture* 7 (2004): 16.

68. From *Collage City* (written in 1973 with Fred Koetter; published in 1975), in *Theorizing a New Agenda for Architecture: An Anthology of Architectural Theory, 1965–1995*, ed. Kate Nesbitt (New York: Princeton Architectural Press, 1996), 288.

69. Koshar, *Germany's Transient Pasts*, 13.

70. Tax Reform Act of 1976 (Public Law 94–455), Sec. 2124.

71. World Commission on Environment and Development, *Our Common Future* (New York: Oxford University Press, 1987), 1, 9.

72. Sim Van der Ryn and Peter Calthorpe, *Sustainable Communities: A New Design Synthesis for Cities, Suburbs, and Towns* (San Francisco: Sierra Club Books, 1986); Sim Van der Ryn, "Eco-Villages: Toward Sustainable Architecture," *Progressive Architecture* 72 (March 1991): 88–90. See also Terry Williamson, Antony Radford, and Helen Bennetts, *Understanding Sustainable Architecture* (New York: Spon, 2003).

73. Freeman Dyson, "The Question of Global Warming," *New York Review of Books*, 12 June 2008, 45.

74. *Our Common Future*, 43.

Chapter Six

1. See, for example, Helena Mattsson and Sven-Olov Wallenstein, eds., *Swedish Modernism: Architecture, Consumption and the Welfare State* (London: Black Dog, 2010).

2. Eric Hobsbawm, "Interview: World Distempers," *New Left Review* 61 (2010): 150.

3. Helga Nowotny, *Time: The Modern and Postmodern Experience*, trans. Neville Plaice (Cambridge: Polity, 1994), 32.

4. Manfredo Tafuri, *Architecture and Utopia: Design and Capitalist Development* (Cambridge, MA: MIT Press, 1976), 137.

5. David Harvey, *The Urban Experience* (Baltimore, MD: Johns Hopkins University Press, 1989), 274; David Harvey, *Paris: Capital of Modernity* (New York: Routledge, 2003), 1.

6. Harvey, *Urban Experience*, 83.

7. Fredric Jameson, "Postmodernism, or the Cultural Logic of Late Capitalism," *New Left Review* 146 (July–August 1984): 86.

8. Ibid., 88.

9. David Lowenthal, "The Heritage Crusade and Its Contradictions," in *Giving Preservation a History: Histories of Historic Preservation in the United States*, ed. Max Page and Randall Mason (New York: Routledge, 2004), 33.

10. White House Press Release, "Private and Public Sector Commitments and Executive Actions Will Create Jobs and Cut Carbon Pollution," 19 May 2014, http://www.whitehouse.gov/the -press-office/2014/05/09/fact-sheet-president-obama-announces-commitments-and-executive -actions-a, accessed 18 November 2014.

11. Bruno Latour, *We Have Never Been Modern*, trans. Catherine Porter (Cambridge, MA: Harvard University Press, 1993), 75.

12. Lord Gowrie, chairman of the Arts Council of Great Britain (1994), quoted in Allen Cunningham, *Modern Movement Heritage* (New York: E & FN Spon, 1998), 4.

13. Quoted in Jeff Byles, *Rubble: Unearthing the History of Demolition* (New York: Harmony, 2005), 298.

14. Town of Lexington (Massachusetts) Annual Report for 2011. See also National Trust for Historic Preservation, "Teardowns by State & Community," 2008.

15. Associated Press, "Atlanta to Demolish Turner Field," http://espn.go.com/mlb/story/_/id/9965245/turner-field-demolished-atlanta-braves-leave-new-stadium-2017-mayor-says, accessed 20 November 2014.

16. Author conversation with North West London Hospitals NHS Trust officials Phil Smith, Alex White, and Nick Hulme, 19 December 2005.

17. Yan Zhang and Ke Fang, "Is History Repeating Itself? From Urban Renewal in the United States to Inner-City Redevelopment in China," *Journal of Planning Education and Research* 23, no. 3 (2004): 288. For recent Chinese urbanism, preservation, and ecological planning, see also Daniel Benjamin Abramson, "The Aesthetics of City-Scale Preservation Policy in Beijing," *Planning Perspectives* 22, no. 2 (April 2007): 129–66; Zhu Qian, "Historic District Conservation in China," *Traditional Dwellings and Settlements Review* 19, no. 1 (Fall 2007): 59–76; Fulong Wu, "Globalization, Place Promotion and Urban Development in Shanghai," *Journal of Urban Affairs* 25, no. 1 (2003): 55–78; Pamela Buxton, "China Blueprint," *RIBA Journal* 116, nos. 8–9 (August–September 2009): 52–56.

18. Thomas Campanella, *The Concrete Dragon: China's Urban Revolution and What It Means for the World* (New York: Princeton Architectural Press, 2008), 165.

19. Byles, *Rubble*, chapter 8.

20. Camilo José Vergara, *American Ruins* (New York: Monacelli, 1999), 11, 206. Also Arthur Drooker, *American Ruins* (New York: Merrell, 2007); Tim Edensor, *Industrial Ruins: Spaces, Aesthetics and Materiality* (New York: Berg, 2005); Harry Skrdla, *Ghostly Ruins: America's Forgotten Architecture* (New York: Princeton Architectural Press, 2006).

21. Andreas Huyssen, "Nostalgia for Ruins," *Grey Room* 23 (Spring 2006): 8; Robert Harbison, *The Built, the Unbuilt, and the Unbuildable: In Pursuit of Architectural Meaning* (Cambridge, MA: MIT Press, 1991), 122. See also Antoine Picon, "Anxious Landscapes: From the Ruin to Rust," trans. Karen Bates, *Grey Room* 1 (Fall 2000): 64–83.

22. Yves Marchand and Romain Meffre, with essays by Robert Polidori and Thomas J. Sugrue, *The Ruins of Detroit* (Göttingen: Steidl, 2014); Richard B. Woodward, "What a Disaster," *ARTNews* 112, no. 2 (February 2013): 66–73; Stephen Cairns and Jane M. Jacobs, *Buildings Must Die: A Perverse View of Architecture* (Cambridge, MA: MIT Press, 2014), 6, 183.

23. Elma Durmisevic and Ken Yeang, "Designing for Disassembly (DfD)," *Architectural Design* 79, no. 6 (November–December 2009): 134–37. See also the open-building principles discussed in Robert Kronenburg, *Flexible: Architecture That Responds to Change* (London: Peter King, 2007), 115ff; and John F. Fernandez, "Diversified Longevity: Orchestrated Obsolescence for Intelligent Change," *Thresholds* 24 (2002): 12–19. For interest in temporary architecture and the ephemeral see special issues of *Architectural Design* 68 (September–October 1998); *Domus* 814 (April 1999); *Quaderns* 224 (2000); *Perspecta* 34 (Spring 2003); *Thresholds* 31 (2006).

24. Thomas DeChant, *Detecting and Preventing Hospital Obsolescence* (Madison, WI: Institute for Health Planning, 1985), 8.

25. Rem Koolhaas, in conversation with Lynne Cooke, "Architecture and the Sixties: Still Radical after All These Years," *Tate Etc.* 2 (Autumn 2004), www.tate.org.uk/tateetc/issue2, accessed 9 July 2009.

26. Kenneth Powell, *Richard Rogers: Complete Works*, vol. 1 (London: Phaidon, 1999), 50; quoted in John Earl, *Building Conservation Philosophy*, 3rd ed. (Shaftesbury: Donhead, 2003), 223.

27. Rem Koolhaas, "Urban Operations," *D: Columbia Documents of Architecture and Theory* 3 (1993): 53. See also Rem Koolhaas, "Paris La Défense," *Arch Plus* (December 1991): 44–50, 110.

28. Rem Koolhaas, "CRONOAOS," *Log* 21 (Winter 2011): 119, 121. See also, under Koolhaas's direction, Harvard Graduate School of Design, *Preservation: Operations and Mechanisms* (Cambridge, MA: Harvard Graduate School of Design, 2008).

29. Hans Ibelings, *Supermodernism: Architecture in the Age of Globalization* (Rotterdam: NAi, 2002), 62.

30. Gehry, quoted in Nancy Joyce, *Building Stata: The Design and Construction of Frank O. Gehry's Stata Center at MIT* (Cambridge, MA: MIT Press, 2004), xii.

31. Cairns and Jacobs, *Buildings Must Die*, 231. See also Karsten Harries, *The Ethical Function of Architecture* (Cambridge, MA: MIT Press, 1997).

32. T. J. Clark, "Modernism, Postmodernism, and Steam," *October* 100 (Spring 2002): 158–59, 166. See also T. J. Clark, *Farewell to an Idea: Episodes from a History of Modernism* (New Haven, CT: Yale University Press, 1999), Introduction.

33. Koolhaas, "CRONOAOS," 119.

34. Daniel M. Abramson, "Obsolescence and the Fate of Zlín," in *A Utopia of Modernity: Zlín*, ed. Katrin Klingan (Berlin: JOVIS, 2009), 167–68.

35. Erich Von Dietze, *Paradigms Explained: Rethinking Thomas Kuhn's Philosophy of Science* (Westport, CT: Praeger, 2001), 40.

36. Le Corbusier, *Towards a New Architecture*, trans. Frederick Etchells (1931; New York: Dover, 1986), 48; Walter Gropius, *The New Architecture and the Bauhaus*, trans. P. Morton Shand. (1936; Cambridge, MA: MIT Press, 1965; first published 1936).

37. Joan W. Scott, "History-Writing as Critique," in *Manifestos for History*, ed. Keith Jenkins, Sue Morgan, and Alun Munslow (New York: Routledge, 2007), 25.

38. Ibid., 28.

39. Jean Baudrillard, "The Environmental Witch-Hunt: Statement by the French Group, 1970," in *The Aspen Papers: Twenty Years of Design Theory from the International Design Conference in Aspen*, ed. Reyner Banham (New York: Praeger, 1974), 208–10. See also Craig Buckley and Jean-Louis Violeau, eds., *Utopie: Texts and Projects, 1967–1978*, trans. Jean-Marie Clarke (Cambridge, MA: MIT Press, 2011), 19, 255–57.

40. Andrew Ross, *Bird on Fire: Lessons from the World's Least Sustainable City* (New York: Oxford University Press, 2011), chapter 8.

41. Adrian Parr, *Hijacking Sustainability* (Cambridge, MA: MIT Press, 2009), 4. See also, on neoliberalism, Michael Hardt and Antonio Negri, *Empire* (Cambridge, MA: Harvard University Press, 2000); Robert Brenner, *The Economics of Global Turbulence: The Advanced Capitalist Economies from Long Boom to Long Downturn, 1945–2005* (London: Verso, 2006).

42. Ellen Grimes, untitled lecture, Future of History Conference, University of Michigan Taubman College of Architecture and Urban Planning, April 2011, https://www.youtube.com /watch?v=u6pcwH300Uw, accessed 21 November 2014. See also Austin Williams, *The Enemies of Progress: The Dangers of Sustainability* (Charlottesville, VA: Societas Imprint Academic, 2008); Panayiota Pyla, "Crisis Spins," *Journal of Architectural Education* 69, no. 1 (March 2015): 8–12.

43. Wolfgang Sachs, "Sustainable Development and the Crisis of Nature: On the Political Anatomy of an Oxymoron," in *Living with Nature: Environmental Politics as Cultural Discourse*, ed. Frank Fischer and Maarten A. Hajer (Oxford: Oxford University Press, 1999), 41. See also Simon Guy and Guy Farmer, "Contested Constructions: The Competing Logics of Green Buildings and Ethics," in *Ethics and the Built Environment*, ed. Warwick Fox (New York: Routledge, 2000).

44. Ulrich Beck, "The Reinvention of Politics: Towards a Theory of Reflexive Modernization," in *Reflexive Modernization: Politics, Tradition, and Aesthetics in the Modern Social Order* (Stanford, CA: Stanford University Press, 1994). See also John May, "Against Sustainability," *ID Magazine* 57, no. 1 (January–February 2010): 20–21; Michelle Addington, "Sustainable Situationism," *Log* 17 (October 2009): 77–81; Frank Fischer and Maarten A. Hajer, *Living with Nature: Environmental Politics as Cultural Discourse* (Oxford: Oxford University Press, 1999).

45. William McDonough, "Design, Ecology, Ethics, and the Making of Things" (1993), in *Theorizing a New Agenda for Architecture: An Anthology of Architectural Theory, 1965–1995*, ed. Kate Nesbitt (New York: Princeton Architectural Press, 1996), 400.

46. See for example "Special Report: Architecture and Ethics," *Architectural Record* (June 2014).

47. Vincent Scully, "Tomorrow's Ruins Today" (1999), in *Building the Nation: Americans Write about Their Architecture, Their Cities, and Their Landscape*, ed. Steven Conn and Max Page (Philadelphia: University of Pennsylvania Press, 2003), 46.

48. Freeman Dyson, "The Question of Global Warming," *New York Review of Books*, 12 June 2008, 45.

49. Michelle Addington, "Sustainable Situationism," 79.

50. Brian Walker and David Salt, *Resilience Thinking: Sustaining Ecosystems and People in a Changing World* (Washington, DC: Island Press, 2006), 32.

51. See notes 50 and 52, and also Tobias Plieninger and Claudia Bieling, eds., *Resilience and the Cultural Landscape: Understanding and Managing Change in Human-Shaped Environments* (Cambridge: Cambridge University Press, 2012); Tuna Taşan-Kok, Dominic Stead, and Peiwen Lu, "Conceptual Overview of Resilience: History and Context," in *Resilience Thinking in Urban Planning*, ed. Ayda Eraydin and Tuna Taşan-Kok, (Dordrecht: Springer, 2013).

52. Michael Quinn Dudley, "Resilience," in *Green Cities: An A-to-Z Guide*, ed. Nevin Cohen (Los Angeles: Sage, 2011), 375–79.

Illustration Credits

0.1.   Source: Reginald Pelham Bolton, *Building for Profit* (New York, 1911).

1.1.   © The Metropolitan Museum of Art. Source: Art Resource, NY.

1.2.   Source: Reginald Pelham Bolton, *An Expensive Experiment* (New York, 1913).

1.3.   Source: Reginald Pelham Bolton, *Building for Profit* (New York, 1911).

1.4.   Reprinted with permission, Building Owners and Managers Association International. All rights reserved.

1.5.   Reprinted with permission, Building Owners and Managers Association International. All rights reserved.

1.6.   Collection of Neil Harris.

1.7.   Reprinted with permission, Building Owners and Managers Association International. All rights reserved.

1.8.   Reprinted with permission, Building Owners and Managers Association International. All rights reserved.

1.9.   Reprinted with permission, Building Owners and Managers Association International. All rights reserved.

2.1.   Source: Boston City Planning Board, *General Plan for Boston: Preliminary Report* (1951), pp. 42–43.

2.2.   Courtesy MIT Museum.

2.3.   Source: *Appraisal Method for Measuring the Quality of Housing, Volume 1,* The American Public Health Association, 1945, Fig. 1; Courtesy: The American Public Health Association/Sheridan Content Services.

2.4.   Source: *Appraisal Method for Measuring the Quality of Housing, Volume 1,* The American Public Health Association, 1945, Fig. 6; Courtesy: The American Public Health Association/Sheridan Content Services.

3.1.   RIBA Library Photographs Collection.

3.2.   Private collection.

3.3.   Courtesy, The Estate of R. Buckminster Fuller; Courtesy of Department of Special Collections and University Archives, Stanford University Libraries.

3.4.   Photo © Tate, London 2014; © 2014 Trustees of the Paolozzi Foundation, Licensed by DACS / Artists Rights Society (ARS), New York.

3.5.   Reproduced by kind permission of Mrs. Mary Banham.

3.6.   RIBA Library Photographs Collection.

3.7.   © 2014 Artists Rights Society (ARS), New York / ADAGP, Paris.

3.8.   © Arata Isozaki; Digital Image © The Museum of Modern Art/Licensed by SCALA / Art Resource, NY.

3.9.   Courtesy, The Bartlett, UCL Faculty of the Built Environment.

4.1.   Photo courtesy of Albert Kahn Associates, Inc.

4.2.   Permission of Foster + Partners.

4.3.   © Heinrich Heidersberger/ARTUR IMAGES.

4.4.   tBP/Architecture, Inc. (formerly William E. Blurock & Associates).

4.5.   Permission of Luckman Salas O'Brien.

4.6.   Architectural Press Archive/RIBA Library Photographs Collection.

4.7.   By permission *The Architects' Journal*.

4.8.   By permission of Renzo Piano Building Workshop and Richard Rogers.

4.9.   © Chicago Historical Society / VIEW.

4.10.   Permission of Llewelyn Davies.

4.11.   Permission of Llewelyn Davies.

4.12.   Photo by author.

4.13.   Photo by Digital Archives for Architectural Space Consortium, Permission of Shinkenchiku-sha Co.

4.14.   Credit: Permission of Ted A. Niederman.

4.15.   Courtesy Fumihiko Maki.

4.16.   Photo by author.

4.17.   Photo © Tomio Ohashi, Use by permission Kisho Kurokawa Architect & Associates.

4.18.   Photo © Tomio Ohashi, Use by permission Kisho Kurokawa Architect & Associates.

4.19.   By permission Kisho Kurokawa Architect & Associates.

4.20.   © Archigram 1964; Image supplied by the Archigram Archives © 2014.

4.21.   © Archigram 1965; Image supplied by the Archigram Archives © 2014.

4.22.   Cedric Price fonds, Collection Centre Canadien d'Architecture/Canadian Centre for Architecture, Montréal.

4.23.   Cedric Price fonds, Collection Centre Canadien d'Architecture/Canadian Centre for Architecture, Montréal.

4.24.   Cedric Price fonds, Collection Centre Canadien d'Architecture/Canadian Centre for Architecture, Montréal.

5.1.   Photo by Walter Daran/Hulton Archive/Getty Images.

5.2.   © Bernd and Hilla Becher; Image copyright © The Metropolitan Museum of Art. Image source: Art Resource, NY.

5.3   Permission of Larry Birch.

5.4.   Photograph by Balthazar Korab courtesy of The Library of Congress.

5.5.   Photo by author.
5.6.   © Peter Cook / VIEW.
5.7.   Photo by author.
5.8.   Photo by author.
5.9.   By permission of Andrew Filarski.
5.10.   Louis I. Kahn Collection, The University of Pennsylvania and the Pennsylvania Historical and Museum Commission.
5.11.   DHK. Suhrawardy Ambulatory 02 by Naquib Hossain is used under CC BY / cropped from original.
5.12.   Courtesy of Peter Eisenman.
5.13.   Photo © Busse, courtesy Sauerbruch Hutton.
5.14.   Courtesy Sauerbruch Hutton.
6.1.   Photo by author.
6.2.   Photo by author.
6.3.   By permission of Camilo J. Vergara.
6.4.   Photo by author.
6.5.   Photo by author.
6.6.   Photo by author.
6.7.   Photo by author.

Index

Page numbers in italics refer to figures.

CPSIA information can be obtained
at www.ICGtesting.com
Printed in the USA
LVHW011720160719
624282LV00018B/1586/P